Hituzi Linguistics in English

No. 4 *A Historical Study of Referent Honorifics in Japanese* Takashi Nagata
No. 5 *Communicating Skills of Intention* Tsutomu Sakamoto
No. 6 *A Pragmatic Approach to the Generation and Gender Gap in Japanese Politeness Strategies* Toshihiko Suzuki
No. 7 *Japanese Women's Listening Behavior in Face-to-face Conversation* Sachie Miyazaki
No. 8 *An Enterprise in the Cognitive Science of Language* Tetsuya Sano et al.
No. 9 *Syntactic Structure and Silence* Hisao Tokizaki
No. 10 *The Development of the Nominal Plural Forms in Early Middle English* Ryuichi Hotta
No. 11 *Chunking and Instruction* Takayuki Nakamori
No. 12 *Detecting and Sharing Perspectives Using Causals in Japanese* Ryoko Uno
No. 13 *Discourse Representation of Temporal Relations in the So-Called Head-Internal Relatives* Kuniyoshi Ishikawa
No. 14 *Features and Roles of Filled Pauses in Speech Communication* Michiko Watanabe
No. 15 *Japanese Loanword Phonology* Masahiko Mutsukawa
No. 16 *Derivational Linearization at the Syntax-Prosody Interface* Kayono Shiobara
No. 17 *Polysemy and Compositionality* Tatsuya Isono
No. 18 *fMRI Study of Japanese Phrasal Segmentation* Hideki Oshima
No. 19 *Typological Studies on Languages in Thailand and Japan* Tadao Miyamoto et al.
No. 20 *Repetition, Regularity, Redundancy* Yasuyo Moriya
No. 21 *A Cognitive Pragmatic Analysis of Nominal Tautologies* Naoko Yamamoto
No. 22 *A Contrastive Study of Responsibility for Understanding Utterances between Japanese and Korean* Sumi Yoon
No. 23 *On Peripheries* Anna Cardinaletti et al.
No. 24 *Metaphor of Emotions in English* Ayako Omori
No. 25 *A Comparative Study of Compound Words* Makiko Mukai
No. 26 *Grammatical Variation of Pronouns in Nineteenth-Century English Novels* Masami Nakayama
No. 27 *I mean as a Marker of Intersubjective Adjustment* Takashi Kobayashi

Hituzi Linguistics in English

25

Makiko Mukai

A Comparative Study of Compound Words

HITUZI SYOBO

Copyright © Makiko Mukai 2018
First published 2018

Author: MAKIKO MUKAI

All rights reserved. Except for the quotation of short passages for the purposes of criticism and review, no part of this publication may be reproduced, stored in a retrieval system, or transmitted in any form or by any means, electronic, mechanical, photocopying, recording or otherwise, without the written prior permission of the publisher.

In case of photocopying and electronic copying and retrieval from network personally, permission will be given on receipts of payment and making inquiries. For details please contact us through e-mail. Our e-mail address is given below.

Hituzi Syobo Publishing

Yamato bldg. 2F, 2-1-2 Sengoku Bunkyo-ku
  Tokyo, Japan 112-0011
Telephone: +81-3-5319-4916
Facsimile: +81-3-5319-4917
e-mail: toiawase@hituzi.co.jp
http://www.hituzi.co.jp/
postal transfer: 00120-8-142852

ISBN978-4-89476-900-7
Printed in Japan

Acknowledgements

The research reported here has occupied me for a number of years, and in that time, I have benefited from the comments, questions, and suggestions of a number of linguistics. I would like to single out in particular the following: Anders Holmberg, Gunlög Josefsson, Heinz Giergerich, Seiki Ayano, Shigeru Miyagawa, Hideki Kishimoto, Youko Matsumoto, Ad Neeleman, Josef Emonds, Andrew Spencer, Melinda Whong, Heather Marsden, and the reviewers for the papers that I have published in the course of this work. I owe a special debt of gratitude to Adam Nichols, Lucy Carey and my father for proof-reading this book.

In addition, I thank all those who have sat through presentations of parts of this material and provided feedback, including audiences at Durham University, Newcastle University, Cambridge University, University of Bergen, the Germanic Linguistics Annual Conference at University of Wisconsin, Word-Formation Theories & Typology and Universals in Word-Formation at Šafárik University of Kosice, the Linguistic Society of Japan at University of Fukuoka, the International Spring Forum at Doshisha University, Morphology Lexicon Forum at University of Kounan, and Tsukuba Morphology Meeting at Tsukuba University.

I am also greatfrul for the following people for native speakers' judgements: Heather Marsden, Melinda Whong, Michelle Sheehan, Michael Barr, Simon Quinlan, Stephen Lyon, Claire George, Adam Nichols, Fiona Robinson, Laura All port, and Matthew Bilnski for English; Anders Holmberg, Gunlög Josefsson and Legolas Svarlsvarr for Scandinavian languages; Chisaki Fukushima, Hitoshi Mukai, Keiko Mukai, and Tomoka Mukai for Japanese.

Last but not least, I would like to thank all my friends and colleagues in Durham in UK and Kochi in Japan for their support. I would like to dedicate this book to my family, Hitoshi, Keiko and Tomoka Mukai, Simon and Sora Quinlan. Without their warm encouragement, I would never have completed this book. I would like to thank all the members of the publisher, Hituzi Syobo for agreeing to publish this research as a book. This publication was supported by JSPS KAKENHI Grant Number JP17HP1234.

Abstract

The aim of this book is to propose a structure for compounds, specifically compound nouns in Japanese, English and Mainland Scandinavian within the framework of Chomsky's Minimalist Program and Bare Phrase Structure (Chomsky 1995). The purpose is to show that words are derived in Narrow Syntax as phrases and that words must have asymmetrical structure, i.e. a head of the word should be determined.

The proposed structure of a compound noun in the languages in question is as follows:

(1)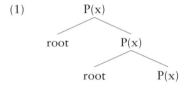

Structure (1) is derived with the following assumptions in mind.

1. The place of Morphology within the Minimalist Program is argued to be outside the Lexicon and after the Narrow Syntax. This has led several linguists to argue that a word is derived in the same way as a phrase. Moreover, linear order is redundant in the Narrow Syntax, since the structure determines the word order. As a result, it is not the Right-hand Head Rule proposed by Williams (1981) which determines the head of a compound word but the structure does. The Right-hand Head Rule may have a place in the phonology, though, in stipulating how a word derived in the Narrow Syntax is spelled out. The rule is formulated by Williams to apply in Morphology. In most current minimalist theories morphology is after spell-out. But the head must be determined before spell-out, since it determines the LF as well as determining aspects of the PF.

2. Nothing prevents us applying Merge at the level of the word as well as the phrasal level. As Williams' (1981) Right-hand Head Rule cannot be used

within the Minimalist Program, Collins (2002) definition of head is used for compound words. According to Collins, a head is a category which has one or more unsaturated features. Another stipulation taken from Collins (2002) is that when a lexical item is chosen from the lexical array and introduced to the derivation, the unsaturated features of this lexical item must be satisfied before any new unsaturated lexical items are chosen from the lexical array. The effect of these two assumptions is that when two categories α and β are merged, only one of them, say α, can have an unsaturated feature (which is not saturated by β), so α will be the head.

The structure (1) shows the following.
- First, a root without word class features is merged with a Property feature, the content of which is given by the root.
- The Property feature is represented above as P(roperty) (x) where 'x' represents the unvalued referential index.
- There are two ways to check P(x): one is assigning x a value, that is an index, and the other is deleting x. Since the P(x) feature is unsaturated in the sense that it needs a referential index from either D or DP, it is a head, and as such it percolates to the dominating node. Then, another root is merged to form a compound word. As P(x) is the only unsaturated feature before and/or after the root is merged, it is percolated and it is the head of the whole compound.

The present theory can account for the syntactic and semantic properties of a wide range of compounds, particularly noun-noun compounds in English, Japanese, and Mainland Scandinavian, within a syntactic theory based on minimalist assumptions.

Contents

Acknowledgements		V
Abstract		VII

CHAPTER 1
Parallelism between Morphology and Syntax within a Generative Framework

1.1	Lexicon and Lexicalisation	1
1.2	Parallelism of morphology and syntax in Word formation	4
1.3	Productivity and recursion in word formation	5
1.4	Why is it necessary to have a structure?	7

CHAPTER 2
Compound Word Formation

2.1	Common features of compound formation	11
2.1.1	Constituents of compound words	11
2.1.2	Bound morphemes and Compound word formation in the three languages	15
2.2	Lexical Integrity in Compound word formation	24
2.3	Phonological properties of compound words	30
2.3.1	Compound Stress Rule and Compound Accent Rule	30
2.3.2	Rendaku in Japanese compound words	37
2.4	Counter-argument for Lexical Integrity?	39
2.4.1	Plural as first constituent and the Lexicon	39
2.4.2	Genitive compound words in the three languages	45
2.4.3	Compound words but not lexical?	49
2.4.4	Phrasal compounds	50
2.5	Copulative (or Dvandva) compound words	53
2.6	Productive compounds in the three languages	56

CHAPTER 3
Structure of Compound Words

3.1	Structures for compound words in the GB framework	63
3.1.1	Transformational account of compound words	63
3.1.2	Lexical account of compound words	67
3.1.3	Lieber (1992)	77
3.1.4	Holmberg's analysis (1992)	84
3.2	Structures for compound words in the Minimalist Programme	91
3.2.1	Spencer's analysis (2003)	98
3.2.2	The theory by Roeper, Snyder & Hiramatsu (2002)	102
3.2.3	Problems of Roeper, Snyder & Hiramatsu's theory	114
3.2.4	Josefsson's (1997) theory	115
3.2.4.1	Lexicon	115
3.2.4.2	Structure	119
3.2.4.3	Non-head of compound words	120

CHAPTER 4
Proposed Structures of Compound Words

4.1.1	The Non-head of compound words in Japanese	129
4.1.2	The non-head of English compound words	131
4.1.3	Affix-driven vs. base-driven stratification of the lexicon	132
4.1.4	Criticism of the Lexicon within the framework of Lexical Phonology	139
4.2	Structure	140
4.2.1	The head of compounds in Japanese	140
4.2.2	Headedness?	144
4.3	Structures	152
4.3.1	Structures for 'cranberry morphemes'	152
4.3.2	Structures for genitive compounds, neoclassical compounds and other complex compounds in Scandinavian and English	152
4.3.3	Adjective-Noun/Adjective-Adjective compounds?	155
4.3.4	Structure for synthetic compounds	158
4.3.5	Recursive compounds	165
4.4	Recursion in other languages for Noun-Noun compound words	171
4.5	Phrasal compounds	188

4.6	Copulative compounds and Dvandva compounds in these languages	194
4.7	Weak points in other theories and analyses solved in my theory	196
4.8	Problems in this theory	197

CHAPTER 5
Conclusion

References	211
Appendix	220
Index	235

CHAPTER 1
Parallelism between Morphology and Syntax within a Generative Framework

The main aim of this study is to find a unified structure for compound noun words in English, Japanese and Mainland Scandinavian languages within the Minimalist Program (Chomsky 1995, 2000, 2001). The main focus of this study is underived noun compound words. The reasons for undertaking this research on compounding are as follows: Existing research includes many studies of compound words in many languages, but a detailed comparison of different languages has not been conducted. In addition, previous theories and analyses of compound words focus too narrowly on a specific language or a specific type of compound words. In this book, on the other hand, I will look at different types of noun compound words, including neo-classical compounds, genitive compounds, phrasal compound words, productive compound words, synthetic compound words, and recursive compound words in English, Japanese and Mainland Scandinavian languages.

This book is organised as follows. In Chapter One, I first discuss some characteristics of the lexicon of a language and ways in which a new word is lexicalised. This is followed by a consideration of the parallelism of morphology and syntax within the generative framework. This chapter will be followed by a detailed discussion of word formation in the languages in question in Chapter Two. Chapter Three criticises previously proposed theories of compound words within the Principles and Parameters approach and the Minimalist Program. Chapter Four presents a new, alternative theory. The conclusion of this book will be a summary of the characteristics of compound words in the languages discussed and the proposed theory which resolves the problems found in the previously proposed theories.

1.1 Lexicon and Lexicalisation

It is well known that the lexicon of a language consists mainly of morphologically simplex and complex words. Additionally, the lexicon consists of syntactic chunks that have unpredictable properties, the idioms of a language (Jackendoff[1] 1997: 161).

Another feature of the lexicon is that it is not a fixed list. One of the main functions of morphology is to expand the fund of lexical items. That is, morphological operations take words (simplex or complex) as their inputs and create more complex words. Most of these words are existing and they are listed in the lexicon. However, non-existing but possible words can also be used as input for word-formation processes.

The operations that create complex words in English, Japanese and Mainland Scandinavian are affixation and compounding. In addition, conversion, the change of the word class of a word without overt phonological effect, is also used to create new words. Other ways of extending the lexicon include acronyms, clipping, and blending[2].

According to Bauer (1983), a new word, whether it is simplex or complex, is coined by a speaker or writer on the spur of the moment to cover an immediate need. Different speakers in the same language community can use the same word on different occasions with different meanings. As soon as the speakers using the new word are aware of using a term which they have already heard, it stops being a new or nonce formation. For example, consider a possible English word *dunch* which was used by a non-native English speaker to cover the concept of a joined meal of lunch and dinner (in analogy with *brunch*), and a Japanese possible compound word, *huru-mori* 'old-forest' produced by a Japanese translator (in analogy of *huru-hon* (old-book) 'second-hand book'). Another type of new word is made up of non-existing words, as mentioned above.

The second stage of a new word is institutionalisation (Bauer 1983; Lipka 2002[3]). In other words, as soon as speakers have accepted the nonce word as a known word, only some of the possible meanings of the forms are used and the meaning must be accepted by speakers in the same language community. For instance, *Indian summer* is not a summer in India, but it is a period of usually warm and sunny weather during the autumn. The phenomenon of institutionalisation also can happen not only for word formation, but also for metaphor (e.g., *fox* can be conventionally used for a cunning person).

Many researchers have argued that the final stage of a nonce word is lexicalisation (Bauer 1983, Downing 1977, Booij 2002, Lipka 2002 and many others). The word is said to be lexicalised when it cannot be productively formed anymore. There are different types of lexicalisation; phonological (change of stress patterns and phonotactic change), semantic, morphological, syntactic and mixed lexicalisation. One can see that a new word is lexicalised when it has changed its stress pattern (see 2.3.1) and segmental features, e.g., a sound change affects a morph either only in isolation or only when it appears in combination with other morphs (e.g., Japanese *rendaku*, see 2.3.2).

Many lexicalised forms are semantically opaque. Even though Bauer (1983) states that opacity is not a necessary prerequisite for lexicalisation, one thing which is clear is that a lexicalised compound is a compound whose meaning is stored permanently in the lexicon. Therefore, the meaning does not have to be computed each time the compound is used. Whether a compound becomes lexicalised depends on its frequency in everyday use and its significance for the hearer. The semantic criterion for lexicalisation has been discussed by many researchers, such as Booij (2002).

Morphological change in a new word is another type of lexicalisation. For instance, linking elements in Scandinavian languages (see 2.1.1 for more details) are sometimes added to a stem when that stem is combined with another one (Bauer 1983). Nevertheless, there are not any firm rules for when the linking element is used except the case when the lefthand constituent is branching (see Chapter 3 and Chapter 4 for more discussion). In addition, in English with a large learned vocabulary from different branches of Indo-European languages, there are a number of derivatives which are closely related semantically and possibly etymologically, but which have different roots. Bauer (1983: 54) cites example pairs like *eat* and *edible*, *legal* and *loyal*, *opus* and *operation*, *right* and *rectitude* and many others. Another type of morphological lexicalised form can be seen in affixes. Similar to linking elements and roots, affixes can cease to be productive, e.g. *–ment* (e.g., *confinement, enlargement*), *-th*[4] (*length, warmth*). There are some constraints governing which roots these affixes can be added to.

The last type of lexicalisation, Bauer discusses, is syntactic in the sense that words are formed in the syntax (see Chapter 3). For example, when the prefix *dis-* is added to the verb *believe*, the resulting word *disbelieve* does not take an object, unlike its base verb. On the other hand, adding the same prefix to the verb *obey* does not change the syntactic function of the resulting word (e.g., *I disobey my parents*). Finally, Bauer argues that new words can be lexicalised with mixed features, including phonological or morphological. For example, the Danish compound word, *jord-e-moder* (earth-mother) 'midwife' is morphologically lexicalised because of the form with the linking element, but also, semantically lexicalised because the resulting word no longer has anything to do with the meaning of earth.

The degree of lexicalisation is discussed in Di Sciullo & Williams (1987) from the lexicalist perspective (see below) and by Baker (1988). Baker states that a high proportion of compounds are generated 'on-line' by speakers but many would say that words such as *outcast* or *navy blue* are more highly lexicalised than *soft fruit* while non-compounds like *hard fruit* or *nice man* are not lexicalised at all. In other words, the former words have a more permanent storage in the brain than the latter words.

In this thesis, I will assume the theory of the lexicon in Platzack (1993) and Josefsson (1997) which is based on Halle (1973). According to this theory, a list of morphemes and lexicons are separated places and all the lexicalised words are listed, including lexicalised compounds and derived words, but also phrasal idioms, and in general everything that is idiosyncratic and has to be learnt. This means it is possible to say that all compounds, productive as well as lexicalised ones are derived in the syntax, as will be discussed in Chapter 3 and Chapter 4.

1.2 Parallelism of morphology and syntax in Word formation

Throughout the history of the generative tradition two main ideas have developed regarding the issue of how to view the parallelism between words and phrases. One school argues that syntactic principles are responsible for the formation of words. This school is called the non-lexicalist school. By contrast, according to lexicalist school, principles governing the syntactic formation of phrases and the formation of words are separate.

From the non-lexicalist perspective, early works such as Lees (1960) claimed that a compound is formed by transformations from an underlying sentence, the main idea being that material in the underlying sentence was deleted (see Chapter 3). However, as the theory developed, the deletion transformation could not be maintained. One of the reasons was given by Chomsky (1965). He stated that a deletion can eliminate only a dummy element, or a formative explicitly mentioned in the structure index (for example, *you* in imperatives) (1965: 144–5). Baker (1988) supported Chomsky's argument of deletion by analysing a number of constructions in terms of syntactic head movement (for example, noun incorporation). Baker argues that there is no independent morphological component and that productive word formation takes place in the syntactic component.

In contrast, in the lexicalist school, a famous article by Chomsky "Remarks on Nominalization" (1970) claimed that idiosyncratic information belongs to the lexicon, and that transformations should deal only with regular correspondences between linguistic forms. In his work, Chomsky exemplified the English gerundive formation, which has the same meaning as the corresponding verb and is therefore assumed to be formed through a syntactic process. In contrast, however, other kinds of nominalisation with idiosyncratic meaning are not considered part of the syntactic process. Other linguists who followed

Chomsky in this tradition were Di Sciullo & Williams (1987). They argued that morphology and syntax should be separated. In this study, as indicated in Section 1.1, the non-lexicalist will be the standpoint that is primarily adopted (see Chapter 2). Therefore all compounding of words is believed to be done in the syntax.

1.3 Productivity and recursion in word formation

As discussed in the above sub-section, this thesis will take the non-lexicalist approach for compound word formation. One reason for this is that in many languages, compound word formation can be productive and recursive, just as phrase formation. Recursion is a fundamental property of human language which potentially differentiates human language both from other human cognitive domains and known communication systems in animals (Fitch, Hauser & Chomsky 2005). Before continuing this discussion it is important to define the term *productive*.

Potential measures of productivity in previous research, such as Aronoff (1976) first had the idea that an index of productivity for a word formation rule could be obtained by counting the number of actually occurring words that are formed by the rule, and comparing this with the number of words that could potentially be formed by that rule. In order to clarify the definition, Lieber (1992: 3) following Schultink (1961, cited in Lieber 1992) says:

> By productivity as a morphological phenomenon we understand the possibility for language users to coin, unintentionally, a number of formations which are in principle uncountable (Lieber 1992: 3).

The main points here are the notions of unintentionality and the ability to coin new words. By unintentionality, Lieber and Schultik mean that the creation of new words can go unnoticed. Speakers of the language are not conscious of using the newly coined words. With unproductive processes, on the other hand, a new word may sometimes be coined but such coinages will always draw attention to themselves and language speakers will find them amusing, odd or even unacceptable.

Plag's (2004) definition of productivity seems to give us a clearer picture. According to this definition, a morphological process is more productive than another if it is more accepted in the language, because it is constrained by fewer linguistic and non-linguistic factors of the language. Plag (2004) argues that extra-linguistic developments in society often referred to as 'fashion' make certain linguistic elements desirable, and therefore, productive to use. A typical example in Japanese is *–mitaina* 'like' which has started to be used by young speakers recently at the end of a sentence. Another example is a word 'sha-mail' which means text-message with a photograph. In English, it is fashionable recently to create computer-related words.

Another constraint is blocking[5]. The existing form blocks the creation of a semantically or phonologically identical derived form. For example, the existing word *thief* blocks the creation of the word **stealer*. Other examples would be optician or *dentist* blocks the compound word formation of *eye doctor* or *teeth doctor*. Also in Japanese, *ganka* blocks the compound word formation of *meisha* (eye+doctor).

In addition, Plag (2004), following Bauer (1983: 86), argues that the new word must denote something nameable. This is a pragmatic constraint. For example, Rose (1973: 516) gives the following example of an unlikely denominal verb-forming category: "grasp NOUN in the left hand and shake vigorously while standing on the right foot in a 2.5 gallon galvanized pail of corn-meal-mash." It is not possible to conceptualise this action in the real world, therefore these can be no such verb. Conceptually impossible words are often different in different cultures.

Moreover, there are linguistic constraints, including phonology, morphology, syntax, and semantics. The new word needs to be sensitive to phonological constraints, which can make reference to individual sounds and to syllable structure or stress. For example, nominal *–al* in English only attaches to verbs that end in a stressed syllable (e.g., *arrive* → *arrival, betray* → *betrayal*, but not *enter* → **enteral*, and *promise* → **promiseal*). Another example of phonological restrictions is that suffixation of verbal *–en* in English is subject to a segmental restriction: the last segment of the base can be /k/, /t/, / θ /, /s/, /d/, /p/ but must not be /n/, /ŋ/, /l/, or a vowel.

According to a morphological constraint, a certain affix is attached to a certain base. For example, every verb ending in the suffix *–ise* can be turned into a noun only by adding *–ation* (e.g., *organise* → *organisation, civilise* → *civilisation*).

Semantic restrictions can also be used on bases and derivatives. For instance, derivatives in *–ee* (*employee*) must denote sentient entities, to the effect that *amputee* cannot refer to an *amputated limb* (see Barker 1998)[6].

Finally, the most commonly mentioned type of constraint is the one referring to syntactic properties. For example, the adjectival suffix *–able* normally attaches to verbs, as in *readable*, but not, for example, to adjectives (e.g., **dirtyable*). In summary, Plag's (2004) definition of productivity is used in this thesis.

In many languages, it is possible to coin a compound noun freely and in principle there is no limit to the number of constituents a compound may have, due to the fact that a compound noun freely becomes the base of another compound noun (Namiki 1988). In this book, a new definition of recursivity will be proposed, based on the definition of Namiki (1988). (Chapter 4). In contrast to what Namiki argues, however, there is a limit for recursivity of compounding (Chapter 4). Another main aim of this book is to understand within the framework of the Minimalist Program why some languages do not have recursive compounding. Before understanding the reason for recursivity within the Minimalist Program, it is necessary to consider some important aspects of linguistics in terms of word formation.

1.4 Why is it necessary to have a structure?

The main goal of this book is to understand why it is possible for human beings to understand compound word formation. In other words, the aim of the book is to explain some properties of word formation within the genetically encoded linguistic structure in the human mind, Universal Grammar (Chomsky 1981). Chomsky claims that every child is born with a Universal Grammar. So with the help from the environment surrounding them, the child develops a language specific grammar. It is evident that since grammars of languages differ considerably, the Universal Grammar structure must be abstract. However, unlike what has been discussed by traditional grammarians within specific languages, the aim of generative linguistics is to find out whether at the appropriate abstract level all grammars share a common structure. Since this common structure is a biological property, grammars are constrained by it.

The basic aim of generative grammar has been to have a balance between explanatory adequacy (to explain how knowledge of the linguistic phenomena arises in the mind of speaker-hearer) and descriptive adequacy (to account for the phenomena of particular languages). In the Principles and Parameters theory, Parameters, such as head-parameters of morphology (Williams 1981, Selkirk 1982), have been proposed (see Chapter 3). For example, a child with Universal Grammar, once exposed to compounds with the head on the left-hand (Romance languages), as opposed to the right-hand (Japanese and Germanic languages), can then set their parameter to the appropriate setting. If so, a single computational system for human language and only limited lexical variety, such as morphological properties, can be assumed. In addition, Chomsky (2000, 2001, 2002) suggests that language is a perfect system with an optimal design in the sense that natural language grammars create structures which are designed to interface perfectly with other components of the mind, speech and thought systems.

The idea of perfection has led Chomsky to propose the Minimalist Program (1993, 1995, 2000). The only conditions are the Bare Output Conditions, eliminating stages such as Deep and Surface Structures[7], unlike in the Principle and Parameters approach. According to Chomsky, Bare Output Conditions are the conditions imposed from "external systems" at the interface, i.e. PF and LF. A syntactic structure, which is combined together by a series of syntactic computations in the syntax, ends up represented at the two interfaces, LF and the PF. Whereas the LF is input into semantic representation, the PF is input into phonetic representation.

In addition, Chomsky suggests that there should not be any new objects added in the course of computations. In particular, there should be no uninterpretable features at the LF interface, such as X-bar level (Chomsky 1981). Elements interpretable at the PF interface are not interpretable at the LF interface or conversely. So there is no interaction between the two interfaces at all[8].

In this thesis, words are assumed to be derived in the same way as phrases. This therefore implies that there is no direct relation between the sound and meaning for word formation either, and that a computation should be involved there before a new word is derived. If words are derived by the same rules as phrases, the resulting word should have an asymmetrical structure, i.e. a head of the word should be determined.

With these assumptions in mind, a structure for compound words in English, Japanese and Mainland Scandinavian languages within the generative linguistics framework is proposed. Knowledge of language, including compound words, relies on the structural relationships in the sentences or words rather than on the sequence of words or morphemes. If no structure is proposed, it is not possible to know how we determine which real-world object, event or concept the compound refers to, i.e. its reference: the compound word must have a head.

Within the Principles and Parameters approach, an X-bar structure is constructed of projections of heads selected from the lexicon. The head of a phrase is projected from X^0 to X' and then X' to XP. On the other hand, within the Minimalist Program, the head (or in Chomsky's (1995) terminology: *label* (Chomsky 1995: 244) is constructed from the two constituents α and β, each of which has a set of features. Chomsky argues that the simplest assumption would be that the label is either:

(1)
       a. the intersection of α and β.
       b. the union of α and β.
       c. one or the other of α, β.

He concludes that (1c) is right, because the options (1a) and (1b) cannot be right. He gives the following rationale: The intersection of α and β will generally be irrelevant to output conditions, often null; and the union will be not only irrelevant but 'contradictory' if α and β differ in value for some feature, which is the normal case. So the head is either α or β. Either one or the other projects and is the head of the new merged element. In this thesis, the issue of whether the head of a compound can be determined using the assumption (1c), as Chomsky claims (Chapter 4) will be discussed.

In summary, this chapter looked at the ways in which a new word is stored in the lexicon. In addition, the two main schools of thought, the lexicalist and non-lexicalist schools were discussed and it was concluded that the non-lexicalist school of thought will be followed within this thesis. This discussion was followed by the definition of the term *productivity* in relation to word formation. The next section looked at several reasons why it is necessary to assume that compound words have structure within the generative grammar, and why a word, like a phrase, also needs to have a head. The next chapter presents a comparative study of compound words in English, Japanese and Mainland Scandinavian.

Notes

1 Before Jackendoff, it was considered that a lexical item has to be a word and the margin of language. Therefore, idioms cannot be in the lexicon of a language, because almost all of them are sentences. However, Jackendoff said that in Lexical Conceptual Structure Framework, every item is linked. The LCS has Representational Modularity; language vs. non-language modular theory. Literal meaning and non-literal meaning, such as idioms are listed in the lexicon. This idea allows lexical licensing by listing and larger than X^0. So lexicon contains all sets of fixed expressions and represents the knowledge of language.

2 Blending can be analysed in the same way as compounding. The only difference is that it is spelled out differently/phonological deletion. Blending is where words that combine two words into one, deleting a material from one or both of the both words. Semantically, lots of resulting words are copulative than compounds. For example, in English, there are *Spanish+English* → *Spanglish* and *science + fiction* → *sci-fi*. And the phonological rules is that AB + CD → AD the first syllable and the last syllable. Clipping; just like truncations, is where the relationship between a derived word and its base is expressed by the lack of phonetic material in the derived word.

3 Lipka (2002) stresses the sociolinguistic aspects of words. In this thesis, Bauer's definition is used.

4 The morphological lexicalisation of affixes has been extensively discussed in the framework of Lexical Phonology (see Chapter 4). However, this is not the main focus of the thesis and so will not be discussed in detail.

5 See Aronoff (1976) and Rainer (1988) for more details on blocking.

6 Barker (1998) argues that the derivation of nominal *–ee* is constrained semantically, not syntactically. For example, it is not grammatical to say 'The doctor amputated John' whereas it is grammatical to say 'the doctor amputated John's leg'. So the *amputee* does not refer to the syntactic object of its verbal stem. The derivation of nominal *–ee* is grammatical as long as

the derived noun is episodically linked to its verbal stem. In other words, the derived noun has to be a member of participants who participates in the event which is characterized by the verbal stem.
7 See Chomsky (1993, 1995) for his conceptual and empirical grounds to eliminate the Deep and Surface Structures.
8 See Section 4.2 for my discussion on the referential index feature.

CHAPTER 2
Compound Word Formation

In the last chapter, the definitions of productivity, headedness within the Minimalist Program and lexicalist and non-lexicalist schools were taken into consideration. In this chapter, the main focuses will be on similar and different features of compound word formation observed in the languages in question, with a particular focus on noun-noun compound formation.

2.1 Common features of compound formation

2.1.1 Constituents of compound words

Roeper & Siegel (1978) (supported by Grimshaw 1990) define root compound words as compound words headed by underived nouns. This kind of compound word is different from the compound words headed by deverbal or deadjectival nouns. The head of the former type does not take an argument whereas the latter does.

As part of expanding the lexicon, word formation in English, Japanese and Mainland Scandinavian involves derivation and compounding. The defining criterion for compounding as opposed to derivation is that compounding is the combination of two independent words, while derivation arises when an affix is added to a base (*care+ful*, *un+acceptable*). Here, the term 'base' can be defined as a morpheme where an affix is added (Katamba 1993). The common feature of derivation and compounding is that they both form a new word from existing words. However, questions should be raised here: do all languages have the same compound word formation and what are the criteria for compounding in these languages[9]?

(2)   black+bird   [E]

(3)   match+box   [E]

In Japanese, compounds can be formed in a variety of ways. For example, constituents of compounds can be merely native words or combinations of words of different origin.

(4)   Native Compounds   [J]
      a. aki + zora   'autumn sky'
      b. hon + bako   'book case'
(5)   Hybrid Compounds   [J]
      a. Sino-Japanese + native: dai+dokoro   'kitchen'
      b. Sino-Japanese + foreign: sekiyu+sutoobu 'oil stove'
      c. foreign + Sino-Japanese: taoru+zi   'towel cloth'
      d. native + foreign: ita+tyoko   'chocolate bar'
      e. foreign + native: garasu+mado   'glass window'
      f. foreign + foreign: teeburu+manaa: 'table manner'

A compound word in English and Japanese is generally formed with two words (Bloomfield 1933: 227 and Bauer 1983: 53 and Kageyama 1999). Here, the term 'word' is defined as 'free morpheme', in contrast to 'bound morpheme'. A 'free morpheme' is a morpheme that need not be attached to other morphemes. In contrast, a 'bound morpheme' is a morpheme that must be joined to other morphemes, such as *un-*. The definition of compound word can be applied in the above examples, (2) – (5). Both words which form the compound word in the examples are free morphemes, on the face of it, as they need not be attached to other morphemes.

However, adjectival and verbal left-hand segments of compound words show different formations in Japanese. For example, see the following.

(6)   a. the verb *odouru* 'to dance'
         odori+ko
         dance+child
         'dancer'
      b. the verb *nagareru* 'to flow'
         nagare+boshi
         flow+star
         'shooting star'
      c. the verb *kuru* 'to come'
         ki+hazimeru
         come+start
         'start coming'

As the above examples (6a) – (6c) show, the left-hand segment of these compound words is different from the free morpheme of the verb. The verbal left-hand segment is not a free morpheme, but *renyookei* or 'an infinitive form' (Kageyama 1983) in traditional Japanese grammar, which needs to be merged with another morpheme to occur independently as a verb.

In addition, adjective- compound words show a similar phenomenon in Japanese.

(7)   a. the adjective *hurui* 'old'
           huru+hon
           old+book
           'second-hand book'
    b. the adjective *yowai* 'weak'
           yowa+ki
           weak+feeling
           'timidness'
    c. the adjective *kirei-na* 'beautiful'
           kirei+dokoro
           beautiful-place
           'Geisha'
    d. the adjective *sizuka-na* 'quiet'
           sizu+kokoro
           quiet+mind
           'mind with which you enjoy the present environment quietly'

The adjectives in (7a)-(7b) are called *i*-adjectives in traditional Japanese grammar and the last morph –*i* is deleted in compound words. It has its own inflectional paradigm for tense. When the past tense morpheme –*katta* is merged, the last morph –*i* is also deleted. It is assumed, therefore, that the morph is an inflectional suffix. Another type of adjective in Japanese is the *na*-adjective. To appear in a compound word, the last morph –*na* is deleted in (7c) and (7d). This type of adjective behaves more similarly to nouns in Japanese in that it does not have its own inflectional paradigm for tense. In general, if an adjective is to occur inside a compound, it cannot be inflected. An uninflected adjective cannot occur as an independent word, and is therefore not a free morpheme.

Scandinavian compound words present a similar phenomenon.

(8)   te+ske   [D]
        tea+spoon
        'tea spoon'
(9)   ord+bog   [D]

	word+book	
	'dictionary'	
(10)	fred+s+konference	[D]
	peace+LINK+conference	
	'peace conference'	
(11)	jul+e+gave	[D]
	Christmase+LINK+present	
	'Christmas present'	
(12)	kyrk+torn	[S]
	church+ø+ tower[10]	

The examples (8) – (9) are similar to English and Japanese compound words in terms of category levels of the constituents. They are free morphemes. In contrast, the examples (10) – (12) show that the left-hand and right-hand constituents of the compounds are different. The left-hand constituent of the compound word has either a linking element (example (10)), or vowel morpheme (example (11)). This is morphological change of lexicalisation discussed in 1.1. In the examples (10) and (11), according to Josefsson (1997), Holmberg (1992) and Mellenius (1997), the –s in the Mainland Scandinavian can be called a linking element or a liaison form and it is a morpheme without independent meaning. There are no firm rules for when the linking element is used, but it is found in the following cases: firstly, according to Holmberg (1992), requiring a linking element in this way is an idiosyncratic lexical property of some nouns, subject to dialectal and idiolectal variation. Secondly, according to Delsing (1993, cited in Josefsson 1997), stems corresponding to old words are more likely to have a linking element when used in the left-hand position of compounds. Examples are the following.

(13)	stol+s+ben,	skov+s+bryn,	sæd+e+mark,
	chair+LINK+leg,	forest+LINK+edge,	grain+LINK+field,
			Danish (also in Swedish/Norwegian)

Another type of compound word in Scandinavian languages is shown in case (12), seen in Swedish but not in Danish or Norwegian. In Swedish, there are two types of nouns, strong and weak nouns. According to Josefsson (1997), weak nouns are defined as nouns ending in –a/-e in the nominative singular, but where the final –a/-e is absent in the left-hand segment position of a compound or derivation. The following pair illustrates this case.

(14)	kyrka	kyrk + torn, kyrk + lig	[S]
	church	church +tower, church +LIG	

```
*kyrka + torn,    *kyrka +lig
hare              har +stek, *hare + stek
hare + roast
```

Josefsson states that the *–a/-e* weak nouns are inflectional, since the *–a/-e* is not allowed in the left-hand position of compounds and derivations, as shown above. If the *–a/-e* is inflectional this is expected, since inflectional features generally are allowed inside words. Other linguists such as Teleman (1969, cited in Josefsson 1997) state that the *–a/-e* is part of the stem. On the other hand, (Holmberg (1992) and Dahlstedt (1965, cited in Holmberg 1992) argue that the *–a/-e* are nominal word markers that encode the feature number.

Thus, in contrast to English, compound words in Scandinavian languages and Japanese are sometimes constituted by bound and free morphemes and elsewhere, two free morphemes.

2.1.2 Bound morphemes and Compound word formation in the three languages

The following examples are 'cranberry' words in English.

(15)   cran+berry
(16)   huckle+berry

If one looks at the surface of these words, they seem to be analysable as compound words, containing the word *berry* as head, preceded by a modifier. The element that precedes *berry* is a noun. In *elderberry*, the noun elder refers to the elder tree that produces *elderberries*; *elder* can be an independent word. Thus, it is a compound.

Nevertheless, it is difficult to analyze *huckleberry* and *cranberry*, since there is no *huckle* or *cran* shrub. The morphs, *huckle* or *cran* only appear in these words. According to Anderson (1992), it is not necessary to assume that *cran* or *huckle* is listed separately as a bound morpheme in the lexicon. It is only necessary to assume that there is a lexical entry for the word *cranberry* and it is a non-canonical example of compound word. Other words containing cranberry morphemes in English include *gruntle* in *disgruntle*, *couth* in *uncouth*, *ept* in *inept*, *shevel* in *dishevel*, *chalant* in *nonchalant*, and *kempt* in *unkempt*.

In Japanese, too, there are so-called cranberry morphemes. The basic unit of word formation is the single morpheme, either native or Sino-Japanese. In the case of Sino-Japanese morphemes, the smallest building block is represented by single Chinese characters like *kuu* and *koo*, which in turn are combined to form a word like *kuu-koo* 'airport'. Examples of 'cranberry morphemes' would be the following. Bolded font identifies the 'cranberry morphemes'.

(17) **ton-bo**[11]
dragon-fly+dragon-fly
'dragon-fly'

(18) mi-**so**
flavour-noisy
'soy-bean-paste'

(19) **na**-su
aubergine-child
'aubergine'

(20) **kai**-chuu
roundworm-insect
'roundworm'

In Scandinavian languages, too, cranberry morphemes are abundant (Josefsson: personal communication)[12],[13].

(21) **körs**+bär
+berry
'cherry'

(22) **vård**+tecken
guard[14]+symbol
'symbol'

(23) **hövit**+s+man
head[15]+LINK+man
'leader, captain'

(24) **ba**+bord
back+board
'starboard'

In Chapter 3, I will argue against Anderson's (1992) assumption that a cranberry morpheme is a lexical entry in the lexicon (see 3.2.4.1 for more discussion).

Another argument against the claim that compounding merges two free morphemes comes from examples of neoclassical compounding in English (Bauer 1983, Plag 2003). Bauer (1983) and Plag (2003) argue that new words can be formed by applying rules to smaller units than words. Bauer also claims the formation of neoclassical compounds is a counter-argument for Aronoff's (1976) word-based morphology (1976: 21). That is to say, a new word is not always formed by applying a regular rule to a single already-existing word. The examples are morphemes, shown in the table below.

Table 1: Neoclassical compounds in English (Plag 2003: 156)

Element	Meaning	Examples
astro-	'space'	astrophysics, astrology
bio-	'life'	biodegradable, biocracy
biblio-	'book'	bibliography, bibliotherapy
electro-	'electricity'	electrocardiography, electrography
geo-	'earth'	geographic, geology
hydro-	'water'	hydroelectric, hydrology
morpho-	'figure'	morphology, morphogenesis
philo-	'love'	philotheist, philogastric
retro-	'backwards'	retroflex, retrodesign
tele-	'distant'	television, telepathy
theo-	'god'	theocratic, theology
-cide	'murder'	suicide, genocide
-cracy	'rule'	bureaucracy, democracy
-graphy	'write'	sonography, bibliography
-itis	'disease'	laryngitis, lazyitis
-logy	'science of'	astrology, neurology
-morph	'figure'	anthropomorph, polymorph
-phile	'love'	anglophile, bibliophile
-phobe	'fear'	anglophobe, bibliophobe
-scope	'look at'	laryngoscope, telescope

The elements are borrowed from Greek or Latin and educated speakers of English know that these elements originally had their own individual meaning. These are often called 'neoclassical elements' (Plag 2003: 74). Although there is a claim that elements in neoclassical elements are affixes (Marchand 1969, Allen 1978, Siegel 1974 and Lieber 1980, Williams 1981), in this thesis, the claim that they are 'neoclassical elements' and not affixes is assumed.

Following Scalise (1984) and Plag (2003), I argue that these elements cannot be considered affixes. They sometimes can be the second element of a word, as in *franco-phile*, but they can also be the first element as *phi-anthropist*. A true affix is not this free; if it occurs to the left it is a prefix, whereas if it occurs to the right, it is a suffix. Furthermore, the items in question can be separated. For example, it is possible to say the following.

(25)   It does not matter if they are pro- or anti-Soviet.   (cf. Scalise 1984: 75)

However, with 'true' affixes, this is not possible to say.

(26)   *I do not know if he should be dis- or en-couraged.   (Scalise 1984: 75)

In addition, the items in question can sometimes combine quite freely with each other as in the followings.

(27)   An Anglo-Soviet production[16].

Again, this is not the case with 'true' affixes.

Moreover, Plag (2003) convincingly argues that neoclassical elements are not affixes. According to him, an affix can combine with a bound root (not an affix and not a neoclassical morpheme) (cf. e.g., *bapt-ism*, *prob-able* which are not neoclassical compounds, but bound-root + affix) but cannot combine with another affix to form a new word (e.g., **re-ism*, **dis-ism*, **ism-able*). Moreover, a bound root can take an affix (cf. e.g., *bapt-ism*, *prob-able* which are not neoclassical compounds, but bound-root + affix), but cannot combine with another bound root (e.g., **bapt-prob*). On the other hand, neoclassical elements can combine either with bound roots (e.g., *glaciology, scientology*), with words (*lazyitis, hydro-electric, morpho-syntax*), or with another neoclassical element (*hydrology, morphology*) to make up a new word.

According to Bauer (1998b), neoclassical compound words show similar semantic behaviour to that of other types of compounds. As Allen (1978) states, compounds are subject to the ISA condition. This condition implies that N1+N2 *is a* kind of N2. For instance, *houseboat* is a hyponym of boat. In neoclassical compounds, the semantic relationship between the two elements shows that of the modifier and the modified. For instance, *hydro-electric* is a hyponym of electricity; *glaciology* is a hyponym of *-logy* which means 'study' in Greek. In contrast, a derivation such as *kind-ness* is not a hyponym of *-ness* or *foundation* is not that of *-ation*.

Another similarity between neoclassical compounds and compounds is that neoclassical compounds have a semantic value or density more similar to that of lexemes than to derivatives. Allen's (1978) Variable R Condition "predicts that the complete semantic content of the first constituent element may fill any one of the available feature slots in the feature hierarchy of the second constituent element, as long as the feature slot to be filled corresponds to one of the features of the filler" (Allen 1978: 93). For example, the compound *fire-man* has a range of possible meanings, such as *man who worships fire, man who walks on fire, man who sets fire, man who puts out fires* and so on, although it has a conventional meaning (Scalise 1984: 91). This is also true in neoclassical compounding. Bauer gives the following examples.

(28)   a. geology   study of the earth
       b. neurogilia   glue that sticks the nerves together
       c. photograph   drawing made by light

d. phytochrome   colour in plants   (Bauer 1998b: 405)

Finally, if the internal constituents of words such as *franco-phile* are labelled as prefix and suffix, respectively, most morphological theories would have problems in deriving the external label adjective. As a result, a structure of this type behaves more like a compound than like a derived word. This can be seen, for example, in cases where an *o* appears in the compounds in (28) as well as in combinations in which the second element is one of the items in question, and in particular, one with the strata feature of [+Greek]. Typical examples are *music +logy →musicology, dialec*t + *logy→dialectology*. Scalise (1984) states that the problem raised here can be easily resolved if we consider the items in question to be 'stems' rather than affixes. For example, it is not necessary to identify that the item such as *phile* is a prefix or suffix. If we consider all of the morphemes in neoclassical compounding as stems, not affixes, we do not have the above problems mentioned[17].

Interestingly, Plag (2003) has found some phonological generalisations for linking elements inside neoclassical compound words in English. For example, he claims that if there is already a vowel in the final position of the first combining form or in the initial position of the final combining form, the linking element does not appear. Typical examples are *tele-scope*, *laryng-oscope* and *polymorph*. In contrast, there is a linking morpheme when the initial combining form ends with a consonant and the final combining form begins with one. *Gastronomy* and *gastrography* are two examples and the alternate of *gastro* is *gastr-*. With the combining form, *gastr-*, there is no linking morpheme, e.g., *gastritis*. However, the generalisation does not work for all combining forms. This is the case, because there are no alternate forms of *bio-* and *geo-*(**bi-*, **ge-*). Thus, Plag concludes that the status of the linking element is not the same in all neoclassical compounding. The phenomenon of overt linking element is not found in other types of English compounding apart from genitive compounds (see 2.4.2 for more discussion).

In general, a characteristic of neoclassical compounding which is different from other compounding is its phonological aspect. Plag (2003) argues that the phonological properties of neoclassical compounds are not the same as those of other compound words; consider the following examples.

Table 2: The phonology of neoclassical compounds in English
astro-phýsics   astrólogy
biodegradable   biócracy
biblio-thérapy   bibliography
electro-cárdiograph
electro-cárdogram

geo-chémist geógraphy
hydro-eléctric hydrógraphy
laryng-ítis
poly-mórph

súicide, génocide
ánglophobe
télescope
ánglophile

(cf. Plag 2003: 157 (31))

The examples in the left-hand column do not show the usual leftward stress pattern, but have their main stress on the right-hand member of the compound. In the column on the right, the first elements have stress, just like compounds in general. This phenomenon happens when the second element is -*logy*, -*cide*, -*scope*, -*phobe*, - *phile*, and -*graphy*.

In Mainland Scandinavian, too, there are a number of neoclassical compound words. The examples are very similar to those in English.

Table 3: Neoclassical compounds in Danish/Norwegian/Swedish

Element	Meaning	Examples
astro-	'space'	astrofysisk, astrologi
bio-	'life'	biografi, biochemi
biblio-	'book'	bibliografi, biblioterapi
elektro-	'electricity'	elektrocardiografi, elektrografi
geo-	'earth'	geografi, geologi
hydro-	'water'	hydroelektrisk hydrologi
morfo-	'figure'	morfologi, morfogenesis
filo-	'love'	filoteist, filogastrisk
retro-	'backwards'	retroflex, retrodesign
tele-	'distant'	television, telepati
teo-	'god'	teokratisk, teologi
*-cide	'murder'	N/A
-krati	'rule'	bureaukrati, demokrati
-grafi	'write'	sonografi, bibliografi
-it is	'disease'	laryngitis, meningitis
-logi	'science of'	astrologi, neurologi
-morph	'figure'	anthropomorph, polymorph
-fil	'love'	francofil
-skop	'look at'	laryngoskop, teleskop

Apart from few neoclassical elements, like –*cide* and –*phobe*, Scandinavian languages show similar elements as found in English. As they are almost the same as the English ones, it is not necessary to test whether they are different from derivational affixes.

Similarly, in Japanese compound words there is a type of compound word which can be considered a neoclassical compound. Both elements in these compounds are bound morphemes. As in English, they are considered compounds in Japanese (Kageyama 1983, Tsujimura 1996). In the case of Sino-Japanese morphemes, the smallest building block is represented by single Chinese characters like *kuu* and *koo*, which in turn are combined to form two-character words like *kuu-koo* 'airport'.

(29) a. min-zoku   to   ka-zoku
        people-family and house-family
        'the nation and family'
     b. *min-to ka-zoku
        people and house-family
(30) a. koku-doo to ho-doo
        country-road and walk-road
        'national road and pavement'
     b. *koku- to ho-doo
        country- and walk-road
(31) a. moku-roku to ki-roku
        eye-record and write-record
        'list and written record'
     b. *moku- to ki-roku

The grammatical examples, (a), show that the two-Chinese-character words stand independently, whereas the (b) examples cannot. Therefore, this type of word formation is similar to English neoclassical compounds in that we are not dealing with the formation of words from other words, but the formation words from morphemes smaller than words.

Moreover, they are similar to English neoclassical compounds, as both elements of the compound are not affixes. They can appear as the first and second element freely (see below), like morphemes in English neoclassical compounds can. Compound words made up of Sino-Japanese words are considered neoclassical compound words in this thesis (see also Mukai 2004). The English neoclassical compounds are called neoclassical compounds, as they used to be compound words in their original languages, such as Greek and Latin. In Japanese, too, the neoclassical compound-type compounds used to be compound words in their original language, i.e. Chinese.

(32) u   -ki
     rain -season
(33) ki   -setsu
     season -season

'season'
(34) setsu -bun
season -division
'the day before the spring day'
(35) ki -setsu
season -season
'season'
(36) hi -kki
pen -record
'writing by pen'
(37) ki -roku
record -record
'record'

The second elements of the examples (32), (34), and (36) are the same as the first elements in (33), (35) and (37), respectively. Thus, in both English and Japanese, the contrast between derivation and compounding is clearly seen in the aspect of neoclassical compounding.

Another similarity between neoclassical compounds and compounds in Japanese is semantic, as observed in English. It is possible to see that the above examples are subject to Allen's Variable R condition. For example, *hi-kki* is a hyponym of *ki* 'writing' (a form of writing by pen) and *u-ki* is a rainy season, so a hyponym of season. The other examples show equal relationships between the two, namely, that of dvandva compounds (see 2.4 for further discussion of dvandva compounds).

As discussed above, in English an affix can combine with a bound root. In Japanese, when a derivational affix (e.g., *oo-* 'big', *ko-* 'small') is combined with a bound root, its pronunciation changes to that of Chinese and thus, becomes like a neoclassical element (e.g., ***dai-gaku*** (big-study) 'university', ***shoo-kan*** (small-officer) 'I'). Further examples are given below in Table 4. According to Tsujimura (1996), bound elements like *oo/dai-* 'big', *ko/shoo-* 'small', *hi-* 'non', *hu-* 'anti-', and *zen-* 'all' are affixes.

Table 4: Japanese neoclassical compounds

Affix	An affix with a stem	An affix with a neoclassical element
oo-	a. oo-daiko 'big-drum' b. oo-ame 'heavy rain' c. oo-yuki 'heavy snow'	a. dai-gaku (big-study) 'university' b. tai-ka (big-fire) 'conflagration' c. tai-ga (big-river) 'large river'

ko-	a. ko-guma small-bear 'little bear' b. ko-tori 'small bird'	a. shoo-kan (small-officer) to call oneself an officer b. shoo-sei (small-student) 'me' (used by a male speaker to be modest) c. shoo-koku (small-country) 'minor state'

Therefore, the 'affix' is more like a bound root, resulting in a neoclassical compound.

In contrast, many 'affixes' in Japanese cannot be combined with each other.

Table 5: Affixes in Japanese

Affix	Combined with another affix
hu-	*hu-hi *'anti-non' *hu-ko *'anti-small' *hi-oo *'anti-big'
doo-	*doo-zen *'the same-all'

Zen-, doo-, dai-, and *shoo*- are considered affixes. Structurally they are similar to compounds in that the morphemes which are attached to can be called roots (bound morphemes. But *doo*- is affixed to a free morpheme and no rendaku, which is one of the main characteristics of compounding in Japanese.

In this section, some characteristics of compound words in Japanese, English and Mainland Scandinavian languages have been discussed. As the comparison between compound words in the languages showed, all of the languages have compound words consisting of free morphemes. However, there are also compounds in Japanese and Mainland Scandinavian languages that have bound morphemes as constituents. In addition, Scandinavian languages provided a linking element. Thus, the criterion of compounding in contrast to derivation is not always that compound words are constituted of what looks like two free morphemes (I will discuss more in Chapter 4) whereas derivation is with affix attached to a base. This argument is supported when we look at 'cranberry morphemes' in English and 'neoclassical compounds' in English, Scandinavian languages and Japanese. Secondly, according to Anderson (1992) 'cranberry morphemes' are listed in the lexicon, not as derivational morphemes, but as parts of compounds (see more discussion on this in 3.2.4.1).

The next section will focus on Lexical Integrity in compound formation in English and Japanese. The main concern will be to discuss whether all compound words in the languages are formed in the lexicon, not the syntax.

2.2 Lexical Integrity in Compound word formation

Are all compounds different from their corresponding phrases? According to Di Sciullo & Williams (1987), there are three ways in which words can be distinguished from phrases. Firstly, a word is a morphological object, constructed out of morphological atoms, i.e. morphemes, by processes of affixation and compounding.

Secondly, according to Di Sciullo & Williams (1987), another criterion for words is that of listed objects. According to Lexical Integrity, no parts of a word can be separated, moved, or deleted by rules of syntax. To describe this idea, Di Sciullo & Williams (1987) coin the term *listeme*. Listemes can be defined as the linguistic expressions memorised and stored by speakers. However, they also admit that just because an expression is listed does not mean that it is a word. There are morphological objects which are formed by a perfectly regular and exceptionless process whose products are not therefore listed. For example, they illustrate the derivational deadjectival nouns formed by *-ness* affixation in English. This affixation is regular and said to be productive. On the other hand, some objects, such as idioms, are listed (Jackendoff 1997), yet, they are not words. They are items governed by syntax. For example, in the Japanese idiom *neko o kaburu* (cat ACC wear) 'pretend to be shy', there is accusative case, so it is a phrase, yet the lexical elements *neko* and *o* cannot be moved from their original positions, because the idiom has Lexical Integrity. For instance, the object *neko* cannot be topicalized.

Thirdly, words are syntactic atoms, i.e. the indivisible building blocks of syntax: Di Sciullo & Williams' Lexical Integrity (1987). According to Lexical Integrity, morphology and syntax are entirely separate domains of inquiry.

The following examples of compounds show that pronominal reference is not allowed in words, i.e. words are anaphoric islands[18].

(38)   blackbird '*turdus merula*'
       → *I wanted to see a blackbird and a blue one.
(39)   black bird 'a bird which is black'
       → I wanted to see a black bird and a blue one.
(40)   car salesman
       → *John went to see a car$_i$ salesman and he did not like any of them.
(41)   a salesman who sells cars
       → John went to see a salesman who sells cars$_i$ and he did not like any of them$_i$.

Examples (38) and (40) are ungrammatical whereas their corresponding phrase examples (39) and (41) are grammatical. Thus, *blackbird* and *car salesman* are compound words, whereas *black bird* and *a salesman who sells cars* are phrases[19].

Let us see more examples of compound words.

(42)   car salesman
       →*[big car] salesman
(43)   White House
       →*very White House

Words are built on a base of words and bound morphemes, not on phrases. This constraint is called the No Phrase Constraint (developed by Allen 1978; the name was introduced by Botha 1981, Roeper & Siegel 1978).

On the other hand, the No Phrase Constraint is violated in the following examples.

(44)   wine glass
       →[red wine] glass
       →red [wine glass]

Red wine glass can mean both a glass for red wine and wine glass which is red. Note that *red wine* has end-stress whereas *wine glass* has forestress (see more on Compound Stress Rule in Section 2.3.1). According to the Compound Stress Rule, *red wine* is not a compound whereas *wine glass* is a compound[20]. However, the string *very red wine* is not grammatical. In addition, *red wine and white one* is not possible, like the example (38). So *red wine* is more similar to a compound than a phrase. Therefore, the distinction between phrases and compounds is not clear-cut in this case.

In Japanese, compound words are formed in the lexicon, therefore a similar test to that used for English compound words is applicable for assessing Japanese compound words also. It is not possible to modify one part of a compound word, as the following examples show.

(45)   a. hansamu na [otoko+onna]
          handsome-ADJ [man+female]
          'a handsome manly female'
       b. *[hansamu na otoko] onna]
          *[handsome ADJ man] female]
(46)   a. ookina [kuruma hanbaiin]
          big   [car   salesman]
          'a big car salesman'
       b. *[ookina kuruma] hanbaiin

*[big   car]   sales-man

The adjective *hansamu-na* cannot modify the noun *otoko* in example (45). Similarly, in example (46), the noun *kuruma* cannot be modified by the adjective noun.

Moreover, in Japanese, too, pronominal reference is not allowed in words, as the following examples show. Note that in example (47), the initial sounds of the second constituents, *sara* 'tray' are voiced when they are combined with another word. This is a clear indication that the construction is a compound (see 2.3.2).

(47) hai+zara 'ash+tray'
    a. otite-iru hai$_i$ o hirotte sono sara ni ire-nasai.
        fallen-is ash$_i$ ACC pick-and ash$_i$ tray in put-IMP.
        'Gather the ashes on the floor and put them in the ashtray.'
    b. *otite-iru hai$_i$ o hirotte sore$_i$-zara ni ire-nasai.
        fallen-is ash$_i$ ACC pick-and it$_i$-tray in put-IMP.

(48) yama+nobori
     mountain+climb
     'mountain climbing'
    a. *yama$_i$+nobori no suki na hito wa soko$_i$ de sinde mo
        mountain$_i$+climb GEN like MOD person TOP there$_i$ at die too
        honmoo da to omotteiru.
        desire   COP COMP thinking
        'People who like mountain$_i$ climbing wish to die there$_i$.'
    b. yama$_i$ ga noboru no ga suki na hito wa soko$_i$
        mountain$_i$ NOM climb GEN NOM like MOD person TOP there
        de sinde mo honmoo da to omotteiru.
        at die too desire COP COMP thinking
        'People who like mountain$_i$ climbing wish to die there$_i$.'

Examples (47) and (48) show that part of a word cannot hold an anaphoric relationship with another item elsewhere.

In contrast, the following examples show that a part of a word can sometimes hold an anaphoric relationship with another item elsewhere. Note that the initial sound of the second constituent, *hako* 'box' is voiced when it is combined with another word.

(49) match+bako 'match+box'
    a. table no ue ni match$_i$ no hako o mitsukete sono$_i$ naka no
        table GEN on DAT match$_i$ GEN box ACC found after that$_i$

ippon   ni   hi o   tuketa.
inside GEN one DAT fire ACC lit
'When I found a box of matches$_i$ on the table I lit one of them$_i$'.
b. table no   ue ni   match$_i$+bako o   mitukete sono$_i$ naka no
   table GEN on DAT match box   ACC found that$_i$ inside GEN
   i-ppon ni   hi o   tuketa.
   one-CL DAT fire ACC lit
   'When I found a match$_i$box on the table I lit one of them$_i$'.

The grammaticality of the sentence (b) might be because the 'anaphor' in this case is not a definite pronoun but an indefinite null noun, with only the classifier pronounced. There are some examples which seem to support this argument.

(50) kasi+bako
      snack+box
      'box for snacks'
      a. kasi$_i$+bako o   mitukete sono$_i$ naka no i-kko   o   tabeta.
         snack$_i$+box ACC found-and that$_i$ inside GEN one-CL ACC ate
         'I found a snack-box and ate one of them'.
      b. kasi$_i$+bako o   mitukete sore$_i$ o   tabeta.
         snack$_i$+box ACC found-and that$_i$ ACC ate
         'I found a snack-box and ate it'.

The sentence (50b) is grammatical but *sore* does not necessarily refer to particular snack, but it can be any snack inside the box.

(51) inu+goya
      dog+house
      'kennel'
      a. inu$_i$+goya no   naka o   mitara   i-ppiki haitteita.
         dog$_i$+house GEN inside ACC looked-and one-CL entered
         'When I looked inside the kennel, one dog was there'.
      b. *inu$_i$+goya no   naka o   mitara   sore$_i$ ga   haitteita.
         dog$_i$+house GEN inside ACC looked-and that$_i$ NOM entered
         'When I looked inside the kennel, it was there'.
(52) yoohuku+dansu
      clothes+wardrobe
      'wardrobe'
      a. yoohuku$_i$+dansu o   akete   i-cchaku o   toridasita.
         clothes$_i$-wardrobe ACC open-and one-CL ACC took-out

'I opened the wardrobe and took one piece of clothing out'.
b. *yoohuku$_i$+dansu o akete sore$_i$ o toridasita.
   clothes$_i$-wardrobe ACC open-and that$_i$ ACC took-out
   'I opened the wardrobe and took one piece of clothing out'.

One finds a similar effect with *one* in English[21]. These examples in Japanese are problems for the Lexicalist school of compound words. This is, however, not unexpected in the proposed theory presented in Chapter 4. Another case which shows this is that of phrasal compounds, such as *a pipe-and-slipper husband*. These will be discussed in Section 2.4. 4.

Since no syntactic operation such as focusing or topicalising can take place inside a word, Kageyama (1983, 1993, 1999) argues that elements, such as *sae* 'even', *mo* 'also' and *dake* 'only', cannot be inside compound words. These elements have the function of focusing or topicalising a phrase.

(53) a. aki+zora mo
       autumn-sky also
       'autumn sky, too'
    b. *aki mo zora
       autumn also sky

(54) a. dai+dokoro dake
       table+place only
       'only kitchen'
    b. *dai dake dokoro
       table only place

According to this test, these compounds are words not phrases since no syntactic operation like focusing or topicalisation should occur inside a word.

Compound words are different from Noun Phrases or Determiner Phrases in Scandinavian languages, too.

(55) te+ske
     'tea+spoon'
     a. *Når jeg fandt en te$_i$+ske   i York kunne jeg drikke den$_i$ efterhånd.
        When I found a tea$_i$+spoon in York could I drink it$_i$ later.
        'When I found a good teaspoon in York I drank it later'.
     b. ske for teen
        Når jeg fandt en ske for teen$_i$ i York, kunne jeg drikke den$_i$
        When I found a spoon for tea$_i$-the in York, could I drink it$_i$
        efterhånd.
        afterwards

'When I found a spoon for the tea in York I could drink it afterwards'.

(56) fred+s+konference
peace+LINK+conference
'peace conference'
   a. Der holdtes en fred$_i$+s+konference i Danmark. *Mange mennesker
      There held a peace$_i$+LINK+conference in Denmark. *Many people
      talte om den$_i$.
      talked about it$_i$.
      'There was a peace$_i$ conference in Denmark. *Many people talked about it$_i$.'
   b. konference til fred
      Der holdtes en konference til fred$_i$ i Danmark. Mange mennesker
      There held a conference for peace$_i$ in Denmark. Many people
      talte om den$_i$.
      talked about it$_i$.
      'There was a conference about peace in Denmark. Many people talked about it'.

In many cases, compounds are more similar to words than to phrases. As discussed in Chapter 1, lexicalisation is the final stage which a new word goes through. Usually, the meaning of the lexicalised word becomes non-compositional or even totally idiosyncratic. Similarly, compounds can have meanings that are related to, but not fully deduced from those of their components. For instance, the meaning of the Japanese compound word, *cha+wan* 'rice bowl' which originally means 'tea-bowl' cannot be deduced from the meaning of its constituents anymore.

Other examples are the following;

(57) te+brev (tea+letter)→teabag, dag+hjem (day+house)→nursery   [D]
(58) hime+yuri (princess+lily) → star lily   [J]
(59) dai+dokoro (table+place)→kitchen   [J]
(60) tsuki+mi+soo (moon+look+grass)→evening primrose   [J]
(61) ge+kkei (month+already)→ menstruation   [J]
(62) black+bird   [E]
(63) spring+roll→pastries filled mostly with julienned vegetables   [E]

However, as discussed in Chapter 1, semantic opaqueness is not a necessary condition for lexicalisation. There are a number of compound words in the languages in question whose meaning can be deduced from that of their components, even though they are lexicalised. For example, the lexicalised meaning of *tea pot*, *match box* or *kitchen equipment* can be deduced from that of its constituents. *Tea pot* is a pot for tea; *match box* is a box which contains matches and *kitchen equipment* is equipment used in a kitchen. Also, the meaning of a compound can be deduced from that of its components in not-fully-lexicalised compounds and the relation between their constituents has to be computable for novel ones (Clark 1993). Examples of this kind of compound will be discussed later in 2.5.

In this section, it has been argued that compounds are more similar to words than phrases according to Di Sciullo & Williams' (1987) Lexical Integrity. However, there are some examples which indicate that Lexical Integrity is not as clear-cut as Di Sciullo and Williams' claim. The lexicality of compound words is also considered in terms of the semantic idiosyncrasy of the word. The meaning of a compound cannot always be deduced completely from its constituents. It is obvious that the meaning of compound words does change over time. In the next section, the phonological properties of compounds in the languages will be compared.

2.3 Phonological properties of compound words

2.3.1 Compound Stress Rule and Compound Accent Rule

It is true of all languages that words also have phonological properties. Many linguists state that a Compound Stress Rule (Chomsky & Halle 1968) can tell us whether the word is a compound or not (in the case of a stress language, such as English and Mainland Scandinavian languages). In English and Mainland Scandinavian languages, for example, the Compound Stress Rule yields a stress pattern with the main stress on the initial element[22].

Compound Stress Rule

(64) bláck+bird   [E]
(65) mátch+box   [E]
(66) té+ske   [D]
      tea+spoon
      'teaspoon'
(67) bóg+reol   [D]
      book+shelf
      'bookshelf'
(68) fréd+s+konference   [D]

peace+LINK+conference
(69) júl+e+gave [D]
Christmas+LINK+present

Similarly in Swedish, compound words are stressed with a particular stress pattern, compound stress. According to Mellenius (1997), Swedish compounds are pronounced with a particular intonation contour, characterised by two peaks. The intonation contour includes two stressed syllables: the first where the stress is placed in the first base of the compound when this is pronounced as an isolated word, and the second at the place of the stress of the last base of the compound, when it is pronounced in isolation. For example:

(70) a. hus+nyckel
        house+key
         ↘ ↗
     b. hus'nyck'el
(71) a. central+lasarett
        central+hospital
         ↘   ↗
     b. centra'llasarett'
        centralhospital

As the examples demonstrate, compound words have the stressed syllable of each constituent of the compound, indicated by '. Moreover, the first stress has a falling tone, marked by a falling down arrow; the last stress has a rising tone, marked by a rising arrow. Scandinavian languages do not seem to show any exceptions in the phonological aspect of compound words (Klinge 2010).

However, the distinction between left-stress and right-stress in English is difficult to apply, and many linguists have discussed how to treat compounds with right-stress (see Lieberman & Sproat 1992, Giegerich 2003, Spencer 2003). In fact, there are compound words in English which have right-stress. Typical examples are *black whale, white noise* and *brown bear* (Giegerich 2003). Lieberman & Sproat (1992) argue that such expressions are N^1 categories. That is, one-bar level categories in the X-bar hierarchy, as opposed to 'well-behaved' compounds such as (64) and (65) which are N^0 categories. Nevertheless, they failed to find evidence supporting the other half of the hypothesis, whereby N^0 constructions, which they crucially but wrongly assumed to uniformly have primary stress on the first constituent, systematically arise in the lexicon.

Another explanation is given by Spencer (2003). Spencer (2003) gives examples such as *cake-* and *street-*compounding: *apple píe, bakewell tárt,* *apricot crúmble,* but *cárrot cake; London Róad, Penny Láne, Peyton Pláce,* but *Óxford Street.* Other good examples are terminology for organisations, such as *World Bánk* and *World Córt* (my analysis). Regarding these compounds with right-stress, Spencer (2003) proposes that stress patterns are determined by semantic 'constructions' defined over collections of similar lexical entries[23]. Below are the examples cited by Spencer. The bolded words have primary stress.

(72)   lexicalised   non-lexicalised
   a. eye+ball   **Capsicum**+ leaf
   b. rice+**pudding**   dingo+**stew**
   c. **toy**+ factory   toy+ **factory**   (Spencer 2003: 6)

Spencer concludes that in English the left-stress tends to be associated with lexicalisation as much as with compounding but that individual words which regularly feature in compounds (especially as heads) can create their own islands of systematicity, sometimes in opposition to a prevailing trend for words of the same semantic field (see the Appendix). However, his semantic categorisations are limited to special fields, such as music, chess, and so on. Many linguists have attempted to systematise semantic fields for compound words, but no one has provided a conclusive result.

Giegerich (2003) states that compound words with primary stress on the second constituent are quite common, which was why Lieberman and Sproat could not provide sufficient evidence of the category of N'. Giegerich states that all fore-stressed N-Ns must be lexical as the semantic relationship between the two elements in this type of construction is not predictable. Typical examples are:

(73)   battle+field   seat+belt
       fruit+market   wind+screen
       glass+case   fog+horn
       hand+cream   hair+net
       milk+bottle   tea+spoon
       tear+gas   mosquito+net
       tooth+paste   shoe+horn
       toy+factory   hair+oil
       sparrow+hawk   brick+yard   (Giegerich 2003: 8)

According to Giegerich, the semantic relationships between the two constituents in these compounds demonstrate the paraphrase of 'N for N'. These compounds have primary stress on the first constituent. Their precise meanings depend on the speakers' real-world knowledge, not linguistic knowledge. For example, *mosquito-net* is a net used to keep mosquitoes out, not to capture them inside the net. So the lexicalised meaning of the compound words above must be listed. According to Giegerich, it is possible to state that none of these compounds have the relationship 'A that is a B'. Moreover, this type of construction is lexical according to Lexical Integrity. For example, it is not possible to have a coordination like: **a hair-net and a mosquito one*.

However, if the constructions have stress on the second constituent, the compounds have an 'A that is a B' relationship (Radford 1988: 197).

(74) sparrow+hawk   'hawk that is a sparrow'
      toy+factory   'factory that is a toy'
      milk+bottle   'bottle made of milk'
      glass+case   'case made of glass'
      tooth+paste   'paste made of tooth'
      hair+oil   'oil made of hair'
      hair+net   'net made of hair'
      tear+gas   'gas made of tears'
      brick+yard   'yard made of bricks'   (Giegerich 2003: 8)

The semantic relationship between the two constituents in these examples is a default relationship and according to Giegerich, it is treated in the syntax, not in the lexicon. Attributive NN constructions, as represented in (74) are those whose relationship between the head and modifier are those of attributes. The test for lexical status from the coordination confirms that the construction (74) is phrasal: e.g., *hair net* (net made of hair), it is possible to say *a hair net and a strong one*.

Giegerich gives other types of examples for attributive N-N constructions: the examples of N-Ns which have end-stress, not fore-stress. Typical examples are *steel bridge, silk shirt, stone wall, aluminium room, plastic lawn, chocolate fence* and *rubber radio* (Giegerich 2003: 5). The semantics of these examples are transparent, and the patterns are completely productive. So these examples are not listed. Secondly, both elements can be modified, so they are not syntactically isolated (e.g. *steel suspension bridge, stainless steel bridge*). Thirdly, co-ordination of these examples is possible: *steel and aluminium bridges, steel and wooden bridges*. Also, the head of the examples can be replaced by 'one' in the second part of the coordination: *a wooden bridge and a steel one*. As a result, Giegerich (2003) claims that these examples are phrasal in nature and probably subject to diachronic lexicalisation. In other words, in time, these examples might become lexicalised[24].

Nevertheless, this model also has exceptions. Giegerich himself admits this and concludes that natural language does have exceptions. I will discuss the implications of my theory for Giegerich's theory briefly in Chapter 4.

Compound words in Japanese also have special phonological properties. The Compound Accent Rule (Kubozono 1993) can tell us whether the word is a compound or not. The accent of the second element remains, whereas that of the first element is eliminated in compound words.

Compound Accent Rule

	Constituents	→compound
(84)	sékiyu, stóove	→sekiyu+stóove
	'oil stove'	
(85)	dài, tókoro	→dai+dókoro
	table, place	
	'kitchen'	

In Japanese, too, there are compound words which do not obey the systematic rules. Kubozono (1993) states that there are two different types of compound words. One is those compounds which fall under the Compound Accent Rule as exemplified in (75) and (76). Another group is those which cannot fall under the Compound Accent Rule. According to Higurashi (1983), this type usually consists of compound words whose second member is shorter than three morphemes. Kubozono also has examples for this type in personal names, when the two constituents show a case relation and also names of organisations. Furthermore, Kubozono claims that accent varies according to dialect and idiolect.

Higurashi (1983) demonstrates some generalisations concerning compound words with the second member shorter than three morphemes. The examples used are:

	Constituents	→compound with an accent
(86)	inaka, míso	→inaka+míso
	country, soybean paste	→countrystyle+bean paste
(87)	sínsyuu, míso→sinsyuu+míso	
	Shinshu, soybean paste→ Shinshu+soybean paste	
(88)	takeya, míso →takeya+míso	
	Takeya brand, soybean paste →Takeya+soybean paste	
(89)	akane, sóra	→ akane +zóra
	red, sky	→ red +sky
(90)	yuuyake, sóra →yuuyake+zóra	
	sunset, sky	

The first group Higurashi describes includes short nouns, consisting of one or two morae whose initial accent survives. According to her, the second constituents, *miso* and *sora*, are included in this group. The above examples show the accentuation pattern of short compounds containing these nouns as their second constituents. From the observation above, both words have their accents on the first mora. Higurashi (1983) notes that compounds with these words as the second member maintain their accents on the first mora. However, as Higurashi states, there are a few exceptions to this generalisation. One of these exceptions is when the first constituent is a word that indicates the colour of *miso*, then the compound as a whole becomes accentless. Tsujimura (1996) notes that the accentuation pattern of *miso* in a compound may depend on the accent and length of the left-hand constituent.

Another class Higurashi discusses includes cases where the accent of the second constituent is lost. Examples are compounds comprising of *huro* 'bath', *ki* 'tree', and *su* 'vinegar' as their second constituents.

(91) ása, huró→ asa+buro   (unaccentuated)
     morning, bath→ morning+bath
(92) huyú, kí → huyu+ki   (unaccented)
     winter, tree →winter+tree
(93) goma, sú→ goma+su   (unaccented)
     sesame, vinegar→ dressing with sesame seeds

Thus, these compound words are unaccented.

Finally, there are compounds where an accent is placed on the last mora of the first constituent regardless of whether or not the second constituent is accented or where the accent is.

(94) ása,   íti   → asá+   iti
     morning, market   → morning market
(95) umá, íti → umá+iti
     horse, market → horse market
(96) setomono, íti → setomonó+iti
     ceramics, market → ceramics market
(97) ása,   kaze   → asá+   kaze
     morning, wind   → morning wind

As a result, in this group, there seems to be no generalisation as to where the accent falls in compound words.

On the other hand, Kubozono (1995) observes more data and has some generalisations. The structure and accent of the second constituent determines the accent of the whole compound. The first rule he proposes is that compounds with its second constituent having one or two morae has its accent on the last syllabus of the first constituent. For example, the following shows this claim is correct.

(89) jinji+ bu → jinji'bu
      human resources + department → 'human resources
(90) amerika + jin → amerika'jin
      America+person → American person
(91) sumida +kawa → sumida'gawa
      Sumida+ river → Sumida River   (Kubozono 1995: 58)

However, this first generalization has some exceptions: the last constituent with –*ka* 'section', *ka* 'department' (university), *toh* 'political party'. This type of constituents makes the whole compound unaccentuated: i.e. *ji'nji+ka'* → *jinjika*, *shingaku +ka'* → *shingakuka*, *shinsei+ to'* → *shinseitoh*, etc.

The second generalization Kubozono has is as follows. Compounds where their last constituent has more than three morae follow the CAR rule on the first syllabus of the last constituent.

(92) shi'n + gakka → shinga'kka
      new+department → new department
(93) salary'man+shi'intoh → salarymanshi'ntoh
      salaried man + new party → Salaried Man Party
(94) soh'sa+ho'nbu → sohsaho'nbu
      investigation+headquarters → investigation headquarters
(95) gaikokugo+ gakubu → gaikokugoga'kubu, pe'kin+genjin
      → pekinge'njin   (Kubozono 1995: 59)

Another generalization is where the second constituent has medially accent. When another word is combined with this type, the first constituent becomes unaccentutated and the second one has the Compound Accent Rule, i.e. keeps its own accent.

(96) ya'mato + nade'shiko → yamatonade'shiko,
      Yamato (ancient Japanese) + pink → humble woman of Japan (Yamato Nadeshiko)
(97) iso'ppu+monga'tari → isoppumonoga'tari.
      Aesop+ story → Aesop's Fables

As a result, the common feature among these is that the length or structure of the first constituent does not change the feature. So if the last constituent has the same accent the same accent is maintained. e.g., *Chiri'jin, indo'jin* (Chille+person), *amerika'jin* (America+person), *indonesia'jin* (Indonesia+person), and *neander'jin* (Neanderthal+person).

The above generalisations all seem to give us clearer picture of CAR in Japanese compounds. However, they all look at particular groups of words, so they are certainly not generalisation for all compound words in Japanese. In this book, I am not going to go further into this. Clearly, more research should be done.

2.3.2 Rendaku in Japanese compound words

As mentioned in Chapter 1, there is another phonological feature of lexicalised words in Japanese. As one of the characteristics of 'one-wordness' in Japanese, compound formation shows a phonological feature which is special only to compound formation. This is *rendaku* or sequential voicing. This phenomenon is characterised by the initial consonant of the second word of the compound becoming voiced. For example, when the two words, *antei* 'stability' and *sho* 'place' are combined together to make a compound word, the initial sound, /sh/ of the second word is voiced, resulting in /dz/. If the second word of a compound begins with a vowel followed by a consonant, however, this phenomenon is not observed (Tsujimura 1996). Although *rendaku* is observed quite extensively with compounds, researchers have noted that *rendaku* applies only under certain circumstances.

Otsu (1980) summarises the relevant conditions for *rendaku* as follows. First, the right-hand member of a compound should be a native Japanese word for *rendaku* to apply. This immediately excludes any second member that is a Sino-Japanese word, i.e. words that are of Chinese origin, or other loan words. Even when the right-hand member is a Sino-Japanese or loan word, Otsu (1980: 209) assumes that the word has become 'Japanized'. The term 'Japanized' is explained in terms of the frequency of its usage and/or familiarity for native speakers of Japanese. Another explanation is 'old'. This means that the word has a long history as part of the Japanese lexicon. Usual cases are loanwords from Chinese and Portuguese. Nevertheless, there are exceptions. Otsu (1980) notes that there seems to be no non-circular way of determining whether an element is 'Japanized', or whether it is *rendaku* that determines Japanization. As a result, Otsu proposes that it is necessary to assign a [+/-Rendaku] feature to each lexical item, regardless of the reference to the lexical strata.

One constraint for *rendaku* is that *rendaku* does not occur when the second member of a compound has a voiced stop, voiced fricative, or voiced affricate. Technically, the rendaku-blocking factor is Lyman's Law cited in Otsu (1980:

210)²⁴. This phonological stipulation states that a lexical item never undergoes *rendaku* if it contains a voiced obstruent (in bold), as seen in examples below.

(98) oo, kata →oo+gata
      big, size →big size
(99) oo, kaze→oo+kaze
      big, wind→big+wind
(100) zyuzu, tama →zyuzu+dama
      rosary, ball → (prayer) beads
(101) zyuzu, tunagi→zyuzu+tunagi
      rosary, sequence→roping together

The pair in (98) and (99) shows that when the second member of a compound contains a voiced obstruent, i.e. the voiced fricative /z/ in (98), *rendaku* does not apply. In contrast, when there is no voiced consonant in the second member, the word-initial voice-less consonant undergoes voicing, as shown in (98). Similarly, the pair (100) and (101) indicates that it does no matter whether the first member of a compound contains a voiced obstruent or not, as shown in (100). The first member of the compound in this example does include a voiced affricate, as well as a voiced fricative and yet, rendaku applies to the initial consonant of the second member, /t/, to yield /d/.

In summary, this section has compared phonological properties of compound words in the languages. All the languages show that most compounds follow a compound-specific rule, namely the Compound Stress Rule for English and Scandinavian languages and the Compound Accent Rule for Japanese. It is, therefore, concluded that compound words behave differently from syntactic phrases. There are exceptions in English and Japanese, however. Although many linguists have attempted to systematise semantic fields for compound words to explain the exceptions, there is presently no conclusive systematisation. Exceptions to the Compound Accent Rule in Japanese indicate that separation of morphology and syntax is not clear-cut. Giegerich (2003) observes that there are some systematisation for exceptions to the Compound Stress Rule in English. The semantic relationship between the two constituents in exceptions is a default relationship.

In addition, the phonological characteristic of Japanese compounds, *rendaku* has also been discussed. The next section will look at some apparent counter-examples to Lexical Integrity in these languages.

2.4 Counter-argument for Lexical Integrity?

2.4.1 Plural as first constituent and the Lexicon

Another characteristic of compounds is that neither a functional category nor a phrase can appear inside them. For example, the pairs of the following examples show the validity of the No Phrase Constraint (see Section 2.2).

(102) [shoe shop] vs. *[shoes shop]
(103) [play boy] vs. *[played boy]
(104) [car salesman] vs. *[big car] salesman

The examples (102) and (103) show that the *-s* and *-ed* cannot appear inside the compound words, *shoe shop* and *play boy*, respectively. Moreover, the example (104) cannot have the phrase, *big car*, embedded inside the compound.

If the above characteristics of compounding in English are observed, compounding seems to be different from the corresponding phrases. However, compounding in English is not that straightforward. The following are some examples.

(105) clothes+shop vs. cloth shop
(106) arms+ race vs. arm race
(107) feet+ massager
(108) mice+ eater
(109) parks+ commissioner
(110) awards+ ceremony
(111) pilots+union
(112) weapons+ inspector
(113) buildings+investor
    (from Brown Corpus data cited in Haskell, et al. 2003, Selkirk 1982 and English dictionary)

It is obvious that the first constituents of (105) – (106) are not plural nouns of a base without the plural inflection. They are plural tantum nouns which lack a base. According to the level-ordering account proposed by Kiparsky (1982), a plural tantum noun should be stored in the lexicon because it is an idiosyncratic form. The following tests will shows that the compound words (105) – (106) can be considered words in terms of Lexical Integrity.

(114) clothes+ shop
    *I went to the clothes$_i$ shop yesterday and found some nice ones$_i$.
(115) shop for clothes

I went to the shop for clothes$_i$ yesterday and found some nice ones$_i$.
(116) arms+ race
*There was an arms$_i$ race. Who was quicker to produce more dangerous ones$_i$?
(117) race to arms
There was a race to arms$_i$. Who was quicker to produce more dangerous ones$_i$?

The examples (114) and (115) constitute another type of compound words in English. The left-hand constituent is an irregular plural. Pinker (1999) and Haskell, Maryellen, MacDonald & Seidenberg (2003) argue that irregular nouns are acceptable as modifiers of compound words, although they are significantly less acceptable modifiers than singular nouns.

The following tests will show that the compounds (107) and (108) are more similar to words than phrases.

(118) feet +massager
*After I bought the feet$_i$ massager SWINGER, they$_i$ are not aching anymore.
(119) massager for feet
After I bought SWINGER, the massager for feet$_i$, they$_i$ are not aching anymore.
(120) mice+ eater
*When the mice$_i$ eater approached they$_i$ ran away.
(121) cat that eats mice
When the cat that eats mice$_i$ approached they$_i$ ran away.

Examples (109) – (113) appear more similar to phrases than to words, because their left-hand constituent has a plural inflection. In the level-ordering account of the lexicon, Kiparsky (1982) claims that compound words with a regular plural inflection are stored at Level 3 (see (122) after compound word formation (Level 2). With this in mind, Kiparsky (1982) and Selkirk(1982) claim that the cases like the examples (109) – (113) are explained by a semantic factor: the left-hand constituent has an 'idiosyncratic' meaning, therefore, the left-hand member is stored in the lexicon. Kiparsky (1982) proposed the following structure for the English lexicon in level-ordering.

(122) English Lexicon
Level 1: irregular inflection as first constituent, including plural tantum and irregular inflection.
Level 2: compound word formation

Level 3: Regular inflection

Level-ordering presents the organisation of derivational and inflectional processes of a language as in a series of levels. Each level is associated with a set of phonological rules. According to this, plural tantum can appear in compound words, as they are irregular plurals, listed in the lexicon at Level 1. Moreover, according to this level-ordering, the plural tantum are marked inherently [+Plural]. However, Kiparsky (1982) admits that not all plural tantum are possible as modifiers in compound words. Examples that are not possible include *trouser press* vs. **trousers press*, *scissor case* vs. **scissors case*, and *spectacle pincer* vs. **spectacles case* (Kiparsky 1982: fn 3). In this case, then, English speakers do need to memorise that the plural tantum counterpart does not exist in their language.

On the other hand, compound words with a regular plural inflection inside are listed in the Level 3. This means that there is no clear boundary between compound words and phrases. Haskell et al (2003) reject Selkirk (1982) and Kiparsky's (1982) hypothesis that cases like (109) – (113) are explained by semantic factors. Instead, they argue that their hypothesis was consistent with some of the exceptions, but it did not explain why some are idiosyncratic and not others. Haskell et al's findings from seven studies show that compounds with regular plural inside compound words are less acceptable to native speakers of English than those with irregular plurals or plural tantum as modifiers.

Alegre & Gordon (1996) also attempt to identify semantic bases for the exceptions of plural inflections inside compound words. Considering the contrast between the examples, *a store carries paint* and *a store carries several paints*, they argue that rather than showing multiple instances, this use of *paints* highlights diversity among the things being referred to. They noted that heterogeneity seems to be a necessary condition for regular plural modifiers to be acceptable. Moreover, they also had abstractness as well as heterogeneity as necessary conditions (also supported by Booij 1993). An example of this would be the compound word *publications catalogue*. In this example, *publications* is highly abstract relative to more specific terms like *book* or *magazine*. However, this argument cannot be true for an example, such as *buildings investor*. *Building* is not abstract but concrete. If one considers that modifiers of compound words in English are not able to have specificity, but only generality, *buildings investor* is acceptable. This claim is true for (110) – (113), as native speakers[25] prefer the compound with a plural marker inside and they all agree that they mean the same as the ones without a plural marker. This is due to the modifier of compound words in English not being able to have specificity, but only generality (also supported by Booij 1993, Agathopoulou 2003)[26]. In other words, the left-hand element with a regular plural marker inside (110) – (113)

does not refer to specific plurality (contra. generic) of the objects. Thus, I propose that the *-s* morpheme is not an inflection, but a linking morpheme (see Chapter 3 for the structure of this type) and in this thesis, I will not follow the lexicon with level-ordering, represented in (122) (see Chapter 3 for more reasons for not taking the theory of the lexicon, using level-ordering).

According to native speakers' judgements (6 native speakers)[27], the example (109) is an exception: both *parks commissioner* and *park commissioner* exist and there is meaning difference between the two compounds. Thus, there is a real plural marker inside this compound. This kind of example with plural meaning is not productive and the example *parks commissioner* seems to be an exception in English compounding (see Chapter 4 for the structure of this type of compound).

It is well known that the equivalent of the singular and plural distinction in English is generally not available in Japanese: that is, there is no plural marking similar to the English ending – *(e)s*. Although the root which means a group – *tati*, as in *kodomo-tati* 'children' and *gakusei-tati* 'students', is available, its use is extremely limited in that it can apply only to human beings (see 4.2.1 for more details) and there are no compounds with this root in Japanese. Therefore, a left-hand constituent with plural marker or plural tantum is out of the question in Japanese compound words. If a lexicon with the idea of level-ordering is taken into consideration, Kageyama's (2001) proposal for the Japanese lexicon can be used. As discussed in the section 2.1, compounds can be formed in a variety of ways which include merely native words or a combination of words of different origin. Using and elaborating on Selkirk's (1982) distinction between the terms Word and Stem, Kageyama formulates a theory of Japanese word formation which sets up three types of building blocks: Root, Stem, and Word. It should be noted that in his paper (Kageyama 2001), he uses only Sino-Japanese words.

(123) Root: single morphemes like *hoo+* 'visit' and *bei* 'America[28]'
(124) Stem: two-morpheme constructs like *hoo+bei* 'a visit to America'
(125) Word: constructs that can be used independently, typically with more than two morphemes (Kageyama 2001: 15)

Based on these definitions above, Kageyama (2001) proposes the following rules of compound formation in Japanese.

(126) a. Root (+ Root) → Stem
 b. Stem (+ Stem) → Word
 c. Word (+ Word) → Word

The representations above show that these building blocks are combined with each other to make larger and larger units. According to Kageyama, the difference between the complex words formed by the rules (126a) or (126b) on the one hand and (126c) on the other is that in the former, Lexical Integrity plays a role, whereas in (126c), it does not. For example, the conjunction *oyobi* 'and' can appear inside Word-level (126c) compounds, but not inside (126a) or (126b).

(127) a. **Root-level**
hoo-bei, hoo-chuu[29]
visit-America, visit-China
'a visit to America', 'a visit to China'
with the conjunction 'oyobi' inside
*[hoo-[bei oyobi chuu]
visit-America and China
'a visit to U.S. and China'

b. **Stem-level**
chuu- goku+ zin, kan- koku +zin
China-country+person, Korea-country+person
'Chinese people', 'Korean people'
with the conjunction 'oyobi' inside
*[chuu- goku oyobi kan- koku] +zin
Chinese-country and Korean-country+person
'Chinese person and Korean person'

c. **Word-level**
hoo- bei+ yotei, hoo-chuu+yotei
visit-America+schedule, visit-China+schedule
'schedules of a visit to U.S.', 'schedules of a visit to China'
with the conjunction 'oyobi' inside
[hoo-bei oyobi hoo-chuu] +yotei
visit-America and visit-China+schedule
'schedules of a visit to U.S. and a visit to China'

The (127a) and (127b) on the one hand and (127c) on the other hand show that there is no clear boundary between 'morphology' and 'syntax'. In fact, the word-level complex words behave more like words than phrases with respect to the following points.

(128) a. **Word-level**
Backward gapping cannot delete part of a word (strike through = gapping).

    *koizumi shusoo   wa [hoo+bei ~~+yotei]~~ ~~o~~ ~~happyoo~~
    Koizumi Prime-Minister TOP[visit+America+schedule] ACC announce-
    ~~si,~~ gaimu daizin wa [hoo+ chuu+ yoteei] o happyoo si-ta.
    do, Foreign Minister TOP [visit+China+ schedule] ACC announce
    do-Past.
    'Mr Koizumi announced his schedule of a visit to America and the
    Foreign Minister a visit to China.'

b. **Stem-level**

    Backward gapping cannot delete part of a word.
    *John wa [chuu+goku+ ~~zin]~~ ~~ni~~ ~~ai,~~ Naomi wa
    John TOP [China+country+person] DAT meet, Naomi TOP
    [kan+koku+ zin] ni a-tta.
    [Korea+ person DAT meet-Past.
    'John met a Chinese person and Naomi, a Korean'.

c. **Root-level**

    Backward gapping cannot delete part of a word.
    *Koizumi shusoo   wa [hoo+~~bei]~~ ~~o~~ ~~happyoo si~~, Bush Koizumi
    Prime-Minister TOP[visit+America] ACC announce-do, Bush
    daitooryoo wa [hoo+nichi] o happyoo si-ta.
    president TOP [visit+Japan] ACC announce do-Past.
    'Mr Koizumi announced his visit to America and President Bush did
    to China.'

    Backward gapping
    ken wa [$_{NP}$ huransu no ~~kuruma] o kai~~, naomi wa [$_{NP}$ itaria no
    Ken TOP [France GEN car] ACC buy, Naomi TOP [Italy GEN
    kuruma] o ka-tta.
    car ACC buy-Past
    'Ken bought a car made in France, and Naomi, one made in Italy.'

The above test shows that just like stem-level and root-level words, backward gapping cannot delete part of the word-level word. Gapping in Japanese deletes one consecutive string.

    In summary, the above evidence suggests that there is phrase-like compounding in Japanese. The boundary between the syntax and the morphology is not clear-cut in this sense. However, the phrase-like type of compound is still a 'word' in some respects, such as gapping.

    On the other hand, in Scandinavian languages, there are no regular-looking plural compound words (see Bauer 1978 on Danish). As a result, if the theory of a level-ordering is taken into consideration, there are only two levels involved in compound formation the Lexicon of Scandinavian languages[30].

2.4.2 Genitive compound words in the three languages

There are genitive compounds in English and whether they are formed in the lexicon or in the syntax is a controversial issue. They are regarded as counter-examples to the generalisation shown below.

(129) No syntactically relevant elements can occur inside a word
(Anderson 1982)

This means that inflection cannot feed word derivation. However, in addition to the compounds with plural discussed in the previous section, there are some compound words which seem to have inflection inside. The following examples are possessive compounds[31].

(130) woman's magazine, women's college, children's book, Mother's Day, collector's item, child's play, spider's web, devil's advocate, driver's license, farmers' association

The expressions can be considered either as phrases or as compounds and the pronunciations differ accordingly. The primary stress lies on the first constituent of the whole word, just like normal compounds. When they are considered compound words, they are words in terms of Lexical Integrity.

Compound
(131) the [torn [woman's magazine]]
Phrase
(132) [the woman's] torn magazine   (Taylor 1996:29, Shimamura 1986)

Thus, adjectives cannot occur inside the compound, in contrast to in its corresponding phrase.

Similarly, considered as compounds the expressions obey the notion of an anaphoric island (like root noun-noun compound words in (2)-(5)).

(133) *I found those [woman$_i$'s magazines], but as far as I know she$_i$ has not read them.
(134) I found [that woman$_i$]'s magazines, but as far as I know, she$_i$ has not read them.   (Taylor 1996: 29)

The anaphoric islandhood of the compound does not allow the pronoun *she* to be coreferential with the noun *woman* inside it.

In that case, what is the level of the first constituent? There are two views.

One is that the first constituent is a maximal phrase and the second constituent is non-maximal. Then, genitive compounds are regarded as incompatible with the generalization that 'no syntactically relevant elements can occur inside a word'.

Taylor (1996) and Shimamura (1986) argue that genitive compounds are similar to compound words. Firstly, they argue that the semantics of genitive compounds follow from their status as a noun, not as a noun phrase. A possessive compound denotes a type of entity, not an instance of a type. Generally, the designated type is a subcategory of the type denoted by the second constituent. Another characteristic is that the –s morpheme is not equivalent to that in prenominal possessives. Shimamura states that it is neither a derivational nor an inflectional suffix. It is not a derivational suffix, as it does not affect the category of the first constituent as a normal derivational suffix does. On the other hand, it is not inflectional suffix, as an inflection cannot go inside a word. Also, the whole compound displays the stress pattern of compounds, namely, with main stress on the initial part.

Similarly, in Scandinavian languages, as discussed in Section 2.1, there are some compound words whose first constituent is marked with the linking element, such as –s or –e. The phonetic form of the linking element corresponds to the possessive marker.

(135) fred+s+conference [D]
(136) peace+s+conference
 'peace conference'
(137) bord+s+lamp [S]
 table++LINK+lamp
 'desk lamp'

The whole compound displays the stress pattern of compounds, namely, with main stress on the initial part.

In Japanese, too, there exists genitive compound words.

 genitive compounds
(138) haha+ no+hi
 Mother+GEN+day
 'Mother's day'
(139) chichi+ no + hi
 Father+ GEN+ day
 'father's day'
(140) ama+ no + gawa
 heaven+ GEN + river

'milky way'
(141) na + no + hana
rape+ GEN+ flower
'rape blossoms'
(142) mago+ no+ te
Grandchild+ GEN+ hand
'back scratcher'

The following examples show that those compounds are considered words in terms of Lexical Integrity.

(143) haha+ no+ hi 'Mother's day'
Watashi no haha wa go-gatu no haha no hi o
I GEN mother TOP May GEN mother GEN day ACC
tanosimi ni siteiru.
look-forward-to.
'My mother is looking forward to Mother's Day in May'.

This sentence is not the same as the following in meaning.

(144) Watashi no haha wa go-gatu no zibun no hi o
I GEN mother TOP May GEN self GEN day ACC
tanosimi ni siteiru.
look-forward-to
'My mother is looking forward to her day in May'.

This test shows that the *haha* in the compound *haha-no-hi* in (138) does not specify someone's mother (my mother) and that the sentence (143) does not mean the same as the sentence (144).
 Consider also the following examples.

(145) genitive compounds
ama+ no+ gawa
heaven+ GEN+ river
'milky way'
*[kirei na ama] no gawa]]
*[beautiful heaven] GEN river]
'beautiful milky river'
[kirei na [ama no gawa]
[beautiful[heaven GEN river]
'beautiful milky river'

The corresponding Noun Phrase of the example (145) is (146).

(146) tengoku + no+ kawa
heaven+ GEN+ river
'river in the heaven'
[kirei na [tengoku no] kawa]
beautiful heaven GEN river
'beatiful river in the heaven'
'river in the beautiful river'

Ama is an allomorph of the morpheme *ten* and in general, it appears in compound words. The initial sound of the second constituent in (145), *kawa* (river) has undergone *rendaku*, which, as discussed, is a particular phenomenon in compounding. This proves that *no* in Japanese is not an inflectional morpheme. The grammaticality contrast between the compound and its equivalent phrase shows that whereas the adjective, *kirei na*, in the phrase can be interpreted as modifying both the words *ama* 'heaven' and *kawa* 'river', it cannot be interpreted as modifying *ama* in the compound word. This shows that the compound word signifies only a general concept.

(147) a. genitive compound
mago+ no+ te
grandchild GEN hand
'back scratcher'
chiisai mago no te
small grandchild GEN hand
*'small grandchild's hand'
'small back scratcher'

In the corresponding phrase, the adjective *chiisai* 'small' modifies both *mago* and the whole phrase *mago no te*.

b. corresponding phrase
mago no te
grandchild GEN hand
'grandchild's hand'
chiisai mago no te
small grandchild GEN hand
'small grandchild's hand'
'grandchild's hand which is small'

The accent of the compound word in (147a) and its corresponding phrase (147b) is different. The phonological difference also shows that the former is a compound word, whereas the latter is a noun phrase. These tests show that these kinds of compounds are also lexicalised words in Japanese as in English.

In conclusion, this subsection has shown some characteristics of genitive compound words in these languages. The left-hand constituent of genitive compound words seems to be always generic, not specific, and this leads me to believe that the genitive marker-looking morpheme is a linking morpheme which has the function of checking a categorical feature on the left-hand constituent (see 4.3.2 for more discussion). In addition, the meaning of these compounds seems to have lexicalised.

2.4.3 Compound words but not lexical?

Contrary to what has been established in the previous sections and what Di Sciullo & Williams (1987) state, it is well known that there are no unequivocal criteria for distinguishing compounds from phrases in English and many other languages. Bauer (1998a) argues that it is not possible to distinguish between a class of noun + noun compounds and a class of noun + noun syntactic constructions by the criteria which were discussed in Section 2.2. Firstly, he argues that the phonological criterion for compound words fail to show the distinction. Some authors, like Fudge (1984) and Ladd (1984) and Lieberman & Sproat (1992) and, as discussed above in section 2.3.1, Giegerich (2003, 2015) argue that stress patterns are associated with particular semantic relationships between the two nouns involved. 'B made of A' as in *stone wall* result in phrase stress, while 'B used for A' as in *pruning shears* results in compound stress. In contrast, Bauer (1998a) states that it is not clear that the semantic relationship between the two constituents would show a distinction between a lexical construction and a syntactic one. Moreover, he questions whether the 'made of' relation is in any sense less lexical than the 'for' relation. So Bauer (1998a) would argue against Spencer's (2003) and Giegerich's (2003, 2015) analyses.

Secondly, it was argued in Section 2.2 that it is not possible to refer back to a constituent of a compound word. Examples of (38) – (39) and (47) are repeated below.

(148) black+bird
 →*I wanted to see a black+bird and a blue one.
(149) black bird (a bird which is black)
 →I wanted to see a black bird and a blue one.
(150) hai+zara

a. otite-iru hai$_i$ o hirotte hai$_i$+zara ni ire-nasai.
      Fallen-is ash ACC pick, and ash+tray in put-IMP.
   b. *otite-iru hai$_i$ o hirotte sore$_i$ zara ni ire-nasai.
      fallen-is ash$_i$ ACC pick, and it$_i$ tray in put-IMP.
      'Gather the ashes on the floor and put them in the ashtray.'

This criterion can distinguish compound words from phrases. Lieber (2005) claims that to distinguish a compound word and phrase, the first stem of a compound word receives a generic interpretation (non-referential). In other words, the left-segment of a compound is not D or DP. That is why a pronoun, such as *it* cannot be substituted for or refer to the left-hand segment. In contrast, a maximal projection can have definite reference (Scalise 1984)[32].

However, according to Bauer (1998a), there are certain examples where 'the letter of the lexicalist hypothesis is broken, even with derivatives' (Bauer 1998a: 72).

(151) ....what sharply distinguishes Chomskyan practice from that of his structuralist forebears is...   (Asher 1994: 5082, cited in Bauer 1998a: 72)

In this example Bauer claims that *his* refers back to *Chomsky*, even though *Chomsky* was the root in a derivative, and argues, following Lieberman & Sproat (1992) and Ward, Sproat & Mckoon (1991) state that there is no grammatical problem with the use of anaphora, but there may be pragmatic constraints which need to be satisfied. Nevertheless, Bauer's argument does not change the fact that the left-hand segment of compounds in the languages in question does not refer to specific elements, in contrast with their corresponding phrases.

2.4.4 Phrasal compounds

Phrasal compounds have been discussed widely in the recent literature on word formation (Wiese 1996a, Selkirk 1982, Kiparsky 1982, Lieber 1992, Lieber & Scalise 2007). NP-N compounds such as the following are words according to Lieber (1992). The Lexical Integrity test for each example is as follows.

(152) English
   a. a pipe-and-slipper husband
      Lexical integrity: *a [pipe-and-slipper docile] husband
   b. a slept-all-day look
      Lexical integrity: *a [slept-all-day-today] look
   c. over-the-fence gossip

CHAPTER 2 COMPOUND WORD FORMATION   51

        Lexical integrity: *[over-the-fence-in the garden] gossip
   d. God-is-dead theology
        Lexical integrity: *[God-is-dead-already] theology
   e. an off-the-rack dress
        Lexical integrity: *an [off-the-rack-in the shop]-clothes
   f. a connect-the-dots puzzle
        Lexical integrity: *[connect-the-dots-on the paper] puzzle
                                         (Wiese 1996a)
   g. the Obscene Publications Act
        Lexical integrity: the *[Obscene Publications in the book] Act
   h. a strict-word-order language
        Lexical integrity: *a [strict-word-order and head-final] language
   i. hot sausage and mashed potato soup
        Lexical integrity: *[hot sausage and mashed potato and chicken] soup
   j. between-meal snacks
        Lexical integrity: *[between-meal and after meal] snacks
   k. the save-the-whales campaign
        Lexical integrity: *the [save-the-whales in the ocean] campaign
   l. 'all-you-can-eat' specials
        Lexical integrity: *[all you can eat for five pound] specials
                                         (Kageyama 1993)

(153) Japanese
   a. i) [huruhonya no nyoobo] gorosi
        [second-bookstore GEN wife] killing
          'killing of the wife in the second bookstore'
      ii) Lexical integrity: *[huruhonya   no nyoobo, goshuzin] goroshi
                            second-bookstore GEN wife,   husband killing
          'killing of wife and husband in the second bookstore'
   b. i) [terebi no supeciaru bangumi] huu
        TV GEN special programme style
          'Special TV programme style'
      ii) Lexical integrity: *[terebi no supeciaru bangumi futsuu hutuu
                            TV   GEN special programme style normal
                            bangumi] fuu
                            programme]style
   c. i) [maborosi no chosha] sagasi
        phantom GEN author research
          'research of an phantom author'   (Kageyama 1993)

ii) Lexical integrity: *[nihon no maboroshi no chosha] sagasi
Japan GEN phantom GEN author research
d. i) [[konpa no sosikiryokou] [bastsugun]] no Y-san
party GEN organising-ability distinguished GEN Mr. Y
'Mr Y who is distinguished in the ability to organise a party'
ii)*[[konpa no sosikiryokou] [batsugun de genki]] no Y-san
party GEN organising-ability] distinguished and cheerful]] GEN Mr. Y
e. i) [[zibun ga motte umareta] sainoo] soooo]] no sigoto
he NOM innately gifted talent suitable GEN job
the job which is suitable to the talent with which he was innately gifted
ii)*[[zibun ga motte umareta] sainoo] soooo, tekioo]] no sigoto
self NOM innately gifted] suitable, appropriate]]GEN job
(Namiki 2001)

(154) Swedish
a. ett jag-längtar-efter-dig-brev[33]
a I long for you letter
'an I-long-for-you-letter'
Lexical integrity: *ett jag längtar-efter-dig hemligt-brev
secret
b. ett skicka-mera-pengar-brev
a send more money letter
'a send-more-money-letter'
Lexical integrity: *ett skika-mere-pengar-eftersänt-brev
forwarded
c. en rakt-på-sak-fråga
a right on issue question
'a question that goes right to the point'
Lexical integrity: *en rakt- på-sak-stor-fråga
big

These kinds of compound words also exist and are quite productive in other languages, including Afrikaans, German, and Dutch. It is important to state that it is always the non-head of compound words which is the phrase and not the head (Namiki 2001). Lieber (1992) proposes to modify the word syntax of compounds. Both words (Y^0) and maximal phrases (Y^{max}) are allowed as non-heads in compounds. The argument that such compounds exist originates from the fact that stress patterns are exactly as expected for phrases and for compounds: the embedded phrases bear the stress patterns exhibited by the same phrases in isolation, and the whole compound displays the stress pattern of compounds, namely, with main stress on the initial part. Another criterion for compound words met by phrasal compounds, as Lieber (1992) notes, is that the interpretation of phrasal compounds parallels that of compounds in general. The rough characterisation that 'A compound XY refers to a Y that is further specified by X' holds for phrasal compounds just as well as for most other compounds.

In summary, this section has discussed compounds, such as compounds with a plural inflection inside in English, genitive compounds, and phrasal compounds. What they have in common is that the left-hand constituent looks like a noun phrase. However, the left-hand constituent does not refer to specific things, and they obey Lexical Integrity. Also, it was argued that the plural affix as the left-hand constituent of a compound is not actually semantically plural, and it was concluded that it was a linking morpheme.

In addition, I have discussed whether it is possible to distinguish between a class of noun + noun compounds and a class of noun + noun syntactic constructions by the criteria discussed in Section 2.2. I have concluded that the left-hand segment of compounds does not refer to specific elements, in contrast with their corresponding phrases.

2.5 Copulative (or Dvandva) compound words

The previous four sections have looked at compound words whose two constituents form a modifier-modified relationship. In this section, by contrast, another type of compound word in these languages is considered. The semantic relationship between the two constituents is that of coordination. In other words, one entity is characterised by both members of the compound. Let us see some examples in Japanese, English and Danish.

(155) Japanese
    a. saru + kizi
       monkey+ pheasant
       'monkey and pheasant'
    b. zisin+ kazi
       earthquake+fire
       'earthquake and fire'
    c. oya+ ko
       parent+child
       'parent and child'
    d. yama+ kawa
       mountain+river

'mountain and river'
   e. ame+kaze
      rain+wind
      'river and wind'
   f. ama+tsuchi
      heaven+earth
      'heaven and earth'
   g. kusa+ki
      grass+tree
      'grass and tree'
   h. ta+   hata
      paddy-field+field
      'paddy-field and field'

(156) English   (from Plag 2003: 146)
   a. mother+daughter relationship
   b. the doctor+patient gap
   c. the nature+nurture debate
   d. a modifier+head structure
   e. the mind+body problem

(157) Scandinavian
   a. moder+datter forhold
      mother+daughter relationship

(158) English
   a. mother+daughter
   b. blue+black
   c. poet+translator
   d. singer+songwriter
   e. scientist+explorer
   f. hero+martyr
   g. dunch (dinner and lunch combined together)[34]

(159) Scandinavian
   a. nord+vest
      North+west
   b. Østrig+Ungarn
      Austria+Hungary
   c. Svensk+russisk
      Swedish+Russian   (Mellenius 1997: 22)
   d. blå+gul
      blue+yellow   (Mellenius 1997: 22)
   e. bonden+advokaten
      farmer-the+lawyer-the   (Mellenius 1997: 22)

These compounds are called copulative (or dvandva) compounds (Bauer 1983, Olsen 2000, Plag 2003). Copulative compounds fall into two types, depending on interpretation. Firstly, as Plag (2003) states, the type represented in the examples (157) – (159) is known as a coordinative compound. There are a number of coordinative compounds in Japanese as the above examples show. They always refer to a set of two (or more) individuals. For example, *oya+ko* 'parent+child' refers to a set of one parent and one child. According to Olsen (2000), the constituents of a copulative combination are marked with the dual inflection and retain their individual accents. Japanese coordinative compounds also have the same accents as those of their individual constituents. The following examples demonstrate the accentual patterns in Japanese.

(160) a. coordinative compound
sa'ru+ kizi
monkey+pheasant
b. corresponding phrase
sa'ru to kizi
monkey and pheasant

(161) a. coordinative compound
zi'sin+kazi
earthquake+fire
b. corresponding phrase
zi'sin to kazi
earthquake and fire

(162) a. coordinative compound
o'ya+ko
parent+child
b. corresponding phrase
o'ya to ko
parent and child

(163) a. coordinative compound
ya'ma+kawa
mountain+river
b. corresponding phrase
ya'ma to kawa
mountain and river[35]

As the above examples show, the accentual patterns in Japanese coordinative compounds (a) are the same as their corresponding phrases (b). Moreover, the example (163a) is clearly coordinative, since the initial sound of the second constituent /k/ is not voiced (see 2.3.2).

On the other hand, there are appositional compounds (Bauer 1983, Plag 2003), shown in the examples (158) and (159). This type refers to an entity with two facets. For example, the compounds such as *mother+daughter* and *poet+translator* refer to one person with two characteristics of being mother and daughter, and poet and translator, respectively. According to Olsen (2000), in English and Scandinavian languages (Germanic) appositional compounds are morphological in nature, as they denote a single entity which can be described in both ways, as opposed to a collective entity (pair). Another reason for these appositional compounds being morphological in nature is that they show similar characteristics to normal lexical compounds. In particular, the plural marker is only on the second constituent only and not on the first. The definite article in Scandinavian languages is only on the third element (e.g., *moder+datter forhold+et* (mother+daughter relationship+the), in contrast to occurring on both elements in the example *bond+en-advokat+en* (farmer-the-lawyer+the). The latter example is a counterexample to Olsen. In other words, this example is an appositional compound but more similar to a phrase than a compound word.

2.6 Productive compounds in the three languages

All of the types of compounds discussed in the previous subsections are productively formed or lexicalised. Some examples of productively formed compounds are shown below[36, 37].

(164) Examples (a) – (d) from Spencer 2003: 2
    a. Chomsky hierarchy
    b. song bird
    c. London bus
    d. capsicum leaf
    e. broom-cupboard baby (Boris Becker's illegitimate baby after him having a relationship in a broom-cupboard) (from a magazine)

The above examples are productively formed. Therefore, it is possible, for example, to say 'a bus which runs in London', 'a bird which sings', 'leaf of capsicum', and so on.

As in English, productive compound words exist in Japanese (Namiki 1988). Examples are presented below and taken from Namiki (1988).

Japanese children
(165) kame+pan   káme no katachi o sita pan

turtle+ bread   turtle GEN shape ACC did bread
'bread in the shape of a turtle'   'bread in the shape of a turtle'

The interpretations for *kuma tokei* and *kuma dokei* are the same.

(166) a. kúma+tokei   kúma no katachi o sita tokei
         bear+clock   bear GEN shape ACC did clock
         'a clock in the shape of a bear' 'a clock in the shape of a bear'
      b. kuma+dokei   (the underlined has undergone *rendaku*)
         bear+clock
         'a clock in the shape of a bear'
(167) húusen+zoosan   húusen de dekita zoosan
      balloon+elephant   balloon in made elephant
      'an elephant made of balloons' 'an elephant made of balloons'
(168) koóri+panda   koóri de dekita panda
      ice+panda   ice in made panda
      'a panda made of ice'   'a panda made of ice'
                                (from Sugisaki & Isobe 2000: 500)
(169) sáme+kan   sáme no kan
      shark+can   shark GEN can
      'shark can'
(170) tára+kan
      cod+can
(171) ebi+kan
      shrimp+can
(172) másu+kan
      trout+ can   (from Miyoshi 1999: 170–172)
(173) gakusei+ eiga+ kurabu
      student+ film+ club
(174) tsuri+baka
      fishing+stupid
      'a person who is keen on fishing'
(175) tori+influenza
      bird+influenza
      'chicken flu'
(176) tairyoo+kagaku+heiki
      mass+ chemical+weapon
      'weapons of mass destruction'
(177) tatari+gami
      curse+ god
      'cursed god'

The following compounds are from Mellenius (1997) and they are all productively formed.

Swedish children
(178) vatten+s+våda, in analogy with eld+s+våda ('fire')
water+LINK+accident   fire+LINK+accident
(179) örn+tross, in analogy with alba+tross
eagle+tross
(180) klack+skav; fot+skav; both in analogy with sko+skav ('chafed feet')
heel+chafed   foot+chafed
(181) fel+ vist, in analogy with rätt+vist ('fair')
wrong+way   right+way
(182) bläks+filibabba, in analogy with mums+filibabba ('yum-yum')
yack+yum
(183) klänning+daler, in analogy with sandaler (sandals)
dress+dals
(184) tejp+skav in analogy with sko+skav (chafed feet)
pain because of tape (on the lips, here)
(185) snö+strumpor
snow stockings
(186) hjärt+ (a) + potatis
heart+ (a) +potato
'potato with funny shape'
(187) kritor+leken
crayons+game-the
(188) spoken+lukken
ghosts-the+smell
'the smell in damp forest'
(189) böter+bilen
fines-car-the
'the car that gives fines'
(190) pengar+lapp
money+flap
'note'
(191) kläder+väska
clothes+bag
'suitcase'
(*resväska* is the word in dictionary)
                                          (all the examples from Mellenius 1997: 63 and 74)

In summary, this chapter has considered some characteristics of compound words in English, Japanese and Mainland Scandinavian languages. Firstly, the constituents of compound words in these languages were compared and it was concluded that, whereas the compounds in English are constituted of what looks like two free morphemes, those in the other languages often are not. Also, the traditional view is that compounds are formed by combining free morphemes, while derivational word formation is attaching an affix to a base (a root or a stem). It was argued that this view is wrong. This argument is supported especially if we look at 'cranberry morphemes' and neoclassical compounds. Some differences between neoclassical elements and derivational affixes were considered in the languages in question.

In addition, this chapter has observed some characteristic differences between compounds and their corresponding phrases with regard to Lexical Integrity. The examples show that compounds are in general more similar to words than phrases. However, these compounds have other properties which show clearly that they really are compounds, not phrases. For example, the left-hand constituent of these compounds never refer to specific things, and they obey Lexical Integrity. In the case of the compounds with a plural affix inside it was argued that apart from one or two exceptions, the affix is not actually semantically plural, and it was concluded that it is not an inflection, but a linking morpheme. This will be further discussed in Chapter 4. I also gave examples of compounds which clearly have a phrase as left-hand constituent and coordinative compounds. All of these show that the borderline between compounds and phrases is not clear-cut. I will come back to these compounds in Chapter 4.

The next chapter will look at previously proposed structures in both the Principles and Parameters approach and the Minimalist Framework approach. After the illustration, a proposed structure for all types of compound words in all the languages in question will be presented.

Notes

9 The data in the languages are all lexicalised, i.e. accepted by the speakers of the languages. Morphological, phonological, and semantic lexicalisations (see 1.1).
10 The symbol ø shows that the last morph of the word is deleted when it is merged with another word (see below).
11 The symbol - shows the boundary between two morphemes, in contrast to two words.
12 I would like to thank Dr. Gunlög Josefsson for the examples in Swedish.
13 There are some other examples, according to Josefsson. They are *be-*, *hisk-*, *-on*, and some others. *Be-* and *–on* do appear in several words, though, such as *bedröva* 'distress', *befrynda* 'find oneself', *begynna* 'begin', *behaga* 'please', *bekymra* 'worry', *belamra* 'cluttered' and *betyga* 'mean'. *-On* in *hallon* 'raspberry' *lingon* 'lingonberry', *päron* 'pear', and *plommon*

'plum'.
14 I would like to thank Dr. Gunlög Josefsson for her comment on this morpheme. According to her, this morpheme is a cranberry morpheme, so the meaning is opaque to everyone except to specialists in etymology.
15 I would like to thank Gunlög Josefsson for her comment on this morpheme. This morpheme is a cranberry morpheme and it does not have a meaning associated with it. Etymologically, however, the morpheme is related to the word *huvud* 'head'.
16 However, it is not possible to combine *dialecto* and *-biolo*. Thus, this kind of combination is limited.
17 Thus, the claim that compound words consist of two free morphemes is not true in this case.
18 I would like to thank five English native speakers (four British and one American), three Japanese native speakers and one Swedish native speaker for their judgments on the data in each language.
19 See Appendix 1 for more example sentences.
20 *Weather warning* is another exception. This compound can have the adjective *severe* to modify the first segment as well as the whole compound (Giegerich 2003).
21 Bare nouns in English or Japanese can occur as agent. 'We linguists like ourselves, don't we'? 'Linguists are clever, aren't they?' These two sentences suggest that the subject we or linguists (generics) have phonologically null D. But as roots, the non-head of a compound should not occur as agent or case-marked.
22 Another argument for a Compound Stress Rule has been given by Lieberman and Prince (1977). They say that in any pair of sister nodes [A B]$_x$ where X is a phrasal category, B is strong. In other words, if the X is not a phrasal category, A is strong.
23 For more examples, see Spencer (2003).
24 Rendaku is blocked also by the compound having a certain morpheme. Some morpheme are said to be immune to rendaku. This factor is discussed more in detail by Vance (2015) and many others.
25 Giegerich's analysis implies that compounds need to be formed both in syntax and lexicon. In this book, as can be seen later, there should not be any distinction between syntax and lexicon. If one word or compound refers to one thing, then, that is a word or compound, whereas sentences or phrases do not. That is the only difference between words and phrases.
26 I would like to thank the 6 native speakers (two American English speakers and four British English speakers) for their judgments on these words.
27 Another possible generalisation is given by Montgomery (2001). This generalisation states that the modifier element in a compound is an abstract, not a concrete noun upon which a count interpretation is imposed. Then, the element takes the plural inflection. The examples are *admissions, departments, promotions, innovations, publications*. However, it is obvious that *park* is not an abstract, but a concrete. Therefore, I do not agree with Montgomery's generalisation.
28 I would like to thank the 6 native speakers (two American English speakers and four British English speakers) for their judgments on these words.
29 Root-level morphemes of course obeys No Phrase Rule, as they are only bound morphemes not free morphemes.
30 These examples are counter-examples of the Righthand Head Rule.
31 For more discussion on Lexical Phonology, see 4.1.3.
32 Frequent use of possessive compounds is seen in popular names of plants: *Old man's beard, goat's beard, traveller's joy, elephant's ear, daisy (day's eye), lamb's lettuce*. Many speakers appear to interpret *cowslip* as *cow's lip* (Taylor 1996).
33 It is not clear why *one* could not refer back to a bare noun (see Appendix 1). Perhaps it can

but the left-hand segment is not a bare noun: it is a root without word class features (see Section 3.2.4.3).
34 I would like to thank Prof. Anders Holmberg for his examples in Swedish.
35 More examples of copulative compounds are in the Appendix.
36 Other examples are in the Appendix.
37 Spencer analyses these examples as compound words in English and some of them are stressed on the 'left-hand' constituent and the others are stressed on the second. For these kinds of words, it is necessary to have tests to see whether they are lexicalised compound words.
38 The examples from Spencer (2003) are in fact lexicalised compounds.

CHAPTER 3
Structure of Compound Words

The last chapter looked at the common and distinct characteristics of compound word formation in Scandinavian languages, English and Japanese and found that there are a number of common characteristics between these languages. I have also shown that neoclassical compounds and cranberry morphemes exist in Japanese and Scandinavian languages, just as in English. One distinction between English on the one hand and Scandinavian languages and Japanese on the other is that the left-hand constituent of compound words in English does look like a free morpheme whereas in the other two languages, it is often not a free morpheme and so cannot appear independently in the syntax.

In addition, the last chapter looked that some examples of compounds in the languages in question show that the borderline between compounds and phrases is not clear-cut, unlike what Di Sciullo and Williams (1987) say.

This chapter is organised as follows. In the first section, structures for compound words proposed by other researchers within the GB framework will be discussed. This section will be followed by a discussion of structures for compound words proposed within the Minimalist Program. The aim of this chapter is to find out which structure is the best for compound words in the languages investigated.

3.1 Structures for compound words in the GB framework

3.1.1 Transformational account of compound words

As discussed in Section 1.2, the first account of compound words in English in a transformationalist framework was given by Lees (1960). However, his analysis of compound words has been rejected by many researchers, including

Chomsky (1970) and Baker (1988). Lees' analysis of compound words is considered first.

Lees analysed compound words in English with their sentential paraphrase as a basis and claimed that compound words derived by transformations from an underlying sentence, the main idea being that material in the underlying sentence was deleted. For instance, the compound word, *steam boat* is derived from an underlying structure, 'steam powers the boat' in the following steps.

(192) a. steam powers the boat →
 b. boat (which is) powered by steam →
 c. steam-powered boat →
 d. steam-boat

This analysis is sufficient in that it provides different deep structures for the same surface form, which accounts for the semantic ambiguity in compound words. Using this kind of derivation, he analyses the relationship between constituents of productive compound words in the following ways, including subject-predicate, subject-middle object, subject-verb, subject-object, subject-prepositional object, object-subject, verb-object, for-adverbial, verb-prepositional object and object-prepositional object. However, if all compound words in English are taken into account, there will be too many semantic relations between the two constituents in compounds (Downing 1977, Lieberman & Sproat 1992). Another criticism is that the relationships between the constituents of some examples of compound words in his analysis are not analyzed correctly. For example, he claims that the compound word, *hardware* is derived from an underlying structure, 'ware which is hard'. However, it is obvious that *hardware* is tools and equipment that are used in the home or garden and it cannot mean ware which is hard. In other words, the meaning of the whole compound is not semantically composed from its constituents. An unusual feature of Lees' theory is that he analyses the genitive construction, as in *John's book* as a compound.

At the time when Lees analysed compound words, no other linguists had claimed that there is a difference between deriving sentences and compound words. Chomsky (1970) concluded that gerundive constructions are formed in the syntax while derived nominalizations are listed in the lexicon. Along with Chomsky (1970), then, Lees would presumably have claimed that his theory is a theory for productive compounding only, and that the lexicalised compounds are listed in the lexicon. They are not derived from sentences in the syntax. However, the lexicalised compounds, although listed, have structure, too. They are constructed in the same way as productive compounds. In Lees' approach, lexicalised compounds are then ignored completely and cannot be derived in the same ways as productive compounds, since they are not derived from phrases.

A similar analysis to that of Lees was proposed by Levi (1978). He claimed that compound words which are semantically transparent can be derived from an underlying structure by deleting a recoverable predicate. For example, the word *malaria mosquito* is derived as follows.

(193)

(194)

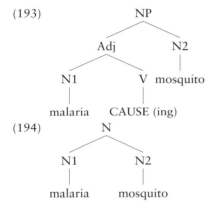

The structures (193) – (194) show that the compound is derived from 'malaria CAUSE mosquito', the Cause being a predicate which shows the semantic relationship between the two constituents, *malaria* and *mosquito*. The predicate CAUSE is deleted. The deleted predicate is recoverable; thus, this process is known as Recoverable Predicate Deletion. Levi has nine predicates which are recoverable, namely CAUSE, HAVE, MAKE, USE, BE, IN, FOR, FROM and ABOUT (Levi 1978: 76). He claims that these are the only predicates which may be deleted in the process of transforming an underlying relative clause construction into the typically ambiguous surface configuration of the complex nominals. Examples of complex nominals derived by deletion of these nine predicates are given in Figure 1. The abbreviation RDP in the first column stands for Recoverably Deletable Predicate.

Table 1:

RDP	N1 < direct object of relative clause	N1 < subject of relative clause
Cause	tear gas disease germ malarial mosquitoes traumatic event mortal blow	drug deaths birth pains nicotine fit viral infection thermal stress

Have	picture book	government land
	apple cake	lemon peel
	gunboat	student power
	musical comedy	reptilian scales
	industrial area	feminine intuition
Make	honeybee	daisy chains
	silkworm	snowball
	musical clock	consonantal patterns
	sebaceous glands	molecular chains
	song birds	stellar configurations
Use	voice vote	————————
	steam iron	
	manual labour	
	solar generator	————————
	vehicular transportation	
Be	soldier ant	
	target structure	
	professional friends	
	consonantal segment	————————
	mammalian vertebrates	
In	field mouse	
	morning prayers	
	marine life	
	marital sex	
	autumnal rains	————————
For	horse doctors	
	arms budget	
	avian sanctuary	
	aldermanic salaries	
	nasal mist	
From	olive oil	
	test-tube baby	
	apple seed	
	rural visitors	
	solar energy	
About	tax law	
	price war	
	abortion vote	
	criminal policy	
	linguistics lecture	

According to Levi, the division of the examples in the Figure 1 into two columns reflects the fact that the prenominal modifiers in these complex nominals can be derived from either the subject or the direct object of the underlying predicate. Thus, *disease germ* is derived from an underlying sentence, 'germ which causes disease' but *birth pains* is derived not from an underlying sentence, *pains which causes birth* but rather from *pains which birth causes*. Levi explicitly rules out the relation 'similarity' because of its pragmatic nature.

However, Levi's analysis of deletion is not compatible with present generative grammar. He states that a predicate such as CAUSE or ABOUT is deleted and recoverable. However, according to Chomsky & Lasnik's (1977) definition of the Recoverability Condition, the predicate should not be deleted. The Recoverability Condition prevents deletion of any element which has semantic content unless there is an antecedent. Moreover, how can the predicate in Levi's structure be recoverable if it is not projected after the deletion? Even in terms of generative grammar of the 1970ies, the structure in question violates the Structure Preserving Principle (Emonds 1970), i.e. all categories presented in the D-structure must be the same in the S-structure. He observes different structures (passive) preposing extrapotation.

Another criticism against the two transformationalist views of the derivation of compound words concerns the headedness of the word. Just like in the case of phrases, it has been argued extensively that it is necessary to have a head in the word, as the head represents the core meaning and the category of the whole word (Williams 1981). In the following subsection, a lexicalist view of compound words will be discussed. Moreover, the important notion of the headedness of compound words will be presented.

3.1.2 Lexical account of compound words

In reaction to the transformationalist account, the argument formed by the lexicalist tradition is that it is necessary to define the head of a word, just like in phrases. If the head is not defined in morphology, it is not possible to interpret what the meaning and the category of the whole word is for compounds as well as derived words. In other words, without any head in morphology, it is not possible to tell for a N-N compound which real-world object the compound refers to, i.e. its reference. Williams (1981) claims that in morphology, it is the right-hand constituent of a complex word that decides the category of the whole word by percolating its features to the dominating node. Williams claims the following.

(195) In morphology, we define the head of a morphologically complex word to be the right-hand member of that word.   (Williams 1981:248)

Thus, in the words below, the element in bold in each is the head:

(196)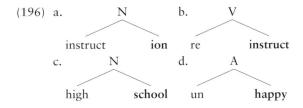

The features of each right-hand element percolate to the node above and decide the category of the word as noun, verb, noun, and adjective, respectively. On the empirical level, compounding in Germanic languages such as English and Scandinavian languages is directly accounted for. Moreover, this can be applied to compound words in Japanese, as well. Japanese, English and Mainland Scandinavian choose the right-most element of a compound as the head (English; Williams 1981, Selkirk 1982, Japanese; Kageyama 1983, Namiki 2001; Mainland Scandinavian languages; Josefsson 1997 and Holmberg 1992)[38].

Namiki (2001) gives evidence for the Right-hand Head Rule with many examples of "reversible compounds" in Japanese and English, such as *hatchi-mitsu* 'bee-syrup' (honey) and *mitsu bachi* 'syrup-bee' (honey bee)[39]. In these cases, they refer to different entities. In either order, the right-hand constituent is the head of the compound. More examples are cited below (the element in bold in each is the head).

(197) Japanese
    a. tsutsumi+**gami**   kami+**zutsumi**
        wrapping+paper   paper+wrapping
        'wrapping paper'   'something wrapped in paper'
    b. mizu+**deppoo**   teppoo+**mizu**
        water+ gun   gun+ water
        'water pistol'   'flash flood'
    c. taru+**zake**   sake+**daru**
        cask+sake   sake+ cask
        'sake in a cask'   'cask for sake'
    d. doku+**gumo**   kumo+**doku**
        poison+spider   spider+poison
        'poisonous spider'   'spider poison'[40]

(199) English
    a. house+**dog**   dog+ **house**
    b. sugar+ **maple**   maple+ **sugar**

Another consequence of the assumed definition for headedness in morphology is given by Williams (1981) and Josefsson (1997). They observe that inflections encoding tense, case etc. are suffixes. This means that they are heads according to the Right-hand Head Rule. And this is a desirable consequence, since tense is a property of the V (and case of the N) from where it percolates to VP (NP) in the syntax.

These structures show that the feature [tense] occurs strictly in head position.

(200)

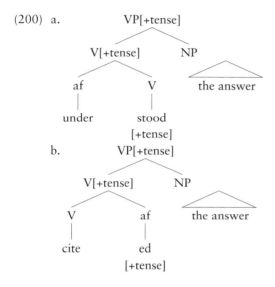

It is a head both above and below the word level; the feature percolation is determined by the RHR up to the word level. Above the word level, it is determined by the rules of syntax/X'-theory. Williams does not clearly say how she determines affix is a head of the word. The feature of the suffix is percolated. The tense is the head, because in gapping, you can only delete a head; eg. *John is reading Shakespeare, Simon is Hardy*. In contrast, it is not grammatical to say eg. *John is reading Shakespeare, Simon reading Hardy*.

In the same way, in Scandinavian languages, too, Williams' Right-hand Head Rule assumes that the inflection both above and below the level of the word is the head.

(201) a.

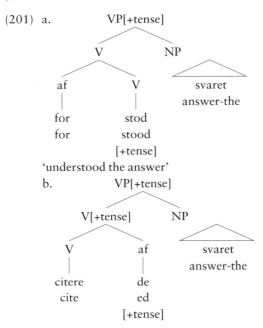

'understood the answer'

b.

In contrast to English, Japanese and Mainland Scandinavian languages, compounding in Romance, Vietnamese and Thai (Lieber 1992) presents another class of rather fundamental problems. They present the left-hand constituent as the constituent which decides the category of the whole compound. Thus, the RHR needs to be somewhat modified. Criticising Williams' RHR, Selkirk (1982) formulates the RHR in a different way.

(202) In a word-internal configuration:

Where X stands for a syntactic feature complex and where Q contains no category with the feature X, X^m is the head of X^n.

According to (202), it is possible that a word has a head which is not the rightmost morpheme. This is when all morphemes to the right of the word lack the relevant features to determine the category of the word as a whole. For instance, in verb-particle sequences such as *grow up* or *step out*, the head is not the rightmost element (i.e. *up* in *grow up* and *out* in *step out*), but it is the verbs, *grow* and *step* which determine the category of the sequences.

In this rule, Selkirk (1982: 21) defines the notion 'head' as follows;

(203) If a constituent α is the head of a constituent β, α and β are associated with an identical set of features (syntactic and diacritic). (1982:21)

Her analysis works with an X-bar rule system, which works in a "top-down" manner. Eventually, it is this top-down property that enables Selkirk to account for category-changing prefixation and a number of Romance compounds. Presumably languages choose either the left- or the right-most morpheme as the head. So (202) applies in languages which have right-headed words. Japanese, English and Danish choose the right-most element of a compound as the head (English; Williams, Selkirk 1982; Japanese; Kageyama 1983, Namiki 2001, Mainland Scandinavian languages; Josefsson 1997 and Holmberg 1992).

In Di Sciullo & Williams' (1987) relativised RHR, they defend another formulation of RHR, based on Selkirk's. This version, too, allows features to come from a morpheme which is not rightmost just in case the morpheme to the right lacks those features. Again, languages with strongly left-headed morphology are not accommodated. Scalise (1988) suggests that the position of the head in compounds is simply stipulated, i.e. Italian compounds are left-headed.

Romance languages (Roeper, Snyder and Hiramatsu 2002: 2, Scalise: personal communication) and Vietnamese (see Gil (2002) to appear on Malayan languages), do not seem to have recursive compound words, whereas English, Scandinavian languages and Japanese do, as do many other right-headed compound word languages. Typical examples of recursive compounds are *restaurant coffee cup* and *student film committee*. Recursive compounds in Romance languages (e.g., * *restaurant café tasse* (French), **teatro billet buro* 'theatre ticket office' in Spanish and *sera computer corso* 'evening computer class' in Italian) do not exist. There might be a correlation between recursiveness of compounding and right-headedness in a given language. Spencer (1991) claims that all of the examples of Vietnamese compounds seem to have the structure of syntactic phrases and lexicalisation of phrases rather than true compounding. Moreover, Romance languages also show similar phenomena. In French, for example, there are two main types of compound-like constructions. One is formed from syntactic phrases, such as *les hors d'oeuvres* (the 'hors d'oeuvre), *le cessez-le-feu* (cease-the-fire) 'ceasefire', and *la mise-au-point* (the put-to-point) 'focus'. The second type consists of a verb followed by its object. Typical examples are *le porte-parole* (carries word) 'spokesman', *le pince-nez* (pinches-nose) 'pince-nez' (Spencer 1991: 312). These constructions in French and Vietnamese might suggest that headedness plays some role in recursiveness of compounding in a given language. However, in Malay (Othman & Atmosumarto 1995), a member of the Indonesian language family, compounding is recursive but is left-headed. Thus, it is not possible to maintain the correlation between headedness and recursivity. Evidently, further research needs to be done to establish whether there is a relation between recursiveness and direction of headedness.

Selkirk has the following structure for compound words in English.

(204) N→N N
       N→A N
(205) N [±Plural]

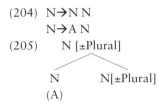

   N   N[±Plural]
  (A)

(205) shows that it is the noun with inflectional features which is the head. The right-hand head's features percolate to the immediately dominating node, and decide the category as Noun. In her work, Selkirk concludes that compound words in English are composed of two words, instead of stems (see section 2.4.1), because of the existence of plural marked constituents inside compound words on heads and non-heads.

This structure seems adequate for English compound words. Even though Selkirk does not consider neoclassical compound, there is no reason not to assume that this type of compound has the same kind of structure as normal compound words. This is especially true in Japanese and English neoclassical compounds, where both constituents are the same. However, some English neoclassical compounds (as discussed in 2.1.2) have a linking morpheme inside them. Thus, there needs to be a projection for the morpheme. Similarly, for genitive compound words in all the language in question, there needs to be a projection for the genitive-like linking morpheme inside the compound word. In both cases, the righthand is the head as it percolates to the dominating node.

Another disadvantage of the structure proposed by Selkirk is that it does not explain why compound words with a plural non-head constituent are in general ungrammatical. Furthermore, as discussed in section 2.4, the occurrence of the plural marker -s found in some English compound words is not actually semantically plural.

Also, neither Selkirk's nor Williams' analysis has phrasal compounds or dvandva compounds, represented in 2.4.4 and 2.4.5, respectively. Phrasal compounds have the rightmost constituent as head and always, the non-head is the phrasal constituent.

Moreover, this analysis does not apply to all compound words in Japanese (contra Kageyama 1993) and Scandinavian languages (see (6) (7), (10)-(12)). There are compounds where the non-head constituent does not look like a free morpheme.

Another criticism of this structure for compound words is that it will massively overgenerate, allowing noun heads in compounds to themselves consist of A-N:

(206) *lion young tamer 'young tamer of lions'
(207) *house incompetent builder 'incompetent house-builder'
(208) *hotel cheap room 'cheap room in a hotel'
(209) *shoe big shop 'big shop for shoes'   (data from Bennet 1996: 1)

The above examples appear to be uniformly excluded, thus adding weight to the view that there should be no such structure as (205).

Lieber (1980) along similar lines as Selkirk and Williams, proposed a somewhat different structure and analysis of compound words. She takes one step further than Selkirk and Williams and proposes that it is not necessary to repeat lexical information like Selkirk's. Unlike Selkirk's analysis, Lieber (1980) argues that free morphemes and affixes alike have lexical entries which show their syntactic category, semantic and phonological representations and subcategorisation frames. Lieber proposes that morphemes are inserted into unlabeled, binary-branching trees according to their subcategorisation frames[41]. Category and other information are then percolated up the structure in accordance with a series of Feature Percolation Conventions.

In this theory, trees are labelled by means of the following four conventions.

(210) Feature Percolation Conventions
Convention 1
All features of a stem morpheme, including category features, percolate to the first nonbranching node dominating that morpheme. For example:

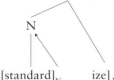

[standard]$_N$ ize]$_V$

Convention 2
All features of an affix morpheme, including category features, percolate to the first branching node dominating that morpheme. For example:

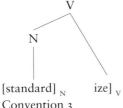

[standard]$_N$ ize]$_V$

Convention 3

If a branching node fails to obtain features by Convention 2, features from the next lowest labelled node automatically percolate up to the unlabeled branching node. For example:

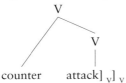

counter   attack]$_V$]$_V$

Where *counter-* lacks a category feature.

Convention 4

If two stems are sisters (i.e. they form a compound), features from the right-hand stem percolate up to the branching node dominating the stems. See the following for derivation of an English compound.

(211)

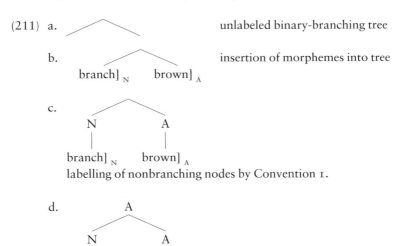

a.   unlabeled binary-branching tree

b.   insertion of morphemes into tree
      branch]$_N$ brown]$_A$

c.
      N   A
      | |
      branch]$_N$ brown]$_A$
      labelling of nonbranching nodes by Convention 1.

d.   A
      N   A
      | |
      branch]$_N$ brown]$_A$
      labelling of branching nodes dominating stems by Convention 4.

Lieber states that convention 4 is language-particular: English, German and other Indo-European languages and languages with right-hand head elements make use of it, but some languages, like Vietnamese and Thai, instead labeling compounds on the basis of the leftmost stem.

Lieber herself admits that her analysis does not limit the type of lexical category which can be inserted into a word tree as a sister to a stem of any other lexical category to form a compound. To apply this framework to compound words in any languages, it is necessary to have strict restrictions for selections in the lexicon for each stem.

In her article, Lieber (1983) considers that the lexical entries of verbs and prepositions contain argument structures and that nouns and adjectives are non-argument taking lexical items.

With this in mind, she proposes the Argument Linking Principle for compound words (Lieber 1983).

(212) Argument-linking Principle
    a. In the configuration $[\ ]_{\{v,p\}}[\ ]_{\{\alpha\}}$ or $[\ ]_{\{\alpha\}}[\ ]_{\{v,p\}}$, where α ranges over all categories, {V, P} must be able to link all internal arguments.
    b. If a stem $[\ ]_\alpha$ is free in a compound which also contains an argument-taking stem, α must be interpretable as a semantic argument of the argument-taking stem, i.e. as a Locative, Manner, Agentive, Instrumental, or Benefactive argument.   (Lieber 1983: 238)

It is necessary to interpret the Argument-linking Principle in connection with the Feature Percolation Conventions given in (212). Given the Feature Percolation Conventions, the right-hand stem of a compound percolates up to the branching node dominating the stems and determines the lexical category of the whole compound. According to the Argument-linking Principle (212), the argument structure of the right-hand stem in the compound is adopted to that of the compound as a whole. For example, a compound *handwash* adopts the argument structure of the verb stem *wash*. Having passed its argument structure onto the compound *handwash*, the verb stem *wash* then usually satisfies its argument structure in a sentence into which the verb *handwash* has been inserted (e.g., *I handwashed my jumper yesterday*). In principle, the Argument-linking Principle is applicable for prepositions as a right-hand stem of a compound word (e.g., A-P and N-P are predicted to be possible). However, such compounds do not seem to exist.

According to (212), the first stem in a compound does not pass any of its features onto the compound as a whole. It is predicted, therefore, that if the first stem is an argument-taking stem, the second stem must satisfy the argument structure of the first. Typical examples of compounds predicted to be possible by the Argument Principle are P-N, V-N and V-A compounds (e.g., *between-class, above-ground, drop-curtain, push-bicycle, be-good, play-dead*). In contrast, it is predicted that P-A compounds would be unlikely. An adjective cannot serve as an argument to a preposition. Thus, compounds like *among-legal* and *during-happy* are not allowed, as predicted.

Moreover, according to the Argument-linking Principle, if the argument-taking stem in a compound lacks an internal argument entirely, it must have a semantic argument interpreted as a Locative, Instrumental, Manner, Agentive argument, etc. For example, N-V compounds are possible only if the N is the internal argument of the V or a semantic argument of the V (e.g., *mallet-crack, knife-slice, steam-wade* where the noun stems can easily be interpreted as Instruments (*mallet, knife*) or as Locatives (*steam*). In contrast, A-V compounds such as **green-dry, *high-walk* and **blue-shave* are predicted to be unacceptable because the adjective stem cannot be given semantic interpretation.

Lieber does not provide an analysis of genitive compound words and Scandinavian compounds with a linking element inside. Nevertheless, it is possible to analyse them within Lieber's theory. As discussed in Section 2.4.2, the case-like linking element in genitive compounds in the languages in question is devoid of features. It is neither a case nor a derivational affix, since it makes the first constituent behave differently from the corresponding NP phrase with a genitive case marker. Under Lieber's Convention 3, if the linking morpheme has no feature, then the features of both of the constituents percolate up to the higher node. The right-hand element is the head by virtue of Convention 4.

A criticism against the Argument-linking Principle is that it is not clear why languages like Japanese, Korean and Chinese allow V-V compound words whereas Germanic languages do not. It is clear that both stems in V-V compounds can be argument-taking. Lieber claims that the Argument Linking Principle can account for the impossibility of transitive-intransitive/intransitive-transitive verb compounds in English. The rightmost argument-taking stem will supply the compound as a whole with its argument structure, and this argument structure will therefore be satisfied outside the compound. In contrast, the leftmost argument-taking stem will have to satisfy its argument structure within the compound. Any V which has an internal N argument is predicted to be impossible in this position. If this type is impossible in English, it should be also in other languages. However, in Japanese this type of compound is productive, especially when the second stem is unergative (Hirakawa 2000). Typical examples of transitive-unergative compounds are *sagasi-mawaru* 'look-go-around' (to look for) and *omoi-komu* 'think-crowded' (to assume) and many others. So the Argument Linking Principle should be re-considered.

Moreover, Lieber does not explain explicitly why plural inflection cannot appear between two constituents. However, she seems to argue that compounding always applies to stems in her Argument-linking Principle. In that case, plural is excluded in compounding.

Also, Lieber's analysis has phrasal compounds or dvandva compounds, represented in 2.4.4 and 2.4.5, respectively. Phrasal compounds have the rightmost constituent as head and always, the non-head is the phrasal constituent.

3.1.3 Lieber (1992)

Lieber (1992) claims that there are some degrees of interaction between morphology and syntax (also discussed in Chapter 2). Rules of word formation must at least be allowed to refer to phrasal categories. Firstly, Lieber states that recursion is allowed at least at the X^0 level. This claim comes from analysing derivation of words in English. Let us look at the following structures.

(213) a.  (Lieber 1992: 35)

It is the case in phrases that 'the head characteristically carries one-bar level less than the phrasal node which dominates it' (Lieber 1992: 35). In contrast, this is not true in words. Therefore, complex words have the recursive structure of (b) rather than that of (a).

b.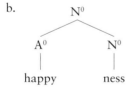

The structure (213b), according to Lieber, is true if we consider prefixation and more complex structure. For prefixation, if a head always has one bar-level less than the node dominating it, then, the following structure should be assumed.

(214)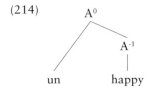

Happy must be A^{-1}, if the structure is to conform to the X-bar template and if *happy* is the head. However, the stem is a free morpheme, so it is most likely an A^0. Lieber claims that there is certainly no evidence that *happy* must be an A^0, so could not be A^{-1}. At the same time, she admits that she is contradicting herself with another claim that the stem *happy* is surely not an A^{-1}, where it is not head[42].

Moreover, there is evidence given by Lieber to suggest that the basic X-bar template below word level becomes even less tenable. That is clear when words that are more complex in structure are considered. For example, the verb *relegalize*, where *–ize* attaches to the A *legal* to create a verb and *re-* to the verb *legalize*. Since *re -* neither changes category nor the argument structure of the items to which it attaches, it is not the head of *relegalize*. As a result, it is clear that the head in the complex word is the form *legalize*, as shown in the structures (215).

(215) a.* 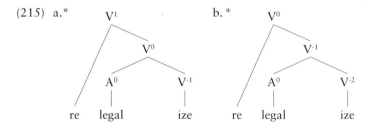 b.*

The above two structures are problematic, since a complex word cannot be V^1 in (215 a). Neither can the suffix *– ize* be a V^{-2} nor the word *legalize* be a V^{-1} in (215 b). In conclusion, it is only possible to permit the following structure (216).

(216)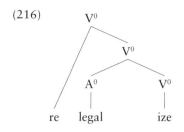

As a result of the problem here, it is necessary to assume recursion in complex words at least at the X^0 level.

(217) a. $X^n \rightarrow ... X^{\{n-1, n\}}...$, where recursion is allowed for n=0.

(Lieber 1992: 37)

As a result, Lieber (1992) revises principles of X-bar theory so that it is possible to generate both well-formed phrasal and well-formed complex words in languages. Based on Stowell's (1981: 87) foundation of X-bar theory and an argument that recursion is allowed for complex words as well as phrases, Lieber (1992: 35) proposes the following.

b. Pre- or post-head modifiers may be X^{max} or X^0. (Lieber 1992: 35)

Based on Stowell's (1981: 87) notions of the foundation of X-bar theory, Lieber discusses the position of complements and adjunct with respect to heads. She notes that it is possible in a language for specifiers and modifiers to appear on one side of the head and complements on the other, or for specifiers to occur on one side of the head and both complements and modifiers on the other. Thus, it appears that we need three separate Head Initial/Final parameters, one concerning the position of complements, a second concerning the position of specifiers, and a third concerning the position of modifiers. These parameters apply at word-level as well as phrasal level.

(218) a. $X^n \rightarrow ... X^{\{n-1, n\}}...$, where recursion is allowed for n=0.
b. Licensing Conditions
 i. Heads are initial/final with respect to complements and adjuncts.
  --Theta-roles are assigned to the left/right.
  --Case is assigned to the left/right.
 ii. Heads are initial/final with respect to specifiers.
 iii. Heads are initial/final with respect to modifiers.
c. Pre- or post-head modifiers may be X^{max} or X^0. (Lieber 1992: 38)

Lieber also defines the terms complement, modifier and specifier. The term *complement* is defined as 'internal argument (in the sense of Williams 1981) obligatorily selected by a verb'. The term *'modifier'* is defined as a constituent which limits potential reference typically of a noun. Lieber argues that there is ambiguity between *'modifier'* and *'specifier'* in X-bar theory and follows Stowell's definition of *'restrictive modifier'*. Stowell defines *restrictive modifier* as follows.

> We can think of a head noun as having an indeterminate scope of reference, ranging over entities or classes of entities. The function of a restrictive clause is to fix the scope of reference of the phrase, narrowing the reference to a specific subset of the referents allowed by the head (Stowell 1981: 278).

According to Lieber, the scope of reference of categories other than N is usually fixed. Therefore, it is typically only Ns that have restrictive modifiers. The term specifier covers determiners, demonstratives, quantifiers and modals within NP structure.

This becomes clear if examples from English are examined. The position of the head in compound words is predicted from the position of head in phrases with respect to the position of modifiers in English. Usually, the setting for the Licensing Condition, (208iii) in English is as follows.

(219) Heads are final with respect to modifiers.

This claim by Lieber is in opposition to Jackendoff (1977) and Stowell (1981)[43].

All modifiers begin in prehead position. The relationship between the two constituents in root compounds is between restrictive modifier and its head. Thus, the third parameter presented above in the Licensing Conditions stipulates that the head is final to restrictive modifiers in root compounds in English. The following examples of English compound words demonstrate the parameters discussed above.

(220) Root compounds
 $[A\text{-}N]_N$ greenhouse, hard hat
 $[N\text{-}A]_A$ sky blue, ice cold
 $[N\text{-}N]_N$ file cabinet, towel rack
 $[A\text{-}A]_A$ red hot, worldly wise
 $[V\text{-}N]_N$ drawbridge, pickpocket (Lieber 1992: 55)

For root compounds, it is possible to tell that they are right-headed, since semantically the right-hand stem determines the object or quality denoted by the compound as a whole. In relation to the head, the complement is the left constituent and it modifies the head. For instance, in the compound word, *file cabinet*, the left-hand stem restricts or limits the reference of the 'right-hand' head. Thus, Lieber's proposal is valid if compound words are considered.

Lieber claims that English allows words to be formed using phrasal bases, i.e. phrasal compounds. The resulting words show that they are right-headed structures. The examples from 2.4.4 are repeated here.

(221) [$_N$ [$_{NP}$ a pipe-and-slipper][$_N$ husband]]
(222) [$_N$ [$_{NP}$ a slept-all-day][$_N$ look]]
(223) [$_N$ [$_{PP}$ over-the-fence][$_N$ gossip]]
(224) [$_N$ [$_{VP}$ God-is-dead][$_N$ theology]]

Thus, the Licensing Conditions are accurate.

The following are examples of compound words in Scandinavian languages.

(225) [A-N]   våd+dragt, små+snak
               wet+ suit, small+talk
       [N-A]   himmel+blå, farve+blind
               sky+ blue, colour+blind
       [N-N]   figen+træ, kontor+tid
               fig+ tree, office+ hour
       [A-A]   lyse+rød
               light+red
       [V-N]   vind+e+bro, køb+stad
               draw+LINK+bridge, buy+place

These examples show that compound words in Scandinavian languages are also right-headed, as semantically the right-hand stem determines the object or quality denoted by the compound as a whole.

As for Japanese, the Licensing Conditions are somewhat hard to state. It is well known that Japanese is a head-final language, in contrast to English and Scandinavian languages. Let us see some examples in phrases and decide the position of head with respect to complements, restrictive modifiers and specifiers.

(226) NP si no hakai
           city GEN destruction
           'the destruction of the city'

PP **ana** no naka ni, **ki** no ue de
   hole GEN inside IN, tree GEN up at
   'in the hole', 'up a tree'
VP **pizza** o tabeta
   pizza ACC ate
   'ate the/a pizza'

The bolded words are complements. They precede their heads in all the phrases in Japanese. Thus, heads are final with respect to complements.

Specifiers, also, uniformly precede their heads in Japanese. For example, subjects of IP and NP come before Infl and N respectively:

(227) **kodomo** tachi ga pizza o tabeta.
      Child- PLURAL NOM pizza ACC ate
      'The children ate the pizza'.
(228) **kodomo** tachi no jujoo no ie no hakai.
      Child-PLURAL GEN up-tree GEN house GEN destruction
      'the children's destruction of the tree house'

The position of restrictive modifiers with respect to the head can be decided from the following examples.

(229) **totemo ookikute sinzirarenaikurai kitanai** inu
      Very big-and unbelievably dirty dog
      'a very big and unbelievably dirty dog'
(230) **betsu ni odorokanai hodo se no takai** josei
      particularly surprising-not extent height GEN tall woman
      'a not too surprisingly tall woman'

The bolded words are prenominal adverbs and adjectives and they modify their heads. Thus, in Japanese, too, like in English, the following parameters are set.

(231) i. Heads are final with respect to complements and adjuncts.
      ii. Heads are final with respect to specifiers.
      iii. Heads are final with respect to modifiers.

The third parameter states, like in English and Scandinavian languages, that the heads are right-headed with respect to modifiers. Root compounds in the examples below show that this is true.

(232) Root compounds

CHAPTER 3 STRUCTURE OF COMPOUND WORDS 83

[A-N]_N   taka+ nami, kirei+ goto
          high+ wave, clean+ thing
          'a high wave', 'whitewash'
[N-A]_A   mimi+ atarasii, kazu+ ooi,
          ear + new, number+ many,
          'novel'   'large number',
[N-N]_N   kitchen+ table, huyu+ gesiki
          kitchen+ table, winter+scenery
                          'winter scenery'
[A-A]_A   aka+ guroi, atsu+gurusii
          red+ black, hot+painful
          'reddish black', 'sultry'
[V-N]_N   agari+guchi, nomi+mizu
          rise+mouth, drink+water
          'doorway', 'drinking water'

It is possible to determine the head since the right-hand head determines the object or quality denoted by the compound as a whole. Thus, Lieber's proposal is valid for compound words in Japanese.

I conclude that Lieber's Licensing Conditions can be applied to compound words in Japanese, English and the Scandinavian languages. The structure of a compound word in these languages is given as follows.

(233)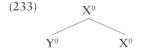

Moreover, Lieber proposes a structure for phrasal compounds. Phrasal compounds in all the languages are assumed to have the following structure.

(234)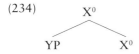

However, one thing needs to be said. In Scandinavian languages, there are two types of compound. As discussed in connection with Selkirk's theory, the compound words, (10) – (12) in Scandinavian languages cannot have this structure. Examples of (10) – (12) are repeated below.

(235)   fred+s+ konference   [D]
        peace+LINK+conference

'peace conference'
(236) jul+e+gave [D]
Christmase+LINK+present
'Christmas present'
(237) kyrk+torn [S]
church+ø+ tower[44]

This is because the levels of the two constituents are not the same, unlike the structure (233). These compounds contain something more than just two N⁰s. There needs to be a projection for the linking morpheme inside compound word in Scandinavian languages.

Also, Lieber's analysis has dvandva compounds, represented in 2.4.5. Dvandva compounds can be analyzed in the same way as normal compounds. Its structure is represented in (233).

3.1.4 Holmberg's analysis (1992)

There needs to be another analysis which can be applied to all the world's languages and to any type of compound words, including neoclassical compounding, compounding with a linking morpheme or vowel morpheme (see 2.1.1), as in Scandinavian languages, and phrasal compound words. Holmberg (1992) analyses compound words in Swedish and English, and thus, includes compound words with a linking morpheme or vowel morpheme. This section will investigate this analysis of compound words.

The main claim in his paper is that for Swedish Noun-Noun compounds, the following generalisation can be made.

(238) The head of a compound is a Word. A non-branching non-head of a compound is either a Root or a Casemarked word, a branching non-head is a Casemarked word. (Holmberg 1992: 1)

As discussed in Section 2.1.1, there are two types of compound words in Scandinavian languages. One is formed with two stems and the other is formed with a root and a stem. Thus, it is possible to see from morphology which is the head of the latter type of compound word in Mainland Scandinavian. Consider the examples in (239) – (240) representing a large class of nouns in Swedish. The left-hand constituent is the same form that is found in combination with derivational affixes: the stem vowel –*a* or –*e* is deleted in compound word as the following shows.

(239) a. skol+a

CHAPTER 3   STRUCTURE OF COMPOUND WORDS 85

       school+a
  b. skol + flicka
       school+ girl
  c. *skol+a + flicka
(240) a. flick+a
       girl+a
  b. flick + skola
       girl + school
  c. *flick+a +skola

The b examples show that the stem vowel –*a* of the left-hand constituent of the compound must be deleted. Holmberg states that the stem vowel –*a* is a word marker which encodes the feature number. Thus, for this type of compound, the structure is as follows.

In the following structures, the Word is represented as W, Root as R and Word Marker as WM.

(241) flick+skol+a
      girl +school+ WM

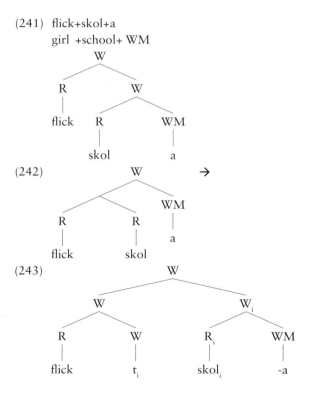

Instead of one simple structure like (241), he states that the structure is derived in a two-step process as shown in (243), just like a phrase is. In D-structure, the two roots are formed as a constituent and the singular word marker *–a* is merged with this constituent at the end. However, following Williams (1981), Selkirk (1982) among others, Holmberg (1992) states that if two roots are merged, all their features will be percolated to the dominating node, resulting in an uninterpretable construction. Thus, in S-structure, one of the roots moves and adjoins to the WM. The index of the Root *skol* percolates to the W immediately dominating R and WM. At S-structure, the tree should be ready for semantic interpretation in the S-structure. The features of the various heads should be appropriately distributed in the tree, each node having features as determined by its head and general principles of feature percolation. The two constituents are constituents ordered in terms of their levels. This structure is based on the assumption that the root in compound word is a maximal category and a Word is a non-maximal category (Muysken 1983, cited in Holmberg 1992).

The following structure, according to Holmberg's (1992) proposal, is not possible for a compound word.

(244)

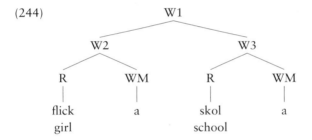

This structure is ungrammatical, as the structure has two heads, W2 and W3, projecting all their features onto W1, resulting in an uninterpretable construction[45].

Another type includes compound words with a linking morpheme (as discussed in Section 2.1.1). Holmberg (1992) claims that this morpheme is a case-marker. With these three types of compound words in Scandinavian languages, Holmberg proposes the following structure for compound words.

(245) stol+s+ben
      chair+Case+leg

CHAPTER 3 STRUCTURE OF COMPOUND WORDS 87

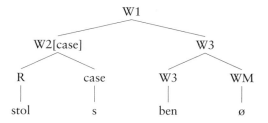

The ø in (245) under the WM encodes the singular form of the word *ben*. In order to prevent the case-feature itself to percolate to W1, Holmberg proposes a mechanism of government by a 'case-assigning head' which in this case is W3. The case-feature is governed by the head, and the W2 is well-formed non-head by virtue of containing a governed case-feature.

When a compound itself is embedded as the non-head of a compound, the stem vowel disappears and a linking morpheme –*s* is attached.

(246) a. *skolflicka + dröm, *skolflick + dröm
       school+ girl+ dream
    b. skol+flick+s +dröm
       school+girl+s+dream

The b example means 'school girl's dream' and it is necessary to have the linking element in order to have the interpretation.

(246b) is represented in the following structure.

(247)

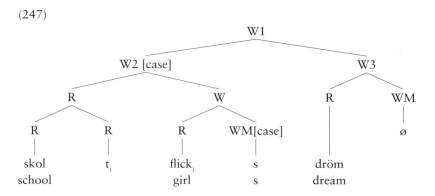

In this structure, the root *flick* moves and adjoins to the linking morpheme. The linking morpheme here is the head of the structure when it is merged with the lexical element *flick*. The case feature on W2 turns W2 into a maximal category, by virtue of containing a governed-case-feature. W3 is the head, since it assigns case.

Let us see if the structure proposed by Holmberg is appropriate for the other two languages. In fact, he discusses the structure of compound words in English. As discussed above in Chapter 2, both segments in compound words are at the same level, unlike in Scandinavian languages. They are, in fact, Word categories in this theory.

(248)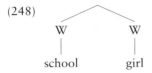

In Holmberg's theory, the non-head of a compound should either be a Root or be case-marked, but there is no morphological evidence that the non-head is a Root in English. The fact that the non-head can be plural-marked (at least phonetically) indicates that it cannot be a Root (Section 2.4.1). If this is true, in the present theory non-heads in English compounds are always expected to have abstract case-marking. In English, it is possible to have genitive on the non-head, like in the compounds such as, *woman's magazine, devil's advocate* and *driver's license*, as discussed in Section 2.4.2. Thus, within this theory, the following structure is possible in English compound words.

(249)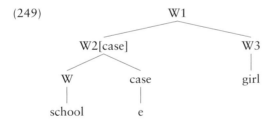

If abstract Case is represented as an empty head, the structure is as above. We can then assume that the phonetically empty Case on W2 is licensed by W3, simply because of W3 governing W2 leftwards in English.

Holmberg also goes on to say that in English compound words, there is no reason not to allow a plural non-head, whereas in Swedish it is not possible at all. In Swedish, the number affix is termed by Holmberg as a word marker. The word marker in Swedish takes a Root or a Stem as a complement. In contrast, however, in English, there is no selection for the plural morpheme. As a result, different structures are formed for compound words in the two languages.

(250)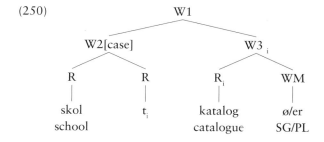

In Swedish, the non-head is a Root. A plural non-head would be a Word. Then, it would require Case. But since word-internal Case is a WM (word marker), it is incompatible with the plural form. Therefore, both *skol-or-katalog* (school-PL-cataglogue) and *skol-or-s-katalog* (school-PL-LINK-catalogues) are ungrammatical.

In English, it is possible to have plural marker inside a compound.

(251)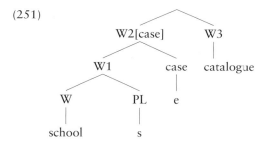

The structure shows that combining a non-head with a plural marker is not a problem in English. It is also possible to combine a plural W with abstract Case since Case is also an adjunct to W. These assumptions are, however, from a structural point of view.

In Japanese, there is no plural marker. Let us assume that a compound in Japanese has the structure (252).

(252)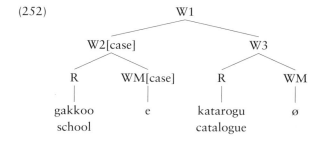

The linking morpheme observed in Scandinavian languages is phonetically empty in Japanese compound words. This structure shows that the left-hand constituent is assumed to be a root and marked by the abstract case marker, whose feature is percolated to W2. However, the phonetically empty word marker on the right-hand constituent is the head, since it governs the phonetically empty case on W2.

Another advantage is that this structure can be applied to genitive compound words in all the languages. Holmberg in fact states that the suffix –s is a case marker in English and Scandinavian languages. Thus, the structure for genitive compound words can be analysed in the same way as that of normal compound words. Japanese genitive compound words are also analysed in the same way.

(253)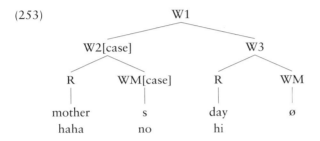

Another advantage of this structure is that the levels of both constituents are marked clearly. Let us see if neoclassical compounds can be analysed in the same way. Neoclassical compounds do not seem to have any case-marking. Spencer (2003) (as discussed in Section 2.1.2), however, states that a special linking element is found in some neoclassical compounds of English, such as *cyt-o-plasm*. This linking element, I propose, is the same thing as the linking element in Scandinavian languages. As in the Scandinavian languages, the possibility of a linking element in neoclassical compound is in complementary distribution with plural-marking. In other words, it is not possible to have a plural marker inside them. Thus, it is possible to assume the same kind of structure for neoclassical compounds as normal compound words. The categorical features represented for each constituent would be Root and Root with WM inside.

There is no linking element involved between the constituents and there is no word-marker inside them in Japanese neoclassical compounds. However, it is possible to assume there is an abstract WM[case]. So the structure (253) is applicable also for neoclassical compounds in Japanese.

One criticism against Holmberg's analysis is that it is not necessary to have such a complicated representation. The next section will discuss a more economical analysis of compound words.

In addition, phrasal compounds and dvandva compounds are not analyzed in Holmberg's theory. There is no reason not to analyze dvandva compounds in the same way as the other types of compounds.

(254)

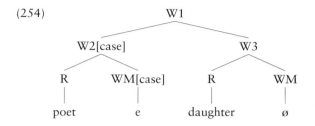

The structure (254) is for the appositional compounds. This structure shows that the case of *poet-translator* in (158c) is not the property of poet or that of translator, but a combination of the two properties assigned to one person. It is possible to assume there is an abstract WM[case]. So the structure (254) is applicable also for appositional compounds. The interpretation of the whole compound would be 'one person with two properties.

(255)

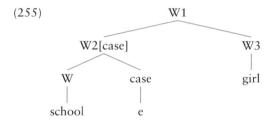

If abstract Case is represented as an empty head, the structure is as above. We can then assume that the phonetically empty Case on W2 is licensed by W3, simply because of W3 governing W2 leftwards in English.

3.2 Structures for compound words in the Minimalist Programme

Before considering structures for compound words proposed within the Minimalist Program, it is necessary first to describe some basic assumptions of the Minimalist Program.

The aim of the Minimalist Program is to answer the question 'How 'perfect' is language?' In other words, we minimalists have to explain how natural language grammars create structures which are designed to interface perfectly with other components of the mind, with speech and thought systems. To answer the question, it is necessary to assume that human language has a single computational system C_{HL} and only limited lexical variety. Differences of language is morphological in character. However, in reality, languages are not 'perfect'. Therefore, there are three choices when encountering the problem. Firstly, we can complicate the computational system, departing from maximal economy in order to accommodate the 'imperfection', concluding that language deviates from 'perfection'. Secondly, we can make the imperfections a responsibility of systems, the two interfaces LF and PF. Finally, we can ignore the 'imperfections' saying that we do not see how to solve the problem.

With these basic assumptions in mind, this programme does require economy in the derivation of human language. Chomsky argues that the basic operation of syntax is that words are combined into phrases. Therefore, a derivation begins with a set N (the numeration) of primitive elements of the language, taken from the lexicon. The primitive operation Merge recursively combines elements of N two by two and eliminates them from N. The interface level PF must interpret the output of Merge as an ordered string of these two merged elements. This interpretation process is called Spell Out. Spell Out occurs at specific points throughout the derivation; in the Minimalist Program there is no level of S-structure that interfaces with PF, but only LF, which interfaces with the conceptual-intentional component, and PF, which interfaces with the articulatory-perceptual component.

Merge is a constituent building operation. Out of the two lexical items from the lexicon, Merge creates a new object, L.

(256)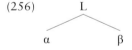

The new object consists of α and β, but, crucially, only one of the two determines the relevant properties of L. It is possible to say that L is an instance either of α or of β, but not of the two of them. The element of which L is an instance is the head of the structure (as discussed in 1.4). As in GB theory, the head gives its part of speech, which is called its 'label' by Chomsky, to the whole phrase or word. The head of the structure projects, i.e. determines the properties of L.

There are two different types of merger proposed by Chomsky (2000), set-merge and pair-merge. Set-merge is defined as a mechanism for structure building by combining categories drawn from the lexicon. It is symmetrical as an operation. In other words, the two lexical elements drawn from the lexicon, α and β, merge with each other and form a set of two elements, but the structure typically has an inherent asymmetry in that the operation is triggered by a selection feature of either α or β, the selector. Chomsky proposes that the selector projects, i.e. it is the head. Triggered by a selection feature, set-merge is obligatory.

On the other hand, pair-merge forms an ordered pair, α and β, and involves at least some cases of movement, i.e. remerge of a category already merged at least once. It is an asymmetrical operation in the sense that α is adjoined to β. By assumption, the target of adjunction projects, labelling <α, β>. There is no selection involved, so the operation is optional. If these two types of merge exhaust the forms that Merge can take, the label of the category formed by Merge is always predictable, therefore redundant. The redundancy of the operation Merge does obey the economy condition in Minimalist Program. If all compounding is pair-merge, it is an ordered pair in the syntax as well as in the phonological component.

The third significant point in the operation of Merge is that the operation only applies to the root nodes of syntactic objects. This is called the Extension Condition (Chomsky (1993, 1995)). A syntactic derivation can only be continued by applying operations to the root projection of the tree. In other words, this condition prohibits setting up syntactic relations between objects which have already been constructed inside a structure. For example, let us imagine the following schematic tree:

(257)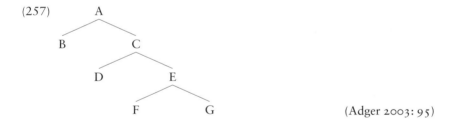

(Adger 2003: 95)

If A is the projection of the head B, it will be possible to set up syntactic relations between B and C for checking purposes. It is also possible to set up syntactic relations between B and F, for example. However, the Extension Condition prohibits syntactic operations, including checking and merging, applying to D, since it is not the root projection of the tree. Any operation involving D must apply before B is merged. In other words, it must apply while D is the head of the root. If it is not a head, it cannot trigger any syntactic operations. Thus, merging of some object with C the category headed by D will disallow checking between D and for example F.

Another important part of Minimalist Program is the operation movement.

In the Minimalist Program, unlike the GB framework, all movements are caused by feature checking requirements; movement is the Last Resort for reasons of economy. The features of lexical constituents consist of three different types: formal features (or syntactic features), such as case, Extended Projection Principle feature (henceforth EPP feature) and semantic features, such as person and number, and phonological features. Semantic and phonological features are considered to be relevant respectively at the interfaces LF and PF. Formal features are the features that cause the movements within the derivation and give rise to the particular patterning of words that we recognise as grammar. Formal features may also be accessed by the rules of morphophonology, giving rise to different morphological or phonological forms. Formal syntactic features may also be accessed by the rules of semantic interpretation. Movement is only necessary to check functional features that are uninterpretable at the LF interface. In other words, movement is regarded as a way to meet the Bare Output Conditions of an interface level.

Let us see how Merge preempts Move (Chomsky 2000). Let us observe the following examples.

(258) a. [T $_{defective}$ thought likely [to be awarded several prizes]
       b. [TP There$_i$ are thought likely [t$_i$ to be awarded several prizes].
       c. Several prizes$_i$ are thought likely [t$_i$ to be t$_i$ awarded t$_j$].
       d. *There are thought likely [several prizes$_i$ to be t$_i$ awarded t$_i$].
   (the derivations of these examples are taken from Radford 2004: 316-321)

When the derivation goes onto the step (a), if the expletive *there* is in the numeration, it is merged at [Spec, TP] to satisfy the EPP feature of the embedded T. Thus, there is no need for the DP *several prizes* to be moved to the position. Example (b) demonstrates this effect. After *are* is merged, the expletive *there* is moved to satisfy the EPP feature on the matrix T. On the other hand, when the expletive *there* is not in the numeration, the DP *several prizes* is another candidate. It is moved to satisfy the EPP feature on the embedded T and moved further to the matrix [Spec, TP] to satisfy the EPP feature on the matrix T, deriving the sentence (c).

The ungrammatical construction of (d) also proves that the operation Merge preempts the operation Move. In this case, the DP *several prizes* is moved to the embedded [Spec, TP] first. Since the expletive *there* is in the numeration, it is also merged at the same place, which results an ungrammatical construction. Thus, Merge wins by economy when the expletive is in the numeration. This is the case Chomsky argues that because the operation Move is more complex than its subcomponent Merge.

Until recently, the Minimalist Program assumed that agreement of T and the subject should take place in the specifier-head relationship (specifier and T). However, this assumption has a number of problems. Firstly, the definition of agreement domain is complicated (Nakamura, Kaneko, Kikuchi 2001: 214). Secondly, there are some cases that the spec-head account of agreement fails to explain, for example: that between the auxiliary *are* and the nominal *several prizes* in passive structures such as below:

(259) There are thought likely to be awarded several prizes.
(Radford 2004: 281)

Since the auxiliary *are* occupies the head T position of TP and the expletive pronoun *there* is in spec-TP, a spec-head account of agreement would lead us to expect that *are* should agree with *there*. However, instead, *are* agrees with the in situ complement *several prizes* of the passive participle *awarded*. How can this problem be solved?

(260)

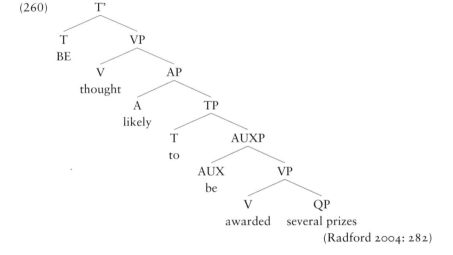

(Radford 2004: 282)

As soon as the main clause *BE* is merged, its features need to be checked. Here, Chomsky (2000) introduces the terms **probe** and **goal.** Probe is a head which searches for a matching lexical item. The term goal, on the other hand, represents a constituent which has features matching with those of a higher head (the probe). By virtue of being the highest head in the overall structure in (260) at this point in the derivation, *BE* serves as a probe which searches for a c-commanded nominal goal to agree with. The goal of the probe is the QP *several prizes*, since the QP is the only nominal projection c-commanded by *BE* with the same set of features, person and number. As a result, the construction is successfully derived. Chomsky proposes the simplest assumptions for the probe-goal system

(261) a. Matching is feature identity.
b. D(P) is the sister of P.
c. Locality reduces to "closest c-command".   (Chomsky 2000: 122)

where P is the probe, and D (P) is the domain where a probe looks for its goal. Moreover, structural case is what makes the goal active. Case-checking renders a DP inactive; the reverse holds for agreement-features.

Another significant point is that Merge does not specify the linear order of the elements that it merges. However, the linear order is important to natural languages in the PF. For example, it is important to determine the difference among the words, *pat, apt,* and *tap* when they are spelled out. It is the order of the words that makes a sentence or a combined lexical element acceptable. Therefore, it is necessary to impose some ordering on the structures built up from Merge in some other way[46]. The parametric differences of word order proposed in Principles and Parameters theory can be explained by movement to check features in Minimalist Program. For example, the contrast between wh-fronting languages like English and wh-in-situ languages like Japanese is explained by the strength of the uninterpretable wh-feature of the wh element. In examples like *what did John buy?*, the dependency between the interrogative C and *what* in the underlying object position is established by a long-distance agreement relation, which checks off the uninterpretable wh-feature of *what* and the uninterpretable [Q]-feature of the probe, C. The reason for the movement is the presence of an EPP feature of the C. On the other hand, in wh in-situ languages like Japanese, the equivalent of *what did John buy?* is as follows.

(262) John ga nani o katta no?
John NOM what ACC bought Q
'What did John buy?'

The complementiser *ka* appears to the right of the inflected verb. The wh-element *nani* is accusative, and appears in just the normal position for an accusative object. In other words, it does not undergo wh-movement. The EPP is weak in Japanese. Accordingly, the relevant feature of the wh-element has a weak EPP feature. Then, the element need not be merged into the specifier of CP, unlike in English, but can remain in-situ. AGREE suffices to check off the uninterpretable features of the probe C and the goal (wh-element), and there is no need to invoke the more complex operation of move (Ochi 2003).

Another important fact in the Minimalist Program which should be discussed is that in the Minimalist Program, each lexical item carries the information necessary for syntactic derivation. That is, the syntactic structure and the derivation of any given sentence are determined by the features on the lexical items used in the derivation. If the lexical items which will be used in the sentence are fixed, it is not too much to state that the sentence structure is decided automatically. The derivation obeys the Inclusiveness Condition proposed by Chomsky (1995: 228). This condition states that no features which are not present in the lexical items may be added in the derivation (as discussed in Chapter 1). Therefore, in contrast to GB theory, projection of X-bar to X" is not possible, because the information about intermediate projection is not part of the lexical entry and to add such information about projection levels during the course of the syntactic computation violates the Inclusiveness Condition. A phrase is by definition derived by merging two categories. There cannot, therefore, be such a thing as an XP or an X' consisting of nothing but an X^0. In contrast, in the derivation which carries information to the PF representation, intrusion phenomena do occur, such as intonation which does not come from the lexical items. Therefore, the PF representation does not obey the Inclusive Condition.

With these basic assumptions in mind, nothing prevents us from applying Merge below the word level too (Josefsson 1997: 17, Roeper, Snyder & Hiramatsu 2002)[47]. To be able to interpret the meaning and the category of the whole word, asymmetry must be obtained as early as possible in the derivation of morphology, since without any head in morphology, it is not possible to tell which real-world object the compound refers to, i.e. its reference. In other words, as discussed in the previous subsection, in morphology as well as in syntax, a complex category must have a head whose features are projected to the node governing the head. It should be noted however, that linear order does not matter in the narrow syntax, but only in the PF. In narrow syntax there is no right and left. Two lexical items are merged without any order. Thus, the Right-hand Head Rule, proposed by Williams (1981), has no place in the narrow syntax. It may have a place in the phonology, though, stipulating how a word derived in the narrow syntax is spelled out. Within the Minimalist Program, therefore, which member is the head must be determined in narrow syntax, because it is essential in LF.

Before discussing how structures for compound words in languages can be presented within the Minimalist Program, let us first consider structures for compound words proposed by researchers in previous works.

3.2.1 Spencer's analysis (2003)

Within the minimalist Bare Phrase Structure (henceforth BPS) (Chomsky 1995), the words project in the following way.

(263)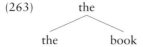

The phrase is built by merging *the* and *book*. Since the determiner selects the noun (not vice versa), *the* projects to become the label of the phrase. As discussed in 3.2, a structure formed in the computational system for human language (C_{HL}) is formed only with the features which lexical items have. For this reason, Spencer states that productive compounds are not different at all from phrases, so the representation of a N-N compound word such as *song bird* is as follows.

(264)

Within BPS, therefore, the two lexical items *song* and *bird* are merged. In this case, *bird* projects and it is the head. Spencer (personal communication) follows the morphological definition of head proposed by Williams (1981). This is inconsistent with the Minimalist Program, and this problem will be discussed below.

Moreover, Spencer analyses productive compound words formed with adjective and noun.

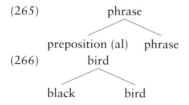

In (265), *prepositional* is the relational adjective from *preposition*. *Prepositional phrase* is generally analysed as a syntactic phrase. However, the meaning is identical to that of *preposition phrase*. Therefore, there is no distinction between the structures of the two constructions in phrase-structure terms. So the difference between the two constructs is phonological.

Another argument for his analysis comes from the analysis of a bare noun modifying an [A-N] phrase. As discussed in 2.2, an adjective which modifies the compound has to be placed outside the compound. However, a bare noun can modify an [A-N] phrase. The examples are as follows.

(267) a. London financial markets
b. An adjunct prepositional phrase
c. Senate Committee internal memoranda

Spencer argues that if *London markets, adjunct phrase* and *Senate Committee memoranda* were compounds formed after the syntactic modification by an adjective, then it is necessary to say that *financial markets, prepositional phrase* and *internal memoranda* are also compounds[48]. Another alternative is to argue that the bare nouns *London, adjunct,* and the compound *Senate Committee* can serve as modifiers in the syntax (Bauer 1998a). As a result, N- N compound words are not distinguished at all from phrases.

Another argument proposed by Spencer follows Lieberman & Sproat's (1992) analysis of stress assignment in syntactic structure. Lieberman & Sproat claim syntactic structure can predict stress and word order. For example, *jar* in *coffee jar* is N^0 and gets left-stress, whereas *jar* in *plastic jar* is N^1 and gets right-stress. For this reason it is possible to say *plastic coffee jar* but not **coffee plastic jar*. In **coffee plastic jar* it is necessary to treat *plastic jar* as an N^0. However, according to Spencer, the real problem with *coffee plastic jar* is that a lexicalised expression is split up. In fact, the string *coffee plastic jar* is perfectly grammatical. It is just that it cannot be related to the non-compositional lexicalised expression *coffee jar*. Notice that it is possible to say *kitchen sink* and *enamel sink* and *enamel kitchen sink* but not *kitchen enamel sink*. This is because lexicalised compounds N^0 cannot be separated by N^1, according to Spencer.

As discussed in 2.6, Japanese compound words are productively formed. Spencer's theory can predict that productive compounds in Japanese have the same structure as English compound words within BPS framework. A Japanese productive compound, such as *kame-pan* 'turtle bread' is structured in the following way.

(268)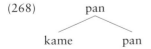

Just as is seen in English compound words, the two lexical items *kame* and *pan* are merged and the right-hand head is projected. This structure is derived with the assumption that the Right-hand Head Rule is correct.

Scandinavian languages also have productive compound words, according to the discussion in 2.6.

(269)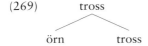

The compound word *örntross* (eagle-tross) is formed by merging the two lexical items and the right-hand head is projected to the first dominating node.

In summary, Spencer's analysis of compound words within the BPS framework has a few advantages. It is economical. There is no movement involved in the structure, but only merging the two lexical elements numerated from the lexicon.

Moreover, what about compound words with a linking morpheme inside and three-member compounds? Do we have the merge operation for three-four member compound words without violating the Extension Condition? With the following examples, I examine whether it is possible to derive four-member compounds within Spencer's analysis.

(270) barn+bok+s+klubb
child+book+LINK+club
'children's book club'

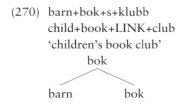

First, the compound word, *barn bok* is derived by merging the two elements. Then, the element, *bok* is the head. Then, another lexical item, the linking morpheme –*s* is merged on the right, and this item is the head by virtue of the Righthand Head Rule.

(271)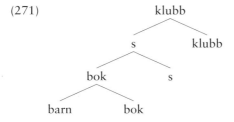

Another lexical item, *klubb* is merged and this item is the head by virtue of the

RHR. In this derivation, the Extension Condition is respected.

Another advantage of this theory is that right-branching compounds can also be analysed. The example (271) is an example of left-branching compound with a linking morpheme inside. The derivation results on a structure with the interpretation 'club for children's book', in contrast to another interpretation, 'book club for children'. The derivation of the compound with the latter interpretation, namely the right-branching compound is as follows.

(272)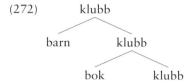

The Extension Condition is respected. By virtue of the RHR, the lexical item *klubb* is the head of the compound.

One question regarding Spencer's analysis of productive compounds is the headedness. In his paper, Spencer assumes that the right-hand element is the head by virtue of the Right-hand Head Rule (Williams 1981). However, if there is no linear order in the narrow syntax, the Right-hand Head Rule cannot determine the head of a compound.

However, one question needs to be raised concerning lexicalised compound words. In personal communication, Spencer claims that the non-head of a lexicalised compound word, such as *blackbird* has no semantic or syntactic features. On the other hand, the non-head of productive compound, such as *London bus*, has semantic and syntactic features. Nevertheless, the present author questions this claim regarding the status of the non-head in lexicalised compound words. It is argued that the non-head of lexicalised compounds is the same morpheme as that of productive compounds. Lexicalised compounds are formed in the same way as productive compounds, and the morphemes involved are exactly the same. This will be discussed in more detail in Section 3.2.4.3.

In addition, another big question to Spencer's theory is Lexical Integrity. He does not say anything about it. There are counter-examples to Lexical Integrity, as discussed in Chapter 2, but on the whole, words are islands to a greater extent than phrases. The question is how to explain that in Spencer's theory.

Finally, how do we determine the types of morphemes involved in the derivation? For example, how do we limit the occurrence of regular plural markers inside compound words in English and Scandinavian languages?

3.2.2 The theory by Roeper, Snyder & Hiramatsu (2002)

Like Spencer (2003), Roeper, Snyder & Hiramatsu (2002) claim that the structure of compound words can be based on the Minimalist Program framework. Their theory is based on the assumption that following Chomsky (1970), Baker (1988) and Lieber (1992), compounds like those in the examples (164)-(191) (e.g., *London bus* in English, *tsuri+baka* (fishing+stupid) 'a person who is keen on fishing' in Japanese, and *örntross* (eagle-tross) in Swedish) are productively formed.

(273) The Root Compounding Parameter (RCP)
Set-merger can (not) combine non-maximal projections.
(Roeper, Snyder & Hiramatsu 2002: 2)

Roeper, Snyder & Hiramatsu (2002) propose the above Root Compounding Parameter (RCP). According to this parameter, some languages permit set-merge of two lexical items *a* and *b* where one is the head and the other a complement and others do not (Chomsky 2000, 2001). According to Chomsky (1995: 246) (see Chapter 1), when *a* and *b* are merged, a is the head if and only if *a* selects *b*. However, it is well known in Generative Linguistic theory that there is no selection by root nouns, unlike verbs, adverbs, determiners, and so on. Therefore, N-N compounds cannot be formed in this way. The alternative which Roeper et al proposes is that N-N compounds are derived by a noun merging with an 'abstract clitic', which may be a noun. For example, the compound word, *coffee cup* can be derived in the following way.

(274)

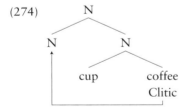

First, the compound word, *cup coffee* is derived by set-merger of the two items. *Coffee* originates in what they call the Clitic position, as in English, RCP is plus, i.e. set-merger can combine two lexical items. (The term Clitic is not the same as 'clitic' as we know it in morphology; see below for a more detailed exposition of the term 'Clitic'.

Then, *coffee* is moved leftward. The trace of *coffee* is deleted. Deletion of trace can occur as long as the trace has no semantic content which needs to be recovered (the Recoverability Condition prohibits deletion of anything which has meaning). Moreover, deletion of trace is constrained by the theta-criterion and the Projection Principle, according to Government Binding theory (Chomsky 1981, Lasnik & Saito 1992). In other words, in the above structure the trace of *coffee* can be deleted as it is not theta-marked or subcategorized, since there are no selectional requirements between two nouns. On the other hand, verb + verb+ verb compound rarely exists, because there is a selection between two or three verbs.

To form a three-member compound headed by *cup* in this case, a new lexical item *restaurant* is inserted in the position of the trace of *coffee* after deleting the trace, and then the new item is adjoined to the compound word already formed, as shown in (275).

(275)
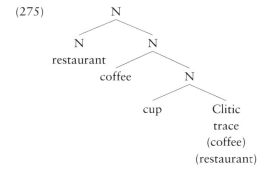

Once the trace of *coffee* is deleted, another lexical item, *restaurant*, is entered in the Clitic position and moved to a higher position to make another projection. As a result, the compound word *restaurant coffee cup* is derived. In this theory, it is possible to derive recursive compound words with an unlimited number of lexical items involved as long as they are nouns. This is due to the fact that there is no selectional requirement for nouns, unlike other lexical categories, including verbs, determiners, adjectives and prepositions. For instance, the trace of a verb is theta-marked and thus cannot be deleted. A noun does not select any lexical categories, thus allowing recursive compound words.

In contrast, in Romance languages for example productive compounds are not allowed, since the Root Compounding Parameter is negative. Typical examples are as follows.

(276) V-Maximal Projection
partir de l'école/*partir d' école
leave from the school/leave from school
(Roeper, Snyder & Hiramatsu 2002: 4)

As the above example shows, French permits only maximal projections as complements to V. The following examples also show that it is not possible to have set-merge of non-maximal projections in French, unlike in English. The preposition *à* on its own is minimal since it is a lexical item and since it has a feature to check. The syntactic object containing *à* and *café* in (277) and *outils* in (278) is maximal since it contains no selectional features, and not minimal because it is not a lexical item.

(277) tasse à café
       cup for coffee
       'coffee cup'   (Roeper, Snyder & Hiramatsu 2002: 7)
(278) boîte à outils
       box to tools
       'tool box'

The same phenomenon can be seen in Spanish and Italian.

(279) caja de herramientas   [S]
       box of tool
       'tool box'
(280) calza di Natale   [I]
       stocking of Christmas
       'Christmas stocking'

The difference between French, Spanish and Italian on the one hand and English on the other hand in terms of productive compound words leads Snyder (1995) to formulate the Compounding Parameter, as following.

(281) Compounding Parameter: The grammar does (not) freely allow open-class, non-affixal lexical items to be marked [+Affixal].   (Snyder 1995: 27)

In other words, in this parameter, languages are different according to whether their substantive categories (noun, adjective, verb, and preposition) are plus or minus [affixal]. Languages such as English whose referential categories can share the [+affixal] property with functional morphemes, N-N compounding and complex predicates are productive. Complex predicates are constructions where a main verb combines with a secondary predicate and are constructions that semantically resemble a single, complex verb (Snyder 1995). These constructions include at least resultative (e.g. *John hammered the metal flat*), verb-particle constructions (e.g., *run up the hill*), *make*-causative, and double-object dative constructions[49].

The Compounding Parameter also accounts for the fact that in languages such as French, Italian and Spanish N-N compounding or complex predication are not productive grammatical constructions. This is because the constituents which are involved in these word formations are not lexically [+affixal]. In these languages, word formation is possible only with lexically [+affixal] morphemes. In other words, in for example, French word formation with the verb stem + *–eur* '-er' is productive, because it has a [+affixal] feature already as part of its lexical presentation. Also, these languages have a case marking using a preposition, as represented in examples (277) – (280), where N-N compounding is preferred in languages such as English, Japanese and Scandinavian languages.

The Compounding Parameter has been shown to be valid as children's age of acquisition of productive N-N compounding and complex predicates are closely intercorrelated (Snyder 1995, 1996). Moreover, the main verb and the secondary predicate in complex predicates must, at some level, constitute a single interpretation; much like the compounding of two lexical items denotes a unified meaning. For example, in the phrase *John painted the house red*, both *painted* and *red* are syntactic predicates, but this sentence denotes only a single event of house painting.

This account of the unproductivity of compound words in Romance languages is similar to the analysis given by Roeper, Snyder & Hiramatsu. The Abstract Clitic position is proposed by Keyser & Roeper (1992). In order to explain a formal relationship between recursive compound words and resultative constructions in a given language (Snyder 1995, 1996, Snyder & Chen 1997, Slabakova 1999, Miyoshi 1999, Sugisaki & Isobe 2000), Keyser & Roeper (1992) proposed the following hypothesis.

(282)   Abstract Clitic Hypothesis
    a.   All verbs in English have an invisible Clitic position that may be occupied by markers such as the one we have called *dative*.
    b.   *Re-*, like *dative*, is one such marker.   (Keyser & Roeper 1992: 91)

According to (282), Keyser & Roeper (1992) argues that in every double object construction that occurs without an indirect object, there is an abstract position in which an invisible indirect object is present. Furthermore, they argue that in the case of indirect object constructions the position they have labeled *Clitic* is occupied by a marker that is called *dative*. The *dative* marker allows indirect objects in constructions like those in *we gave him money* or *he left me a note*.

The Clitic position has little to do with what we know of clitics in morphology. This hypothesis is based on the incompatibility of *re-* and compound words, indirect objects, particles, idioms and resultative constructions. The meaning of the prefix is approximately 'to do action of some verb over again' (Keyser & Roeper 1992: 89). The following examples represent the incompatibility of *re-* and some of these constructions.

Verbs that take double NP objects

(283) a. We gave him money.
　　　b. *We regave him money.

Verbs that take double NP objects may not take the prefix *re-*. In the double object construction, according to Keyser & Roeper, there is an abstract position in which an invisible indirect object is present. As a result, the above sentences have the following Structure form:

(284)　we [$_{VP}$[$_V$[$_V$ give] Clitic]money]

As there is this abstract position in double object construction, it is impossible to also include the suffix *re*, since the position cannot be occupied by both of the lexical elements. They are in complementary distribution with one another. This is true in the following constructions.

The double object construction
(285) a. He rediscovered an island.
　　　b. *He refound an island.
　　　c. He repurchased a car.
　　　d. *He rebought a car.
　　　e. He re-exhibited his paintings.
　　　f. *He reshowed his paintings[50].　　(Keyser & Roeper 1992: 91)

Examples (b), (d), and (f) are ungrammatical. As the following sentences show, whether a sentence in (285) is ungrammatical or not correlates with whether or not its verb may take the double object construction:

(286) a. *He discovered me an island.
　　　b. He found me an island.
　　　c. *He purchased me an island.
　　　d. He bought me an island.
　　　e. *He exhibited me his paintings.
　　　f. He showed me his paintings.　　(Keyser & Roeper 1992: 92)

So the correlation between the sentences shows that the existence of the dative marker assigned to *me* blocks the prefix *re-*.

Let us see some examples with particles and *re-*.

Particles and re-

(287) a. *He regave himself up.
   b. *He repushed his plan forward.
   c. *He resold his friend out. (Keyser & Roeper 1992: 92)

The ungrammacality of these sentences show that as with indirect objects, the particles, *up*, *forward* and *out*, and the prefix are complementary distribution with one another.

The following phrases represent examples of idioms.

Idioms

(288) a. *relose touch
   b. *relose face
   c. *retake risks
   d. *retake advantage of (Keyser & Roeper 1992: 91)

For idiomatic expressions, too, the same is true. In other words, the prefix and the lexical items, *face*, *risks* and *advantage of*, are in complementary distribution. However, the following idiomatic expressions can take the prefix *re-*.

(289) a. reopen a can of worms
   b. rereinvent the wheel
   c. redivide the whole pie (Keyser & Roeper 1992: 93)

This is due to the fact that these idioms contain a full NP direct object with an accompanying specifier (e.g. NP direct object in (a) is *a can of worms* and the specifier within the NP is the indefinite article *a*). This separates the idioms in (288) from those in (289). The full NPs are not in the Clitic position and therefore allow *re-*. In contrast, the bare NPs in (288) are in the Clitic position and therefore disallow the prefix.

As predicted, resultatives also prohibit the prefix.

(290) Resultative constructions
   a. *He redrove the man crazy.
   b. *It remade my friend sick.
   c. He made my daughter well for me.
   d. *He remade my daughter well.
   e. He broke the stick up.

f. He broke the stick in half.
g. *He broke up the stick in half.
h. He broke up the stick into halves.   (Keyser & Roeper 1992: 98)

If sentence (a) is grammatical, it means that he drove the man crazy on more than one occasion. It is ungrammatical, because the position of *re-* is already filled with the word *crazy*. Example (g) is resultative and cannot occur with the particle *up*, whereas example (h) is a prepositional phrase and does not disallow the particle *up*.

Roeper, Snyder & Hiramatsu (2002) argue that the set of categories which can take a Clitic position should be expanded to include all lexical categories, including nouns, adjectives and prepositions. Therefore, derivation of all kinds of compound words can occur taking the Clitic position as a complement.

Another important point in their theory is that by stipulation recursion of compound words can occur only with elements of the same type. For instance, it is not possible to have verb-noun-noun or preposition-noun-noun as a recursive compound. Thirdly, only non-maximal projections can appear in the Clitic position (*contra* Keyser & Roeper's (1992) claim). Finally, following Kayne's (1994) and Chomsky's (1995) antisymmetry theory, all movement is leftward.

In Roeper, Snyder & Hiramatsu's theory, another type of productive compound words in English can be formed by inserting a compound into the Clitic position. It is, therefore, possible to derive a left-branching compound word as well as right-branching. The difference in the branching corresponds to the meaning difference (see also 3.2.1). For example, the above example, *restaurant coffee cup* means 'a coffee cup for restaurant'. In contrast, the left-branching compounding *gourmet coffee cup* is a cup of the kind associated with gourmet coffees.

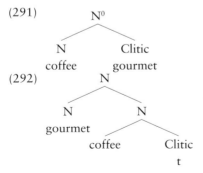

(293)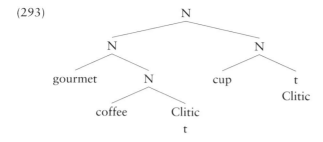

The above derivations show that we first create the compound *gourmet coffee*. Then, the result is inserted into the Clitic position of the N *cup*, to obtain the meaning of 'gourmet coffee cup', or 'cup of the kind associated with gourmet coffees'. Then, the compound in the Clitic is moved.

The final type of compound Roeper et al discuss is synthetic compounding, such as *pen-holder*, where the deverbal noun *holder* takes a complement *pen*. In this case, in contrast to the root compounding discussed above, the derivation does not involve the Clitic position, as the Clitic position is only for a non-argument. The derivation is as follows.

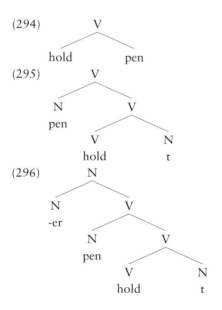

(297)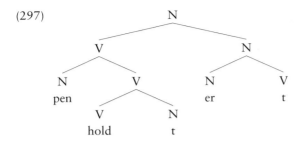

In (274) the complex V *pen-hold* is derived first. The N *pen* is the complement and logical object of the V *hold*. Then, the compound formation rule applies to move and adjoin *pen* to the left of *hold*. The trace left by *pen* is an argument trace. Following Keyser & Roeper (1992), Roeper, Snyder & Hiramatsu (2002) assume that this trace is undeletable. In the structure shown in (297) the resulting complex V is inserted as the complement to the nominal suffix *–er*. Once again, the compound-formation rule applies, and the form *pen-holder* is derived. However, there is no Clitic involved in these structures. This is because the Clitic is associated specifically with modifiers, rather than arguments. The V *hold* takes the N pen as an argument. Similarly, the suffix *–er* takes complex V *pen-hold* as its argument. Thus, the Clitic is not there at all in this derivation.

An advantage of their theory is that both right- and left-branching compound words can be analysed in English, as the above argument demonstrates. The analysis is applicable for compound words in Japanese and Scandinavian languages in the following ways. As discussed in Section 2.4, Japanese allows productive compound words. There are also recursive compound words in Japanese (Namiki 2001), for example, *gakusei eiga kurabu* 'student film club'. Consider first the derivation of the two-member nominal root compound *eiga kurabu*.

(298)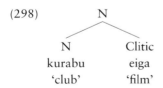

First, *eiga* is inserted in the Clitic position, since *kurabu* does not have any selectional requirements. Then, as the following structure shows, *eiga* is moved and adjoined to make a compound word, *eiga kurabu*.

(299)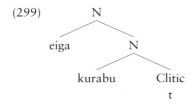

After the lexical element, *eiga* is moved, leaving its trace in the Clitic position, the trace is deleted. To form the three-member compound word, *gakusei eiga kurabu* 'student film club', the new lexical item, *gakusei* 'student' is inserted in the position of the trace of *eiga* after the trace is deleted. Then, *gakusei* is adjoined to the compound word *eiga kurabu*. As a result, the compound word *gakusei eiga kurabu* is derived.

This derivation yields the interpretation 'film club for students', in contrast to the interpretation, 'club for student films'. The latter interpretation has a different derivation, just like the one in the example *gourmet coffee cup*. This demonstrates that Japanese allows insertion of a compound word in the Clitic position.

First, *gakusei* is inserted in the Clitic position, since *eiga* does not have any selectional requirements.

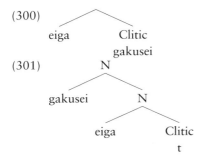

Then, *gakusei* is moved and adjoined to make a compound word, *gakusei eiga*.

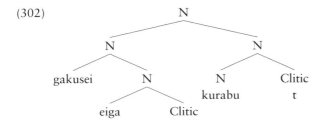

Finally, as the above structure shows, the compound *gakusei eiga* is inserted into the Clitic of the N *kurabu*, to obtain the meaning 'student film society or 'society for student films'. Then, the compound in the Clitic is moved.

In Scandinavian languages, too, it is possible to derive productive recursive compound words (Roeper & Snyder 2002). For example, it is possible to derive the compound word *barn [bok klubb]* which means book club for children.

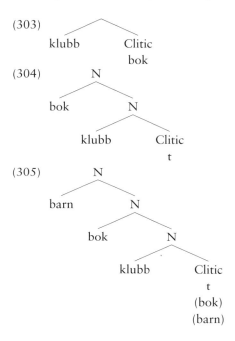

Precisely as in the English and Japanese derivations, the trace of *bok* is deleted and the Clitic is used again to introduce the lexical item modifier *barn* in Roeper et al's terms[51]. In Swedish a left-branching three-member compound always has a linking element usually –s, between the second and the third member (see 1.1). Compare (306) and (307):

(306) a. vin + glass
wine glass
b. boll + plan
ball pitch
'playing field'
c. skåp + dörr
cabinet + door
(307) a. röd + vin + s + glas

CHAPTER 3 STRUCTURE OF COMPOUND WORDS

red + wine + LINK+ glass
b. fot +boll + s + plan
foot ball LINK pitch
c. kyl + skåp + s + dörr
cool + cabinet+ LINK + door
'refrigerator door'

Root compounds in this language are strictly right-branching. Thus, only one interpretation is possible. To obtain the other interpretation, which is 'club for children's books', the linking element –s must be used after the compound word *barn bok*. This interpretation is derived in the following way.

(308)

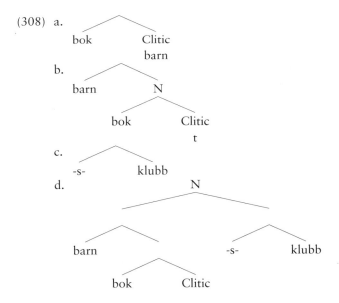

The compound *barnbok* is constructed in a parallel derivation combining *klubb* with the linking element –s-. The linking element requires a second argument, and the compound *barnbok* is inserted into its external argument position. It is important to notice that the only Clitic involved in this derivation in that of the N *bok*, and its only occupant is the lexical element *barn*. The –s- selects two lexical elements and this is why there is only one Clitic position involved in this derivation.

3.2.3 Problems of Roeper, Snyder & Hiramatsu's theory

It seems that compound words in all the languages in question can be derived by this theory. However, this theory has some serious problems. First, the operation movement in the Minimalist Program should be caused by feature checking requirements involving a functional category. However, in Roeper et al's theory, there is no feature to be checked or a functional category involved in the derivation of compounding. Nor does the noun which originates in the Clitic position have any semantic or syntactic features which should be checked by another noun in the course of the derivation.

The second problem is related to the first one. The moved noun is merged twice with the same head noun. For instance, in the derivation (308), the noun, *bog* is merged with *klubb*. Although Roeper *et al* do not discuss headedness (see below) the idea clearly is that *klubb* is the head of the compound. Then, the N *bog* is merged again with the same head, *klubb* (see the explanation under (275)). And this is the same for all the cases.

Another criticism is that this operation violates the Extension Condition (see Section 3.2). The Extension Condition prohibits using the Clitic position to introduce another modifier to derive a compound word. For example, the derivation of a compound word *restaurant coffee cup* by first forming *coffee cup*, then moving *coffee*, and then introducing the new lexical item *restaurant* in place of *coffee* violates the Extension Condition. As a result, their analysis certainly does not adhere to the Minimalist theory of phrase structure rules.

Next, this analysis does not tell us anything about occurrence of regular plurals between the two constituents of the compound words (e.g., *Christmas-es cookie). However, they could claim that the lexical element in the Clitic is a root, not a stem with an inflection, for two-member compounds. However, for three-member left-branching compounds, such as *gourmet coffee cup*, the Clitic cannot be a root, since the Clitic is a compound word.

There is also a problem in determining the head of a noun-noun compound word. Let us assume for the sake of the argument that Chomsky's (1995) definition of headedness being the selector is correct. Recall that deletion of the trace of the moved noun, which was crucial in recursive compounds, was possible because the moved noun (the Clitic) was not selected. So Chomsky's definition of headedness does not work.

3.2.4 Josefsson's (1997) theory

3.2.4.1 Lexicon

Like Roeper, Snyder and Hiramatsu, and Spencer (2003), Josefsson (1997) claims that compound words are derived in the same way as phrases are.

Before analysing structure, it is important to describe the lexicon which is used by Josefsson in her theory. To derive a word, a number of items, X and Y, are enumerated from the triune lexicon, a model by Platzack (1993). This lexicon is modelled as follows.

(309) LIST OF MORPHEMES

PF
LF

(Josefsson 1997: 50)

In this system, the syntactic component has access to the *List of Morphemes* of Halle (1973). All different types of morphemes, including linking morphemes, constituents involved in neoclassical compound words, 'cranberry morphemes' and many others are listed in the List of Morphemes. Another important fact is that there is no information about the phonetic or semantic aspects of morphemes, but only formative aspects. Josefsson (1997) argues that different languages have a different List of Morphemes, which results in different words including compounds in different languages.

Josefsson (1997) and Platzack (1993), as non-lexicalists, state that it is also necessary to assume that the component *List of Morphemes* exists where words, compounds, derived words, collocations, and idioms are stored. The existence of the component is necessary, because all the elements listed may acquire a special meaning, which is not possible to be computed from the meaning of the parts.

Let us demonstrate the derivation of cranberry in this theory. First, from the List of Morphemes, cran and berry are taken. Then, they are merged together. Later, in the LF-lexicon, the cranberry is listed, but the meaning is not there. The LF does not see the meaning of it. In the PF-lexicon, the whole word is there and it is pronounced at the spell-out.

According to Platzack (1993), in this system, only the morphemes are affected by the computational system. The derivational part of the computation performs the process of structure building, building words and phrases by means of generalised transformations Merge. At some point in the derivation, the split-off point is reached, where one part of the derivation goes to PF and one part goes to LF. The former part access the PF-lexicon, the other part the LF-lexicon.

In the LF lexicon, meaning is assigned to the syntactic constituents. The connection between the LF representation of a derivation and the syntactic structure is hierarchical, going from the top of the tree downwards:

> The lexicon mediating between LF and Conceptual Structure works in a top-down fashion: it gives precedence to the entry corresponding to the largest X^0 before it envokes [sic] elements below this level. (Platzack 1993: 310)

In other words, in a derivation, the LF system scans for a concept related to the highest X^0 node. For instance, for ordinary words, the search for a connection between word A and concept A takes place. If concept A is found, then a word-meaning pairing occurs. In the case of a compound, the system scans for a connection between the whole compound and a concept, i.e., the highest node, as a first option. If there is no matching between concept and compound, the procedure of scanning for a matching takes place one level down in the hierarchy and the matching scanning begins all over again. If a connection can be established between the syntactic constituents and the conceptual system the meaning is read off.

In this system, Platzack states that 'cranberry morphemes' which are found in the lexicon as parts of full words (as discussed in Section 2.1.2), are represented as separate morphemes in the list of morphemes. This means that the syntactic system has access to them, but they are not represented in the LF lexicon as separate entries, only as a part of the full word.

Following Halle & Marantz's (1993) Distributed Morphology, Josefsson's claim is that all generalised transformations are assumed to be of the same kind, showing that they take place in a single module. Thus, there is no single place called a 'lexicon' distinct from syntax where some generalised transformations take place. Another point is that only formative aspects of morphemes, but not phonological aspects, are contained in the list of morphemes.

As in theories proposed in the GB framework, the hierarchical head-modifier structure is certainly important in this Minimalist theory of the lexicon. The relation between the head and modifier is an input to compositional process. This process connects the meaning of the constituents to a meaning of the whole. According to this system, the meaning which is appropriate for the actual context is provided by the conceptual system[52], not the syntax.

This type of lexicon seems non-redundant and capable of accounting for any kind of morphemes, including neoclassical compounds, 'cranberry morphemes', productive compound words, idioms, and lexicalised compound words which may have both an idiosyncratic and a compositional reading. To my knowledge, this has not been achieved by other researchers. The theory proposed by Platzack will be assumed in this thesis.

Let us see how the triune lexicon can be applied to compound words. Take the word *pancake*. The compound is constructed by merging the words *pan* and *cake*, taken from the List of Morphemes. Then, the entry for the conventionalised meaning of the lexicalised compound word, *pancake* is searched for in the LF-lexicon. The conventionalised meaning is 'a thin, flat, circular piece of cooked batter made from milk, flour, and eggs' (Collins Cobuild English Dictionary 2001), not 'a cake made on a frying pan'. The conventionalised meaning is there in the LF-lexicon. If it is not, then the literal meaning can be deduced. The difference between the meanings depends on the context where the compound appears. As for a productive compound which does not have any conventionalised meaning, the lexical entry for the meaning is not present in the LF-lexicon. Therefore, it is necessary to rely on lexical entries corresponding to parts of the whole word. For instance, the meaning of the productive compound word *London bus* is absent from the LF-lexicon. Therefore, only the meanings of the parts of the compound word, *London* and *bus*, are in the LF-lexicon and these meanings are relied on for the meaning of the whole compound word.

It is proposed in this thesis that the idea of scanning for meaning can be applied to neoclassical compound words, like Josefsson proposes about cranberry morphemes. Take for instance the word *philosophy*: neither *philo* nor *sophy* mean anything on their own. Yet, since they both occur in various compounds (see Chapter 2), they are listed in the List of Morphemes. The compound is derived by merging *philo* and *sophy* taken from the List of Morphemes, however, it is possible to assume that for a normal speaker of language, unless he/she is highly educated or a linguist, parts of meaning of neoclassical compound words do not usually have a meaning. It is, however, necessary to assume a lexical entry in the LF and PF lexicon for this type of compound word, as is assumed for 'cranberry words'.

This system can be also applied to neoclassical compounds in Japanese. Take for example the neoclassical compound, *kuu-koo* 'air-port' (airport). First, *kuu*, which means 'sky' and *koo* 'port' are taken from the List of Morphemes and merged to make the compound. The LF-lexicon scans for a connection between the whole word, *kuu-koo* and the concept 'airport' as a first option. The concept and the compound are matched, since the meaning of the whole word *airport* is present in the LF-lexicon.

Josefsson briefly discusses the nature of the PF-lexicon. The phonetic properties of the lexical items involved in the generalised operations are assigned at the PF-lexicon, not the LF-lexicon. Contrary to Lieber (1992) (see 3.1.3), linear order is important in PF, so Josefsson assumes that the PF-lexicon contains principles of mapping of the hierarchical structure to a linear one, as exemplified below.

(310)

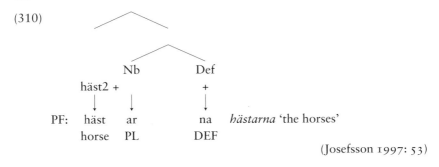

hästarna 'the horses'

(Josefsson 1997: 53)

According to Josefsson (see in Section 3.2.4.2 for the discussion of how the derivation takes place in the syntax), the inflectional features, number and definiteness, could be described as features with binary values. The gender/declension of the stem (declension 2 for this example) is stored in the PF lexicon, or is assigned according to rules of default. As a result, the word *hästarna* is spelled-out in the string order. The spell-out of inflectional features is dependent on the string order, rather than the hierarchical structure.

As for cases without one-to-one mapping from the abstract morphological representation to the phonetic representation, such as cases of ablaut and umlaut[53], Josefsson states that the PF-system is assumed to allow for operations like Fusion and Fission, as proposed in Halle & Maranz (1993).

Rendaku, sequential voicing in Japanese, (as discussed in Section 2.3.2) also takes places in the PF-lexicon. Take, for example, the derivation of the compound *match-bako* (match-box) in Japanese.

(311)

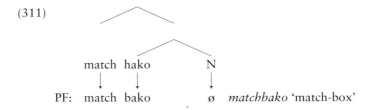

matchbako 'match-box'

As the above derivation demonstrates, the lexical item *hako* is merged with an N feature and then another lexical item *match* is merged (See below for the syntactic derivation). After the syntactic derivation is finished, the initial segment of *hako* /h/ becomes voiced in the PF-lexicon (by Lyman's Law, as discussed in 2.3.2) and the word *matchbako* 'match-box' is Spelled Out. Josefsson does not represent LF lexicon in the derivation.

3.2.4.2 Structure

With this system of LF-lexicon, Josefsson proposes structures for word and compound word in Swedish in the following way.

(312) Swedish

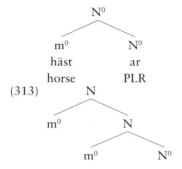

(313)

In these structures, the m⁰ indicates a stem without word class feature (see below for the discussion of word class features). Josefsson (1997) defines non-affixal morphemes as 'stems'. So one can presume that m⁰ can be either a stem or a root in the traditional sense. In addition, Josefsson argues that the inflection is the only source for word class and is therefore referred to as N⁰. Inflections are carried by words, and if the inflection is a suffix, it is the head of the word. Inflections host features like number and gender, and these features are what makes a stem a noun.

The structures (312)–(313) are constructed by the operation Merge under the approach of the Minimalist Program (Chomsky 1995). First, morphemes, m⁰ and N⁰ are merged together to form a word. When two zero level elements are allowed to merge, only one projects. As discussed in Section 3.2, a basic characteristic of language is the asymmetry of syntax. In the case of (312) the inflectional affix (e.g., *-ar* '-'-es') projects its features and will act as the head of the structure.

The strictly configurational definition of head, complement and specifier in Chomsky (1994) is adopted in Josefsson's theory. Chomsky's configurational definition is as follows: "the head-complement relation is the 'most local' relation of an XP to a terminal head Y, all others within YP being head-specifier (apart from adjunction)" (p.11). The following structure shows this.

(314)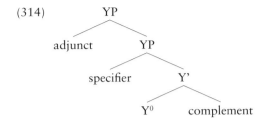

According to Josefsson, Chomsky's definition allows us to assume that the head of the word is the inflection itself (in (312) and (313), it is N^0), and that the stem m^0 is the complement. The inflection selects a stem in Josefsson's terms, although it is unclear what it selects since the m^0 is not a category.

After the merge of the inflectional affix and the complement stem, another stem is merged to form a compound word. This is what the structure (313) shows. Following Kayne (1994) left adjunction is allowed at X^0 level, too. So another stem is merged, forming the more complex structure.

3.2.4.3 Non-head of compound words

It is important to note that neither lexical element involved in a two-member compound word carries word class features in the traditional sense. This idea was suggested in Chomsky (1970: 190), where pairs like *refuse-refusal* are discussed. He proposes that *refuse* is a lexical entry with fixed selectional properties, but which is free with respect to the categorical features [noun] and [verb]. Following Chomsky, the proposal that roots (Marantz 1997, Arad 2003) have no category is widely accepted within minimalism and distributed morphology.

Following Josefsson (1997) (c.f. Marantz 1997, Arad 2003), it is claimed in this thesis that, as a root (in the traditional sense)[54], the 'left-hand' element of a compound word does not have any word class features. The traditional criteria for determining the word class of a word are meaning, morphology and syntactic function. Firstly, the meaning criterion states, for example, that nouns are thing-words, adjectives are property-words, and verbs are event words. However, there are, for example, abstract nouns, and those which denote events or properties, not things, and verbs which do not denote events but states. Thus, the conclusion Josefsson reaches is that the meaning criterion is not useful in deciding the word class of roots, in her terms stems.

Moreover, Josefsson claims that in cases where a noun, a verb and/or an adjective is derived from the same root, it is difficult to decide the word class of the left-hand segment of compounds with zero morphemes, for example *res* + *väska* (trip/travel + bag) 'suitcase' and *res* + *pass* (trip/travel + order) 'order to leave' in Swedish. Thus, the meaning criterion is not useful in deciding the word class of roots.

Another criterion is morphology. According to this criterion, nouns are words that carry nominal inflection; verbs are words with verbal inflection, etc. By this criterion the non-head of a compound is not a noun or verb etc., as it usually does not take any inflection, and as discussed in 2.1.1, the non-head of a compound in Scandinavian languages is not a free morpheme.

The third criterion is syntactic function. For example, nouns function as complements of D. Again, this criterion is not applicable for 'left-hand' segments of compound words and derivations in Scandinavian languages but only for full words. Josefsson concludes that none of the three criteria provide a way of deciding the word class of roots functioning as left-hand segments of compounds and derivations.

This analysis enables us to rule out the inflected forms like *hästar +gård (hose.pl + guard) as opposed to the grammatical form häst+ gård (hose.sing+guard) 'horse guard', and *sockret+ skålen (sigar-def.+bowl) as opposed to the grammatical form sockr+ skålen (sugar+bowl)(Josefsson 2005). The non-head cannot have a definite feature, since this feature needs to be checked by a D. Similarly, the non-head cannot have a plural feature, since it keeps percolating (the number feature being an interpretable feature) and the whole compound gets number from the non-head.

As a result, Josefsson claims that the 'left-hand' segments of derivation and compound words, m^0 in the structures (312) and (313), are morphemes without word class features. In her thesis, she establishes the relation between word classes and conceptual categories, which fall into a finite number of major ontological categories (Jackendoff 1985). Jackendoff claims that ontological category features are visible to the syntax-semantics interface unlike most descriptive features of concepts, so they play an important role in grammar as well as perception. According to Jackendoff (1985), the world is understood in categories like [THINGS], [PROPERTIES], [EVENTS], [DIRECTIONS], [PLACES], etc and there are some differences between the world as we understand it (the projected world, experienced world, or phenomenal world) and the true world. The major ontological categories are prototypically represented in the word classes; Things are nouns, Events are verbs, Properties are adjectives.

Josefsson discusses the relation between the major ontological category [THING] and the word class noun. For example, the stem *tvätt-* (wash) in Swedish is used in different contexts:

(315) a. Olle tvätt-ar.
           Olle wash-PRES
           'Olle washes'.

b. Olle sorterade tvätt-en.
   Olle sorted wash-the
   'Olle sorted the laundry'.

In the examples in (315), it is clear that in (315a), *tvättar* denotes the action/event of washing and on the other hand, *tvätten* in (315b) denotes an object, i.e. the laundry.

In contrast, the distinction of denotation is less clear. It is necessary for *tvätt* in *tvätt* + *korg* in (316c) to denote the object laundry, since baskets are designed for containing concrete objects. Similarly, *tvätt* - in (316e) denotes the event or activity of washing. However, for the other compounds, the major ontological category is difficult or impossible to determine. A root like *tvätt* is apparently able to denote both an event/activity and an object, or to 'oscillate' between the two possibilities.

(316) a. Vi har köpt en tvätt-maskin.
         We have bought a wash-machine
         'We have bought a washing machine'.
      b. Vårt tvätt-medel är slut.
         Our wash-agent is out
         'We are out of washing powder'.
      c. Lägg dina smutsiga strumpor i tvätt-korgen.
         Put your dirty socks in wash-basket-the
         'Put your dirty socks in the laundry basket'.
      d. Vi fick ingen tvätt-tid den här veckan.
         We got no wash-time this week-the
         'We got no washing time this week'.
      e. Tvätt-processen tog två timmar.
         Wash-process-the took two hours
         'The washing took two hours'.

With these interpretations of the root in mind, the structure for the Danish word *klub* 'club' is derived in the following way.

(317)

This structure shows the cognitive/semantic structure. The overall meaning of the noun is that of a Thing, with descriptive features relating to the concept

CHAPTER 3 STRUCTURE OF COMPOUND WORDS   123

#*klub*# 'club'. The notation # is used by Jackendoff (1985) to refer to the projected world, i.e. the world as we understand it. The true world is outside the embedded bracket. According to Jackendoff, the true world is not directly related to the language. The overall Thing classification derives from the inflectional part of the word, descriptive features from the root. The fact that the prototypical meaning of the concept #*klub*# is that of a Thing makes *klub* a prototypical noun.

It is not generally argued in the field of semantics that nouns ever refer to Things. The alternative is that they refer to properties, for example, the property of being a club (Higginbotham 1985, Chierchia 1998 (cf. Di Sciullo & Williams 1987). However, in Josefsson's model N can perhaps be thought of as the morpheme which turns a property-denoting root into a thing-denoting nominal category.

Then, the stem *bog* 'book' is taken from the List of Morphemes and merged with [$_N^0$ *klub* N^0] to form a more complex structure as follows.

(318) $N^{0[thing[\#thing: klub\#]]}$

In the above structure, the morphemes *bog* and *klub* have no word class features. This implies that the structure has only one set of word class features, the ones represented by N^0. The interpretation in terms of major ontological category is not determined either, as long as the morphemes *bog* and *klub* in the structure do not have any inflectional features. *Klub* thus refers to a macroconcept for which the Thing interpretation is the prototypical one, which is assumed to be invoked unless an unprototypical reading is forced by the morphological context (Josefsson 1997: 56).

As a result, with both syntactic and semantic features presented, the structure for the compound word in Danish is as follows.

(319) $N^{0[thing[\#thing: klub\#]]}$

The nominal inflection feature and the semantic feature Thing are percolated to the higher nodes dominating the morphemes. These features decide the categorical and semantic features of the whole compound word.

It is important, at this point in the discussion, to investigate whether Josefsson's (1997) theory is applicable to lexicalised compounds. Josefsson, following Platzack, argues that if there is no matching between concept and compound, the procedure of scanning for a matching takes place one level down in the hierarchy. For example, the Swedish word, *tebrev* literally 'tea-letter' i.e. 'teabag' is derived in the same way as the productive compound shown above. First, the lexical item *brev* is numerated from the List of Morphemes and merged with the inflection and the semantic category, Thing. Then the lexical item *te* is numerated from the List of Morphemes and merged to form a compound word. This compound has a matching concept listed in the LF-lexicon. Therefore, there is matching between concept and compound in the highest node and the non-compositional reading is derived. The connection between the syntactic constituents and the conceptual system is read off in the LF-lexicon.

In this framework, it is possible to analyse a wide range of compound words.

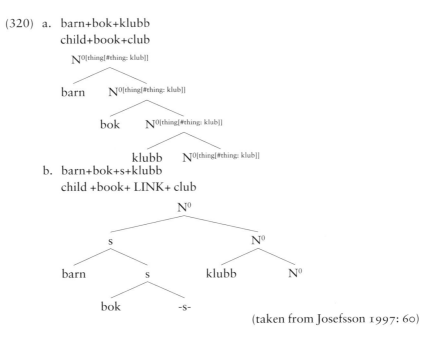

(taken from Josefsson 1997: 60)

The structure in (320a) indicates that the compound word has no linking element and the translation would be 'book club for children', whereas the structure (320b) has a linking element, which is required for the reading 'a club for children's books' (see 3.2.2).

CHAPTER 3 STRUCTURE OF COMPOUND WORDS

As discussed in 2.1.1, the linking morpheme also exists in some compound words which consist of two constituents.

(321) stol+s+en,   skov+s+bryn,   sæd+e+mark
       chair+LINK+leg, forest+LINK+edge, grain+LINK+field Danish (also in Swedish)

The structure for this type of compound words, which is called a simple mediated compound by Josefsson (1997), is different from the one for compound words with a linking morpheme, like the example (320b) (see more about the linking morphemes in Section 4.3.2 and 4.3.5). Josefsson does not propose a structure for compounds such as (321). Therefore, it is necessary to propose a new one in this thesis (see 4.3.2 for the proposed structure).

In summary, this chapter has discussed previous theories for compound words proposed by other researchers within the GB and Minimalist frameworks. It has been discussed that none of them is good enough. They seem to follow the Righthand Head Rule (Williams 1981) for the head of a compound word. In addition, they focus too narrowly on specific types of compound words or languages. I have analysed these theories for the languages in question and other types of compound words, not only noun-noun compound words. As a result, I have concluded that none of them will be sufficient enough.

In contrast, Josefsson's (1997) theory seems applicable to various kinds of compound words in Mainland Scandinavian. One type of compound word which is not discussed by Josefsson is neoclassical compounds. Josefsson states that word class features of roots involved in compounding are not specified. In this thesis, it is proposed that there are no syntactically relevant differences between the constituents involved in the different types of compounding. Distinctions between these can be made, but they are not relevant for how words are constructed.

The next chapter will discuss how to determine the non-head of compound words in English, Japanese and other types of compounds in Mainland Scandinavian. Then, I will discuss whether Josefsson's structure for Swedish compounds is applicable in English and Japanese compounds.

Notes

38 The relation between the elements of compound words can be defined in terms of semantics, according to Allen (1978)'s IS A condition: $N_1 + N_2$ is a kind of N_2 (see 2.1.2). Allen's condition is proposed in reaction to Levi and Lees' claims concerning the semantic

relationship between the two constituents of compound words. By the condition, Allen means that there is a semantic relationship, but not a clear-cut one.

39 The initial sound of *hachi* 'bee' is voiced when it is merged with another word and it occurs as a second element of the compound word.

40 For more examples in Japanese, see the Appendix.

41 Lieber (1980) proposes that all morphemes, including words, affixes, and roots, and lexicalised words and idioms are listed in the lexicon. Each lexical entry has its syntactic category (e.g. verb), its Lexical Conceptual Structure (e.g. EVENT or THING) (Jackendoff 1990), Predicate Argument Structure, which gives the mapping between Lexical Conceptual Structure and syntactic structure. Bound morphemes have their morphological subcategorisation (i.e. the category of the items to which they attach) (e.g. the affix *un-* attaches to an adjective). Also, she assumes that bound roots like neoclassical elements (see Chapter 2) have lexical entries, too.

42 For the structure (206); Lieber claims that there is no certainly no evidence to suggest that happy can be an Ao. What does she actually say is that there is no evidence that happy must be an A°, so could not be A-1. This contradicts but that is what she says.

43 Stowell's claim is that restrictive modifiers follow the head and that certain types of modifiers, specifically bare adjectives are cliticised to the head noun. He also claims that there is a movement of the modifiers to the position before the head. In contrast, Lieber states that prenominal adjectives are not like clitics in Romance languages. Whereas clitics in Romance languages are closed class items, prenominal adjectives are open class items. Secondly, clitics are limited in number and phonologically part of the words which they are attached to, whereas adjectives are never part of the word. Jackendoff argues that restrictive modifiers follow the head and are generated in a position after the head, arguing against an analysis of relative clauses in Smith (1964, cited in Jackendoff 1977). Smith states that restrictive relative clauses are generated prenominally as part of the Determiner position in NP. However, Jackendoff (1977) concludes that PP modifiers and restrictive modifiers should be generated after the head, looking at the examples like *the old Paris, the Paris of my dreams, a cold manner* and *the manner of his arrival*. In contrast, Lieber says that the cooccurence restrictions between determiners and restrictive modifiers only show that all restrictive modifiers behave alike. They do show that restrictive modifiers should not be regarded as part of determiners, but it is not necessary to follow Jackendoff's theory that modifiers follow the head. Thus, Lieber's third Licensing Condition is true.

44 The symbol ø shows that the last morph of the word is deleted when it is merged with another word (see below).

45 Word consists of a root and a word marker in Swedish.

46 Another way of imposing order on the structure is Linear Correspondence Axiom (henceforth, LCA) (Chomsky 1995, following Kayne 1994). The LCA takes a hierarchical structure and produces a linearization of its constituents, i.e. the sentence or the structure is pronounced at PF in the order dictated by the LCA.

47 Kayne (1994) claims that left adjunction can be applied below the word level, too.

48 NAN compounds (to say that they are not different from phrases) are compounds. The A is derived from its N base. There are many of them in English: *social page, liberal democratic party, financial market, royal authority* (*royal* can be a noun). This is because the adjective between the two nouns is relational adjective, i.e. it is derived from its corresponding noun (Shimamura 2015).

49 Snyder (1995) argues that in English, 'the compound' of the two heads *hammer/flat* in the resultative construction and *run/up* in the verb-particle construction are not visible in the PF, since they are separated by the lexical item *the metal* and *hill*, respectively. However, the

interpretation of these constructions is of a single predicate.
50 This sentence is fine if it is in passive: e.g. *these paintings will be re-shown in the summer exhibition*. I would like to thank Prof. Maggie Tallerman for her comment on this point.
51 In Norwegian and Danish, there is a linking morpheme in some compounds, but the occurrence is not as strict as in Swedish. The fact that Danish and Norwegian pattern like Swedish but only in part is a problem for the theory of Roeper et al.
52 Similar ideas are presented in Jackendoff (1997) and Chomsky (1993). They consider that conceptual structure must provide a formal basis for rules of inference and the interaction of language with world knowledge. Jackendoff claims that there has to be some level of mental representation at which inference is codified and it is conceptual structure, a level that is not encoded in narrow syntactic terms. See the further discussion on the complexity of the syntactic structure-conceptual structure interface in Jackendoff (1997).
53 *Ablaut* is a vowel change accompanying a change in grammatical function. e.g. the vowel change in English from *i* to *a* to *u* in *sing, song* and *sung*. *Umlaut* is a special kind of vowel modification. The process of umlaut is a modification of a vowel which causes it to be pronounced more similarly to a vowel or semivowel in a following syllable. e.g. tooth/teeth, foot/feet, man/men, goose/geese
54 As discussed in the previous sub-section, Josefsson (1997) claims that 'stems' are involved in compounding. In her thesis, she defines the term 'stem' as a non-affixal morpheme. In this thesis, the term 'root' is used instead of Josefsson's term 'stem' to avoid the confusion. Here, the term 'root' is defined as a morpheme with semantic content that cannot be analysed further. On the other hand, the term 'stem' is usually used for a root with derivational affixes (cf. Plag 2003: 11).

CHAPTER 4
Proposed Structures of Compound Words

The last chapter considered the previously proposed theories for compound words within the GB and the Minimalist Program frameworks. I have found out that none of them is good enough, especially with respect to headedness of compound words. In most current minimalist theories morphology is after spell-out. However, it is necessary to determine the head before spell-out, since the head needs to be interpreted in the PF. In this chapter, I will propose an alternative theory of compound words within the Minimmalist Program, showing that the head of a compound is determined in the narrow syntax.

This chapter is organised as follows. In the first section, following Josefsson's (1997) theory of non-head in Scandinavian languages, that of Japanese and English will be discussed within the Minimalist Program. I will compare the theory with the Lexical Phonology with regards to the non-head of a compound word in the languages in question. This will be followed by a proposed structure of compound words in the languages in question within the Minimalist Program. I will argue that the proposed structure is applicable for a wide range of compound nouns and different languages. Then, a structure is proposed for phrasal compounds and copulative compounds, respectively in the languages in question. I conclude the chapter by discussing the weak points in the other theories and how my proposed theory solves the problems.

4.1.1 The Non-head of compound words in Japanese

The observation of Japanese compounds in 2.1.1 leads me to think that the left-hand element of compound words in Japanese does not have word class features, as in the case of the Scandinavian languages. Firstly, the meaning criterion states that nouns are thing-words, adjectives are property-words, verbs are event words, etc. As in Scandinavian languages, in Japanese compound words, the left-hand segment can be a deverbal noun, such as in *odori-ko* (dance-child) 'dancing child', *odori-kuruu* (dance-crazy) 'become crazy in dancing'. There is no straightforward way to determine the word class of compound words when the left-hand segment is a deverbal noun.

As in Scandinavian languages, in Japanese compounds it is also not easy to determine the word class of compound words according to the morphological criterion. The morphological criterion is not useful for the non-head of compounds and derivations in Japanese because it is not a free morpheme. The following examples illustrate this.

(322) a odouru 'to dance'
odori+ko
dance+child
'dancer'
b nagareru 'to flow'
nagare+bosi
flow+star
'shooting star'
c hataraku 'to work'
hataraki+bachi
work+bee
'worker bee'
d kesu 'to erase'
kesi+gomu
erase+rubber
'eraser'

As discussed in 2.1.1, the 'verbal' left-hand segment in these examples is not a free morpheme, but *renyookei* 'an infinitive form' in traditional Japanese grammar, which needs to be merged with another morpheme to occur independently as verb. 'Adjectival' compound words are similar in Japanese:

(323) a hurui 'old'
huru+hon
old+book
'second-hand book'
b yowai 'weak'
yowa+ki
weak+feeling
'timidness'
c. kirei-na 'beautiful'
kirei+dokoro
beautiful+place

'Geisha'
d. sizuka-na 'quiet'
   sizu+kokoro
   quiet+mind
   'mind with which you enjoy the present environment quietly'

The adjectives in (a) and (b) are called *i*-adjectives in traditional Japanese grammar. In these examples, the last morph *–i* of the adjective is deleted in compound words. Another type, shown in examples (c) and (d) in Japanese is the *na*-adjective. To appear in a compound word, the last morph *–na* is deleted[55]. Thus, adjectives and verbs as left-hand elements of compound words in Japanese show a similar phenomenon to the left-hand noun in some noun-noun compound words in Scandinavian languages. In fact, I will argue that the non-head element in Japanese compounds is never a free morpheme. In summary, the morphological criterion is not useful in deciding the word class of roots.

The third criterion is syntactic function. For example, nouns function as complements of D. Again, this criterion is not applicable for left-hand segments of compound words and derivations in Japanese, only for full words. Thus, as in Scandinavian languages, it is concluded that none of the three criteria provide a way of deciding the word class of roots, including roots functioning as left-hand segment of compounds in Japanese.

4.1.2 The non-head of English compound words

In English, as discussed in Section 2.1.1, it looks like compound words are composed of two free morphemes. Let us see if the morphemes have word class features. As in the other languages, the meaning criterion is not applicable in this case. One phenomenon found in English but not in Scandinavian languages or Japanese, which has led several scholars, such as Selkirk (1982), to believe that non-heads in compounds are (free) words, is the regular plural marker. However, with some exceptions, the left-hand segment does not have any regular plural inflection. When there is what looks like a regular plural inflection (as discussed in Section 2.4.1), it does not refer to a plurality. For example, in compounds such as *awards ceremony* and *publications catalogue,* the left-hand segment does not necessarily refer to a plurality of publications or awards. So the *–s* is not a plural inflection, but it is a linking morpheme (see below in Section 4.3.1). Thus, the morphological criterion cannot be used in English either. There is one exception: *parks commissioner*. In at least some native speakers' lexicons, both *parks/park commissioner* exist and there is a semantic difference between them, i.e. a *parks commissioner* is a commissioner who looks after several different parks whereas a *park commissioner* is one who looks after parks in general. So the structure of this compound is different.

In addition, as in Scandinavian languages and Japanese, it is difficult to determine the word class of the non-head segment of compounds with zero morphemes, like *travel agent, work camp, dance hall* and so on. The other criterion, syntax, is not applicable, since the non-head of a compound cannot take part in any syntactic operations. As a result, it is assumed that the left-hand segment of English compounds does not necessarily have any word class features either.

If Japanese V-N compounds are translated into English, it is necessary to have derivational suffixes attached to the verbs, such as *–ing* or *–er* to appear as the constituent in compound words. Typical examples are *washing machine* and *fighter bomber*. In these cases, the 'left-hand' element is a full word, not a stem without word class features. Thus, the structure for this type of compound is different from those of N-N compounds (see Section 4.3).

4.1.3 Affix-driven vs. base-driven stratification of the lexicon

Within the framework of Lexical Phonology[56], instead of the affix-driven stratification of the lexicon (Giegerich (1999), Wiese (1996b) and Montgomery (2001) propose base-driven stratification of the lexicon, where the English lexicon has only Root and Word strata whereas German has three strata, Root, Stem and Word (following Selkirk 1982). These categories are the bases which affixes attach to, and Giegerich (1999) gives the following definitions for these categories: the term Root is defined as a morphological category that is not specified for lexical category; stem is defined as a morphological category which is specified for lexical category but subject to further (for example, inflectional) affixation; word is a morphological category that is free as well as fully specified for lexical category. Let us see some of the characteristics of Stratum-1 and 2 affixations within the affix-driven approach and then examine the changes in the base-driven approach before discussing whether this approach can give us a clearer picture of criteria for the non-head of compounds in the languages in question.

Siegel (1974) hypothesised that in English, every affix is firmly associated with one and only one of the two classes of affixes and that a lexicon needs to be stratified. The first boundary or class of affixes, Stratum-1 affixes (for example, *–ion, -ity, -ate*, etc) are attached before the operation of the stress rules. In contrast, the second, Stratum-2 affixes (for example, *-ness, -ly, -like*, etc) are attached after the operation. In addition, another difference between Stratum-1 and 2 affixes is that the former can be attached to bound or free morphemes (in the traditional sense) whereas the latter can be attached only to free morphemes. Thirdly, affixation on stratum 1 is claimed to be less productive than that on stratum 2 (Kiparsky 1982). Along the same line affixation on stratum 1 is more likely to be semantically non-compositional than affixation on stratum 2. The important characteristics of the affix-driven approach are the Blocking Effect and the Affix Ordering Generalisation. The Blocking Effect is achieved automatically in a stratified lexicon. For example, the ungrammaticality of *warm-ness (-ness is a Stratum-2 affix) is accounted for because of the existence of warm-th (-th is Stratum-1). In relation to the Blocking Effect, the output of Stratum-1 affixation tends to be less productive than Stratum-2 affixation due to the Blocking Effect. Finally, the Affix Ordering Generalisation states that, given that both types of affixation are recursive, stratum-2 cannot be 'inside' stratum 1-affixation (e.g. homelessness, tonicity and tonicness are well formed, but *homelessity is not)[57].

In contrast, after careful scrutiny of the affix-driven approach, Giegerich (1999) argues for the base-driven approach. The base-driven stratification of lexicon is proposed due to several shortcomings of the affix-driven stratification. According to Giegerich, there are a number of affixes which cannot be pinned down to a single stratum (those which have dual membership). Moreover, there has never been a consensus as to how many strata the English lexicon should have. Thirdly, the claim that stratum-2 cannot be 'inside' stratum 1-affixation cannot be upheld for cases like - (u) ous and –ize which are both stratum 1 affixes. For example, the word *sens-ous-ize is ungrammatical. So the Affix Ordering Generalisation is not correct in this case.

Instead, Giegerich proposes Root-to-Word Conversion. There must be one class of morphological operations whose inputs are roots and whose outputs are words. In the absence of such a process, no lexical item could transit from stratum 1 to stratum 2. The following rule is proposed.

(324) Root-to-Word Conversion
  $[\ ]_r \rightarrow [[\ ]_r\ ]_L$ (L = N, V, A)   (Giegerich 1999: 76)

Also, following Lieber (1981) and Kiparsky (1982), Giegerich argues that all affixation rules have the form (325) below. This rule is applied to any kind of affixation.

(325) Insert A in the environment $[Y\_\_Z]_L$

In rule (325), L is the lexical category specification of the base. According to '[Y Z]' in (325), any further details of the subcategorisation frame limit the attachment of the affix A. Some examples of such frames are given in (326) below:

(326) a. matern →-al
       →-ity
    * →ø
       moll →-ify
       →ø
       gorm →-less
    * →ø
    b. serene →-ity
       →-nade
       →Adj
       nation →-al

The roots of the frames (326a) are bound forms. The examples in (a) cannot be derived without any further affixation, because the morphemes are roots not free morphemes. Then, there is no lexical category as a result. However, *maternal* is adjective as a result of affixation. Every root is marked, or not, to undergoing (324). One of the operations available is to attach *-al]* to *[matern]*, where 'attach' is taken to mean the placement of a pair of brackets round the concatenated form: [[*matern*] *al*], the same can be said for the operation deriving [[*matern*] *ity*]. Also, the operation (325), *Insert [matern] to rule (324)*, takes place, represented as *matern→ø* in (326a). The resulting derivation is ungrammatical, as predicted.

In contrast, the roots of (326b) are free roots. Contrary to example (326a), the roots of example (326b) are marked for undergoing rule (325). Thus, it is possible to have the operation, *Insert [serene] to rule (324)* and assign the lexical category Adjective[58].

Based on these assumptions, Giegerich (1999), Wiese (1996b) and Montgomery (2001) claim that German should have another stratum apart from Root and Word. Giegerich gives examples of adjective-forming *–bar* 'able', attaching to transitive verbs. Giegerich gives the following examples of noun-forming affix *–ung* '-ing' which is attached to transitive and intransitive verbs (Giegerich 1999: 89) (see Table 2). The suffix is productive and attaches only to a verbal base, so it is not a Stratum-1 affix according to the affix-driven approach. However, its base is not a Word, so there needs to be another category apart from Root or Word in affixation in German. The form in parenthesis is the infinitive form of the verb.

Table 2: Derivation in German

| trinkbar | 'drinkable' | schöpfung | 'creation' |
| (trinken) | | (schaffen) | |

essbar (essen)	'edible'	zündung (zünden)	'ignition'
Brauchbar (brauchen)	'useful'	lesung (lessen)	'reading'
Lesbar (lessen)	'legible'	trennung (trennen)	'separation'
analysierbar (analysieren)	'analyseable'	filtrierung (filtrieren)	'filtration'
opearierbar (opearieren)	'operable'	finanzierung (finanzieren)	'funding' (N)

The bases of both –*bar* and –*ung* are roots in the definition given by Matthews (1991: 64). Matthews' (1991) definition for the term *stem* is that it is morphologically complex and it underlies at least one paradigm or partial paradigm. According to Giegerich (1999), Wiese (1996b) and Montgomery (2001), the bases of the affixes are members of the lexical category Verb but lack the inflection that would enable them to enter the syntax as free forms. These bases of the affixes can be identified as verbs, because they are selected by the affix, -*bar* or - *ung*. These affixes cannot select other lexical categories. The same range of stems occurs in the first elements of verb-noun compounds. The following are examples.

(327) a. Trink+Wasser 'drinking water'
b. Trenn+Wand 'dividing wall'
c. Senk+Fuss 'flat foot' (the verbal root is *senken*)
d. Lauf+Bahn 'career'
e. Fahr+Schule 'driving school' (the verbal root is senken)
f. Filtrier+Werk 'filter station'

The above examples show that German morphology has a stem-based stratum. The stem stratum follows the root stratum. The suffix, –*ier* in (327f) is a root-based derivational suffix deriving a verbal stem. The stem stratum needs to exist, because the outputs of these derivations are subjected to further affixation in order to occur independently in the syntax as a Word.

As already discussed above, Scandinavian languages show a similar pattern in derivation. The following examples clearly demonstrate this. The form in parenthesis is the infinitive form of the verb, and the L in the gloss represents a linking morpheme.

Table 3: Derivation in Scandinavian languages

English	Danish	Swedish	Norwegian
drinkable	drikk+e+lig drink+L+able (drikke)	drick+bar drink+able (dricka)	Drikk+e+lig drink+L+able (drikke)
edible	spis+e+lig eat+L+able (spise)	ät+bar eat+able (äta)	spis+e+lig eat+L+able (spise)
useable	brug+e+lig use+L+able (bruge)	använd+bar use+able (använda)	anvend+e+lig use+L+able (anvende)
readable	læs+e+lig read+L+able læs+bar read+able (læse)	läs+bar read+able (läsa)	les+e+lig read+L+able (lese)
analysable	analyser+e+lig analyse+L+able (analysere)	analyser+bar analyse+able (analysera)	analyser+e+lig anlayse+L+able
operable	anvend+e+lig use+L+able (anvende)	använd+bar use+able (använda)	anvend+e+lig use+L+able
creation	skab+lse create+NOM[59] (skabe)	skap+else create+NOM (skapa)	skap+e+lse create+L+NOM (skape)
separation	adskill+e+lse separate+L+ NOM (adskille)	skill+nad separate+NOM (skilja)	atskill+e+lse separate+ L+NOM (atskille)
ignition	tænd+ing light+ing (tænde)	tänd+ning light+ing (tända)	antenn+e+lse light+L+ NOM tenn+ing light+ing (antenne, tenne)
feeling, marking, sensation	mærk+ning feel+ing (mærke)	märk+ning feel+ing (märka)	merk+ing[60] feel+ing (merke)
worthwhile	mærk+bar, feel+able	märkvärdig feel+worth	merk+bar feel+able
mark-day	mærk+e+dag mark+L+day	bemärkelse+dag notice+ day	merk+e+dag notice+L+day
splashing	plask+ning splash+ing (plaske)	plask+ning splash+ing (plaska)	plask+ing splash+ing (plaske)
splashing rain	plask+regn splash+rain	plask+regn splash+rain	plask+regn splash+rain
measureable	mål+bar measure+able (måle)	mät+bar measure+able (mäta)	mål+bar measure+able (måle)
measuring	mål+ing measure+ing	mät+ning measure+ing	mål+ing measure+ing
measuring tape	mål+e+bånd measure+L+tape	mått+band measure+tape	mål+e+bånd measure+L+tape

stretching	stræk+ning stretch+ing (strække)	sträck+ning stretch+ing (sträcka)	strek+ning stretch+ing (strekke)
stretchable	stræk+bar stretch+able	sträck+bar stretch+able	strek+bar stretch+able
Stretch	stræk+march stretch+march	sträck+marsch stretch+march	strek+mars stretch+march
Christmas present	jul+e+gave Christmas+L+present	jul+klapp Christmas+present	jul+e+gave Christmas+L+present
church tower	kirk+e+torn church+L+tower churchtower	kyrk+torn church+tower (kyrka)	kirk+e+torn church+L+tower
hare roast	hare+steke hare+roast	har+stek hare+roast *harestek	hare+steke hare+roast

As in German, the outputs of these derivations in all the Scandinavian languages are subjected to further affixation in order to occur independently in the syntax as a Word. However, in Danish and Norwegian, sometimes the left constituent is the same as the infinitive of the verb with the vowel morpheme, -e, and this looks like a problematic case. The –e is not the infinitival suffix, however. This is shown by the fact that roots which do not occur as verbs also take the –e in compounds, for example, *dreng-e-tøj* (boy-L-clothes) 'boy clothes' (Danish), *gutt-e-klubb* (boy-L-club) 'boy club' (Norwegian) and *hund-e-kjeks* (dog-L-biscuit) 'dog biscuit' (Norwegian). *Drenge, gutte* and *hunde* are morphologically possible verbs, but this possibility is not realised. Therefore, it seems clear that the –e is a linking element. Moreover, nominal compounds in these two languages sometimes have a linking morpheme between the head and the non-head, as in Swedish. It seems that these languages have a three strata lexicon as German does.

On the other hand, as discussed in Chapter 2, except for cranberry words and neoclassical compounds English compound words always appear to consist of two free morphemes. Therefore, in English, unlike in German and Scandinavian languages, there is no need to postulate the category Stem, because a bound root can be converted to Word and the morpheme can enter the syntax independently. So unlike in German and Scandinavian languages, Giegerich and Montgomery claim that the English lexicon has only two strata, Root and Word. The regular inflection of present-day English is entirely word-based while the bases of irregular inflection are adequately analysed as roots.

I will now examine whether Japanese has a three or two strata lexicon. The ones in parenthesis are the 'non-past tense' and 'root' of the verb in traditional sense (Tsujimura 1996: 128). The term root here refers to a meaningful unit which cannot be given further morphological analysis, not the Root category defined by Giegerich (1999).

Table 4: Derivation in Japanese

English	Japanese
a) drinkable	nomeru (nomu =to drink, nom=root)
b) edible	taberareru (taberu= to eat, tabe=root)
c) useable	tsukaeru (tsukau=to use, tsuka=root)
d) readable	yomeru (yomu=to read, yom=root)
e) separation	ware+me break+eye 'separation' (wareru=to break, ware=root)
f) measurable	hakarareru (hakaru=to measure, haka=root)
g) eating habit	tabe+guse (taberu=to eat, tabe=root)
h) stretching exercise	nobi+taisoo (nobiru=to stretch, nobi=root)
i) whitewash	kirei+goto (kirei-na =beatiful)
j) wintry sky	samu+zora (samui=cold)
k) highwave	Taka+nami (takai=high)

As in German and Scandinavian languages, Japanese seems to have three strata in the lexicon, because the bases of the affixes are traditionally taken to be members of the lexical category Verb but lack the inflection that would enable them to enter the syntax as free forms (in terms of Giegerich) (the examples (a) – (h). The bases of the affixes can be identified as verbs, because they are selected by the affix, for example, *-eru* or *–rareru*. For example, the suffix *–eru* can only be affixed to bases which can occur as verbs, when affixed with a verb-inflection. In addition, the observations of some A-N compound words in the examples (i) – (k) demonstrates that the adjectival element lacks the inflection that would enable it to enter the syntax as free form (also see 2.1.1).

In summary, the categorical features of the non-head of compound words in the languages in question have been discussed. By Giegerich's analysis, there are three strata in the Scandinavian and Japanese lexicon but only two in the English lexicon.

4.1.4 Criticism of the Lexicon within the framework of Lexical Phonology

If Giegerich's claim that the English lexicon only has two strata is correct, the non-head noun in a Noun-Noun compound is a Word. However, the Lexical Phonology does not provide further information as to how to limit the occurrence of a plural inflectional marker in compounds and in derivation in the languages in question. If either the Stem in Scandinavian languages, German and Japanese or the Word category in English is involved in compounding or derivation, it should be possible to have inflection markers, such as plural and tense inflection markers, inside compounds or derived words. Thus, examples such as *ate-able* or *computers technician* in English, **tabe+ta+kata* (eat+Past+way) or **tabe+ru+rareru* (eat+ Present+able) in Japanese and **mærk +ede+bar* (mark+Past+able) or **kirk+e+r+torn* (church+LINK+Plural+tower) in Danish are wrongly predicted to be well formed[61].

An argument in favour of Giegerich's theory is that there are affixes which appear to select verbs and nouns etc. For example, in Danish, the affix *–bar* appears to select a verbal element (e.g. *læs+bar* read+able 'readable'), not a nominal element nor any other element. However, the selection of a specific lexical category contradicts the argument that the base is not specified for a lexical category. So according to Giegerich, it is not possible to know that the base selected by the affix *-bar* is a 'verb', for example. Bases in compounding will be discussed further below.

Another criticism of Root-Stem-Word conversion comes from the theory of the lexicon within the framework of Lexical Phonology. The theory has some advantages in connection with derived compound word formation, such as the blocking effect (see the previous sub-section[62]). In addition, the relationship between morphology, the lexicon and phonology is established successfully with some exceptions in this framework. However, there is no established relationship between word formation and meaning. It is clear that when one considers productivity of compound words, it is necessary to consider the connection between meaning, sound and the derivation in a non-redundant fashion. Furthermore, when lexicalised compound words are considered, the meanings of compound words are not always compositional from those of their constituents. This is successfully shown in the triune lexicon of Platzack (1993), proposed because word derivation cannot escape the rules of syntax or conceptual structure. In this book, as the idea of the triune lexicon is assumed, it is redundant to assume that there are strata in the lexicon. For this reason, I propose to use the word class feature criteria, observed in Section 4.1.1 and 4.1.2.

4.2 Structure

4.2.1 The head of compounds in Japanese

The non-head of a compound in Japanese and in English does not have any categorical features, as discussed in 4.1. However, it is still not clear if the structure of compound words in these languages is similar to that of the Scandinavian languages or not. The following is the structure of the Japanese compound *tenisu kurabu* 'tennis club', modeled on Josefsson's analysis of Swedish compounds:

(328) *tenisu kurabu* in Japanese

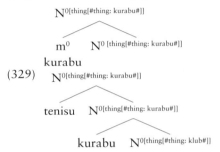

(329)

Let us see if the structure (328) is applicable to compounds in Japanese first. As discussed in Section 3.2.4.2, Josefsson seems to assume that a noun is number merged with a root, so the inflection is the head (Josefsson 1997: 35). However, this analysis cannot be applied to Japanese since there is no number inflection which can be merged with a stem or a root to make it a noun (e.g. *koppu* 'cup' can mean either 'one cup' or 'five cups' according to the context). There is an important candidate, though, for the inflectional suffix in Japanese, *-tachi*, which can be considered the equivalent of the English plural marker – *(e) s*. Let us examine the properties of this suffix in Japanese to see if it can be considered a head in the present analysis.

Firstly, unlike the English plural marker *-s*, the plural marker *–tachi* attaches mostly to animate nouns.

(330) a. gakusei+tachi
student+PL
'the students'
b. inu+tachi
dog+PL

CHAPTER 4 PROPOSED STRUCTURES OF COMPOUND WORDS 141

    'the dogs'   (Ishii 2000: 1)
(331) a. *kuruma+tachi
    car +PL
    'the cars'   (Ishii 2000: 1)
  b. *tsukue+tachi
    desk +PL
    'the desks'

Another difference between the plural marker –*tachi* in Japanese and the English plural marker – *(e) s* is that the Japanese plural marker can attach to pronouns and proper nouns.

(332) watasi+ tachi, anata+ tachi, kanojo+ tachi,
    I+ PL, you+PL, she+PL
    'we/us', 'you' 'they/them(fem.)'
(333) yamada sensei wa taroo+ tachi o syokuzi ni syootai sita.
    Yamada teacher TOP Taroo+PL ACC meal to invited
    'Professor Yamada invited Taroo and those in his group'.
   *'Professor Yamada invited people all named/all with the characteristics
    of Taroo'.

As the translation of the example (333) shows, when added to a proper noun, the suffix yields the reading of a specific group of people including Taroo, and does not mean two or more people named Taroo (Ishii 2000).

 In addition, a pronoun or proper noun with – *tachi* can be followed, but not preceeded by a quantity expression (number + classifier). The following examples support this argument.

(334) yamada sensei + tachi san+nin ga resutoran ni itta.
    Yamada teacher +PL 3+CL NOM restaurant DAT went
    'Professor Yamada and two other people went to a restaurant'.
(335) *san+nin yamada sensei tachi ga resutoran ni itta.
    3-CL Yamada teacher PL NOM restaurant DAT went
(336) watasi+ tachi san+nin wa nihon kara kimashita.
    I +PL 3+CL TOP Japan from came
    'We three came from Japan'.
(337) *san+nin watasi+ tachi wa nihon kara kimashita.
    3+CL I +PL TOP Japan from came

Moreover, another characteristic of the Japanese plural marker can be seen in the following examples.

(338) yamada sensei wa gakusei+ tachi san+nin o syokuzi ni syootai sita.
Yadama teacher TOP student+PL 3+CL-ACC meal to invited
'Professor Yamada invited the three students for dinner'.

(339) yamada sensei ga syokuzi-ni syootai-sita no wa gakusei+ tachi
Yamada teacher NOM meal-to invited- NL-TOP student+PL 3+CL
san+nin da.
COP
'The ones who Professor Yamada invited for dinner were the three students'. NL=nominalizer

(340) *yamada sensei ga syokuzi-ni syootai-sita no wa san+nin gakusei
Yamada teacher NOM meal-to invited- NL-TOP 3+CL student
- tachi da.
-PL COP

The above examples show that common nouns are followed by a classifier, not vice versa.

The suffix – *tachi* is attached to a phrase and it is a phrasal suffix (Ishii 2000). The following examples can support this argument.

(341) [taroo to hanako] + tachi.
'Taroo and Hanako (and those in their group)'
(342) [san-nin no taroo] + tachi
3-CL GEN Taroo PL
'the three Taro's

Moreover, if the suffix –*tachi* selects a bare nominal, and a compound word-like element is formed as a result, the initial element of *tachi* should be voiced according to Lyman's Law (see Section 2.3.2), since it is an obstruent. However, when it acts as a plural marker, as argued, it never is voiced. Thus, the following examples are ungrammatical with the voiced initial element.

(343) *jon+dachi
*gakusei+dachi
student +PL

Therefore, some of properties of the *tachi* are:

(344) –*Tachi* is suffixed to pronouns, proper names, and some common nouns.
  a. Common nouns with –*tachi* must be interpreted as definite.
  b. Attachment of –*tachi* to proper nouns yields only a collective

reading.

    c. A pronoun/proper noun with *–tachi* can be followed, but not preceded, by a quantity expression (number + classifier). In the cases with proper nouns, only the collective reading is possible. Common nouns can also be followed by a quantity expression.

    d. It selects a NP, not a bare noun.   (cf. Ishii 2000: 10)

As a result, if one is to argue that *–tachi* is an affix, it must be identified as a phrasal affix as it selects a NP, not a bare noun, (Klavans 1982: 1985[63]). It does not have a plural syntactic feature, but only a semantic one: i.e. it means 'collective' or 'group'. It is argued here that the suffix is not a proper candidate for an inflection which turns a stem (or a root) without word class features into a word, as the plural marker in the Scandinavian languages does, according to Josefsson. Thus, the crucial feature should be more general than number.

Another candidate for the head of a noun in Japanese is the numeral classifier. As Japanese is a classifier language, numerals are not able to combine directly with nouns: a classifier is necessary to individuate an appropriate counting level. So in Japanese, one cannot say 'two boys', but needs to say 'two portions of boy'. Let us see the distribution of numeral classifiers and their associated NPs in Japanese (all the examples are taken from Kawashima 1994).

(345) san+nin   no gakusei ga hon o   katta.
     three+CL GEN student NOM book ACC bought
     'Three students bought a book'.

(346) gakusei ga san+nin   hon o katta.
     student NOM 3+CL   book ACC bought
     'Three students bought a book'.

(347) *gakusei ga   hon o san+nin katta.
     student NOM book ACC 3+CL bought
     'Three students bought a book'.

(348) gakusei ga hon (o) san+satu katta.
     student NOM book ACC 3+CL bought
     'A student bought three books'.

(349) gakusei ga san+satu (no) hon o   katta.
     student NOM 3+CL (GEN) book ACC bought
     'A student bought three books'.

(350) hon o gakusei ga san+satu katta.
     book ACC student NOM 3+CL   bought
     'A student bought three books'.

(351) gakusei ga san+nin to sensei ga yo+nin kita.
     student NOM 3+CL and teacher NOM 4+CL came

'Three students and four teachers came'.

(352) gakusei ga hon o san+satu to nooto o ni+satu katta.
student NOM book ACC 3+CL and notebook ACC 2+CL bought
'A student bought three books and two notebooks'.

(353) yakuza ni nagurareta no wa tsuukoonin ga san+nin da.
gangster by hit-COMP-TOP passerby NOM 3+CL COP
'It was three passer by who were hit by gangsters'.

(354) gakusei ga katta no wa   hon o san+satu da.
student NOM bought-COMP-TOP book ACC 3+CL COP
'It was three books that a student bought.'

The above examples (345) – (350) show that the subject cannot be separated from its numeral classifier whereas the object can be. Examples (346), (348) – (350) show that the numeral classifier attaches to a NP. This argument is especially true when one considers the phonological criterion of a syntactic phrase distinct from a lexical element. In (348) – (349), even when the accusative case-marker and the genitive case-marker are optionally not assigned to the associate NP of the classifier, there is a pause, indicating the presence of a null case particle. Thus, the classifier selects a case-marked nominal, i.e. a DP, not a bare N. Also, in the examples (352) – (354), the classifier takes an NP with case as complement. I conclude that the classifier in Japanese cannot be the head of a noun either.

4.2.2 Headedness?

Josefsson's theory of INFL works if the head of the compound word is a verb or adjective. The verbal or adjectival inflection can be merged with a verbal stem, in Josefsson's term, and the category of the whole compound word is verb. For instance, Josefsson assumes without further discussion that a Swedish verb is derived in the following way.

(355)

'bend'   (Josefsson 1997: 46)

The verbal stem, in Josefsson's term, *böj* is merged with the infinitive affix *–a*, which is a kind of tense affix. The value of the infinitival tense is unspecified, but it is interpreted in conjunction with the tense of the selecting verb.

In the same way, this structure, I argue, is applicable for a Japanese verb. For example, a verbal stem, in Josefsson's terms, *age* 'give' is merged with the inflectional marker *–ru* (non-past form in traditional Japanese grammar). Since *–ru* selects the verbal element, *-ru* is the head of the word and its [+tense] feature percolates up.

(356)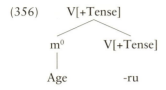

The allomorph of the suffix *–ru* is *–u*. If the verbal root ends in a vowel (except for *–a*), it is merged with *–ru* and if it ends in a consonant, it is merged with *–u*. Also, the idea that the head is an inflection is applicable in the derivation of Japanese adjectives. Similarly to the formation of verb, an adjectival root is merged with an inflection.

Josefsson claims that X is a head if and only if X has a word class feature (a non-head lacks a word class feature, as discussed in section 2.1.1.3). However, this argument cannot hold for phrasal syntax. The complement NP of a verb is not a head even though the NP as well as the head V has a word class feature. Thus, there should be another way to determine the head. Moreover, the way to determine the head should be the same for all lexical categories, and for word syntax as well as phrasal syntax.

In this thesis, Collins' (2002) definition of head is extended to compound words. The following points discussed by Collins (2002) are assumed in this thesis.

(357) a. A head is a category which has one or more unsaturated features.
b. If a lexical item is chosen from the lexical array (Chomsky 1995) and introduced to the derivation, the probe/selectors of this lexical item must be satisfied before any new unsaturated lexical items are chosen from the lexical array. If not, the derivation will be cancelled.

As discussed in 3.2, Chomsky (2000) introduces the terms 'probe' and 'goal'. According to Chomsky, a 'probe' is a head which searches for a lexical item which has matching features, called a 'goal'. The probe has one or more uninterpretable and/or unvalued features, and needs the goal, which has corresponding interpretable, valued features, to assign values to these features, or in some cases, typically the EPP feature to check and delete the feature. With these definitions in mind, Collins (2002) proposes that a head (or a probe) needs to have its features valued or checked before another lexical item chosen from the lexical array is introduced in the derivation. To put it simply, a probe is a lexical item which looks for another lexical item to check its features during the course of derivation.

As an example of assumption (b), Collins states that the combination of a complementiser with Infl' as a constituent [CP Comp Infl'] is impossible, since the EPP feature has not been satisfied when Comp is chosen from the lexical array. This is demonstrated in the following structure.

(358) *

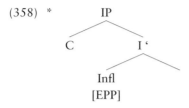

Consider compounds: in the compound *teacup*, *cup* is the head. What unvalued feature does it have? One feature which NPs or DPs have, which is valued and checked when they are merged with a verb, is Case. This suggests that Case is the crucial feature. However, verbs and adjectives occur as heads of compounds but do not have case. They do, however assign theta-roles. This can be expressed as an unvalued theta-feature, which is valued by the argument to which the role is assigned (represented in this thesis as Theme (x) (see 4.3.4 for discussion on the Theme (x) feature). In other words, for compound words with verb or adjective as head, respectively, case cannot be the unvalued feature, but the theta-feature can.

Before continuing to argue that the head of a compound can be a theme feature, it is necessary to discuss whether theta roles can be features or not within the Minimalist Program. Chomsky (1995) argues that theta-roles are not features and further assumes that all movement is restricted to nonthematic targets. In addition, theta-roles are not checkable features. In short, the Minimalist Program retains the theta-criterion of the Government Binding theory.

On the other hand, Hornstein (1999), after having discussed control and raising issues in the Minimalist Program, concludes that theta-roles can be features on verbs. A D/NP receives a theta-role by checking a theta-feature of a verbal or predicative phrase that it merges with. Also, he argues that theta-feature is required if movement to a theta-position is to conform to the principle of Greed. In this paper, I take Hornstein's claim of theta as a feature in a course of a derivation.

According to Higginbotham (1985), discharging a theta-role from simple nominals is also possible, since simple nominals also serve as predicates. He claims that simple nominals have a position accessible to a Specifier, which either receives the theta-role or acts as a binder of it. This means that the relation between the verb and its thematic object is parallel to that between the article and the noun. The article serves the role of saturating the open place that every common noun has and by virtue of which it denotes. For example, a simple nominal like the word *dog* has a thematic grid as part of its lexical entry 'dog, -V, +N, <1>', where the position 1 is accessible to a Specifier. This may be a possessor DP, as in *John's dog*, in which case *John* receives the theta-role, or it may be a determiner, as in *the dog* in which case the determiner binds the theta-role. In this thesis, it is assumed that the theta-role discharged from a simple nominal is the unvalued feature which needs to be assigned a value by a DP or by a D. Thus, all the lexical categories have an unassigned theta-role feature which has to be somehow saturated. I will say that the theta-feature is valued when it receives a referential index from a DP (as in the case of *John's dog*), or from a D (as in *the dog*).

With the assumptions that have been made so far, a word would be derived as follows, taking the Japanese compound *tenisu kurabu* 'tennis club' as example.

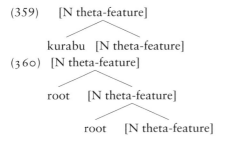

(359)   [N theta-feature]

      kurabu   [N theta-feature]

(360)   [N theta-feature]

      root   [N theta-feature]

            root   [N theta-feature]

In (359) a root *kurabu* without a word class feature is merged with a theta-feature and an N categorical feature. Since the theta-feature is unsaturated when [N theta-feature] is merged with the root, it percolates until the theta-role gets checked by another category, such as D or DP[64]. In the terminology of Chomsky (2000) the head provides the 'label' of the category it heads. I will use the traditional term 'percolation' for the relation between the head and the category dominating the head: The features of the head 'percolates' to the dominating note. As discussed above, Higginbotham (1985) claims that simple nominals also discharge a theta-role to a DP, or have the theta-role bound by a D. In the present analysis, Higginbotham's claims imply that [N theta-feature] merged with a root percolates its theta-role feature until the theta-role feature gets checked by a D or DP[65]. Checking of the features here means that the theta-role feature needs a referential index from either D or DP. Also, checking should occur in a sister-relation. Thus, the category of the whole word *kurabu* in the structure (359) is a Noun with a theta-role feature.

The structure (360) is derived as follows: First, a root is merged with a theta-role feature and an N-feature, and these features percolate. Then, another root is merged, and again, the theta-role feature and the N-feature percolate, so that the category of the compound is [N theta-role].

What differences are there between nouns and verbs? In her thesis, as discussed in 3.2.4.3, Josefsson (1997) establishes the relation between word classes and conceptual categories, making use of a finite number of major ontological categories (Jackendoff (1985). Jackendoff claims that ontological features are visible to the syntax-semantics interface unlike most descriptive features of concepts. So they play an important role in grammar as well as in perceptions. The world is understood in categories like [THINGS], [PROPERTIES], [EVENTS], [DIRECTIONS], [PLACES], for example, and there are some differences between the world as we understand it (projected world, experienced world, or phenomenal world) and the true world. The major ontological categories are prototypically represented in the word classes; Things are nouns, Events are verbs, Properties are adjectives.

In this case, how does one characterise the differences between the categories? Josefsson states that inflection superimposes a different major ontological category. However, as we have seen that number cannot play any such role in Japanese, there should be another criterion which distinguishes ontological categories. Let us see if it is possible to use the argument-taking properties of each category first.

There are different types of nouns. One type of noun is nouns denoting complex events. These nouns often have a corresponding verb with which they share complement-taking properties. This was first established by Chomsky (1970) and developed in Grimshaw (1990) and Kageyama (1993) for Japanese. Grimshaw argues that it is obligatory for them to take the same arguments as the ones taken by their corresponding verbs, whereas it is not for other types of nouns, such as simple and result nominals. Therefore, obligatory means the same for nouns as for verbs: capable in principle of being obligatory but perhaps subject to lexical variation. As examples of complex event nominals, Grimshaw presents the following[66].

(361) The felling *(of the trees) [E]
(362) kyonen no *?(ki no) bassai [J]
last-year GEN *(tree GEN) felling
'the felling of the/a tree last year'
(363) Fældning-en *(af træ-et) [D]

felling-the *(of tree-the)
'the felling of the trees'
(364) They felled *(the trees). [E]
(365) Kyonen *?(ki o) bassai-sita. [J]
last-year (tree ACC) felling-did
'last year I/we felled the trees'.
(366) De fælde-de *(træ-et). [D]
They fell-Past *(tree-the).
'They felled the trees'.
(367) The destroying *(of the city) [E]
(368) kyonen no *?(sono si no) hakai [J]
last year GEN *(that city GEN) destruction
'the destroying of the city last year'
(369) Destruering-en *(af by-en) [D]
Destroying-the *(of city-the)
'the destroying of the city'
(370) They destroyed *(the city). [E]
(371) kyonen *(sono si o) hakai-sita. [J]
Last year *(that city ACC) destroy-did
'They destroyed the city last year'.
(372) De destruerede *(by-en). [D]
They destroyed *(city-the).
'They destroyed the city'. (Grimshaw 1990: 50 for the English data)

As the above examples have shown, in the case of Japanese, what linguists like Grimshaw call Light Verbs take the obligatory arguments if the corresponding verbs do. Moreover, the above examples have shown that in Mainland Scandinavian languages and in English, gerundive nominals take obligatory arguments if the corresponding verbs do. There are some complex event nominals which are ambiguous between the class of nominals that take arguments and nominals that do not. However, it is possible to disambiguate these nouns as certain modifiers occur only with the event interpretation of particular nouns. The other reading is a result reading. For example, the modifier *frequent* forces the event reading of *expression* in the following. Once they are disambiguated, it is possible to see that the object of the event nominal is obligatory:

(373) The expression is desirable. [E]
(374) sono hyoogen wa motomerareteiru. [J]
That expression TOP desirable.
'That expression is desirable'.
(375) Udtrykk-et er ønskeligt. [D]

Expression-the is desirable.
'That expression is desirable'.
(376) The expression (on her face) [E]
(377) (kanojo no kao no) hyoogen [J]
(her GEN face GEN) expression
(378) Udtrykk-et (i ansigt-et) [D]
expression-the (in face-the)
'the expression on her face'
(378) *The frequent expression is desirable. [E]
(379) *sono hinpan-na hyoogen wa nozomareteiru. [J]
That frequent expression TOP desirable.
(380) *Gentaget udtryk er ønskeligt. [D]
repeated expression is desirable
(381) The frequent expression of one's feelings is desirable. [E]
(382) hinpanna kanojo no hyoogen wa nozomareteiru. [J]
Frequent her GEN expression TOP desirable
'The frequent expression of her feeling is desirable'.
(383) Gentaget udtryk af ens følelse er ønskelig. [D]
repeated expression of one's feeling is desirable
'The frequent expression of one's feeling is desirable'.
(384) We express *(our feelings). [E]
(385) watasitachi wa *(kanjoo o) hyoogen-suru. [J]
We TOP *(feeling ACC) express-do
'We express our feelings'.
(386) Vi udtrykker *(vores følelser). [D]
We express *(our feelings).
'We express our feelings'.   (Grimshaw 1990: 50 for the English data)

The following is a more appropriate structure for compound words.

(387)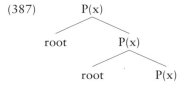

Jackendoff's semantical and conceptual category is not taken in my theory, because Japanese cannot use the theory of inflection as head. Instead of Jackendoff's Thing, I propose that a 'noun' denotes a property the content of which is given by the root (Chierchia 1998, Higginbotham 1985). This is derived by merging a root with a P(roperty) (x) feature[67]. The above structure is constructed as follows: First, a root without word class features is merged with a P (x). There are two ways to check P(x): one is assigning x a value that is an index, and the other is deleting x. Since the P (x) feature is unsaturated in the sense that it needs a referential index from either D or DP, it percolates. Then, another root is merged to form a compound word. As P (x) is the only unsaturated feature before and/or after the root is merged, it percolates and it is thereby the head of the whole compound. As a result of merging after root after root with a P(x), the Extension Condition (Chomsky 1993, 1995; See 3.2) is respected in the structure above, since another modifier is numerated from the lexicon and merged at root with the other two merged items.

As discussed in 1.4, in the Minimalist Program, Chomsky suggests that there should not be anynew objects, particularly no indices should be added in the course of derivations. The referential index proposed in my theory is not a problem for Chomsky's suggestion. The referential index is not the same as Chomsky's indix in that it is a feature necessary during the course of the derivation of a 'noun'.

In the present theory, a noun in traditional sense is a root merged with P(x). It does not refer to a thing. It refers to a thing only when combined with a determiner. Nouns are different from adjectives, which also denote properties. Baker's (2003) idea that nouns have an identity feature (in addition to P(x)) may be what makes nouns different from adjectives. I leave this question for future research.

Although I object to a linear definition of heads in morphology, from looking at compounds in English, Japanese and Mainland Scandinavian, the head almost always 'follows' non-head constituent, as observed in (2) and (3) and many others. According to the structural definition of headedness of Collins (2002), the 'right-hand' is the head of a word or compound word, since that element is merged with a categorical feature. In the PF, this linearization must be specified, so that the words derived can be acceptable when spelled out.

In summary, I concluded, following Josefsson's (1997) work on Swedish, that in Japanese and English as in Scandinavian languages, the 'left-hand' constituent of compound words does not have word class features. I rejected the theory of lexicon within the framework of Lexical Phonology and argued for the triune lexicon. Another proposal is that the head of a compound is a theta-feature, not inflection. The structure (387) is applicable for Japanese, Scandinavian languages and English compounds, since the non-head of compound word does not have any word class features. Structures for English compound words and genitive compound words and other types of compounds, such as neoclassical and 'cranberry morphemes' and finally, recursive compounds in English, Japanese, and Scandinavian languages will be proposed in the following section.

4.3 Structures

4.3.1 Structures for 'cranberry morphemes'

The proposed structure is applicable for 'cranberry morphemes' in the languages in question. As discussed in 2.1.2, 'cranberry morphemes' only appear in words. Unlike what Anderson (1992) claims, I follow Josefsson's (1997) claim that cranberry morphemes are represented as separate entries in the list of morphemes. It is proposed that the constituents involved in cranberry 'compounds' are roots without word class features, like the normal type of compounding. The derivation is the same and the only difference is that a root does not have meaning of its own, so the LF-lexicon accepts the meaning after the derivation. As a result, D or DP can assign a referential index to the resulting 'word'.

4.3.2 Structures for genitive compounds, neoclassical compounds and other complex compounds in Scandinavian and English

In this thesis, the following structure is proposed for genitive compounds in Scandinavian languages, Japanese and English.

(388)

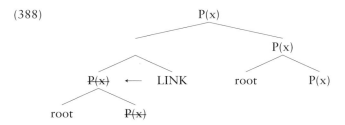

As discussed in 3.2, the linking morpheme in *fred-s-konference* (peace+LINK+conference) 'peace conference' is a morpheme that lacks an independent meaning and thus is similar to a 'cranberry morpheme'. It contributes to the meaning of the whole, though. The phonetic form of the linking element corresponds to the possessive marker, in both old and modern Swedish (Josefsson 1997: 65). Similarly, in the examples (130), (135) – (142), the *–s* morpheme is a homophone of a genitive marker in each language. Thus, I propose that genitive compounds in the languages in question have the above structure, the linking element having the function of checking the P(x) feature[68].

The structure (388) is derived in the following way. Two roots are merged

CHAPTER 4 PROPOSED STRUCTURES OF COMPOUND WORDS 153

with a P(x). They cannot be merged directly because the two P(x)s both percolate, and it is not possible for a structure to have two heads. Instead, one of the two [root, P(x)] trees is merged with a linking element. This morpheme checks the P(x). Then, the two trees are merged. Because the P(x) which has not been checked by the linking morpheme is still unsaturated and needs a referential index from D or DP, it percolates. Thus, the head of the structure (388) is the unchecked P(x). The effect is that the compound is interpreted as denoting a property with the content of the root first merged with the head P(x), but modified by the other root.

The proposed structure (388) is applicable to neoclassical compounds in the languages in question, such as *astrofysisk* 'astrophysic', *television* 'televison' in Scandinavian languages; *geology, photography* in English; *kisetsu* 'season' and *uki* 'rainy season' in Japanese. As discussed in Section 2.1.2, the constituents involved in neoclassical compounds in the languages in question do have semantic value, like those involved in normal compounding. Moreover, it was argued that neoclassical compounds behave more similarly to compounds than to derivation. It is proposed in this thesis that the constituents in neoclassical compounds do not have word class features either. The 'right-hand' constituent is merged with a P(x) and these features percolate to the dominating node.

This structure (388), it is proposed, is also correct for English compounds with a 'left-hand' element which has a derivational suffix, such as *–ing, -er* or *–ion*. For this type of compounds, the derivational suffix supplies a P(x). Synthetic compounds will be discussed in detail in Section 4.3.4. There needs to be a linking element merged to check these features.

On the other hand, the regular plural inflection itself is a linking element. Compounds with a 'plural morpheme' –s on the 'left-hand', such as *awards ceremony* are represented as follows[69].

(389)
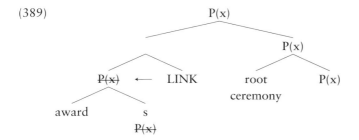

A similar structure is applicable to the compounds which have end-stress (e.g. *sparrow+hawk, toy+factory*) (see 2.3.1). The semantic relationship between the two constituents is that of attribution. I propose the following structure for this type of compounds.

(390)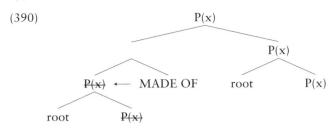

The MADE OF is similar to the LINK in the structure (388) and checks the P(x) feature which is merged with the 'left-hand' root. The 'right-hand' element is the head, and the existence of the category MADE OF in this structure makes it different from a compound which has fore-stress (see 2.3.1 for the differences between the two types of compounds).

Also, a similar structure is applicable to the following type of compounds in Scandinavian languages.

(391) a. e+poster vs. *poster
e+messages vs. messages
'email messages'
b. høver vs. *hest+e+høver
hooves vs. hors+LINK+hooves
'hooves' vs. *'coltsfoot' but 'horsehoof'
c. *hov vs. hest+e+hov
hoof vs. hors+LINK+hooves
'coltsfoots' (Johannessen 2001: 75-76)

The righthand constituent of the type (391a) of a compound word can take a plural inflection whereas as a single word, it cannot. This is explained if there are two lexical items *post*. One of them is a mass noun meaning 'mail', and as such does not have a plural form. The other is a cranberry morpheme, lacking any meaning (that is to say, it has no corresponding concept in the LF-lexicon). When merged with the root *e*, another cranberry morpheme, the resulting compound has a corresponding concept in the LF-lexicon: 'e-mail message'. This compound is a count noun with a regular plural form.

(392)
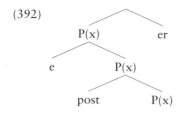

In contrast, in (391b, c) there are two lexical items *hov*. One means 'hoof'. When merged with [Plural] the resulting word is assigned the form *høver* in the PF-lexicon. When combined with another root, for example *hest* 'horse', the result receives a compositional reading. The other item *hov* is a cranberry morpheme. When combined with *hest* (which requires the LINK *–e-*), the resulting compound is assigned the meaning 'coltsfoot' in the LF-lexicon. When this compound is merged with [plural], the resulting word is assigned the form *hestehov* in the PF-lexicon.

(393)
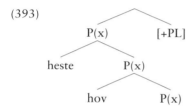

4.3.3 Adjective-Noun/Adjective-Adjective compounds?

'Adjective-noun' (e.g., *blackbird* in English; *højskole* 'high school' in Scandinavian languages; *huruhon* (old-book) 'secondhand book' in Japanese), and 'adjective-adjective' (e.g., *white-hot* in English; *tvärbrant* 'abrupt steep' in Scandinavian; *atsukurushii* (hot-strenuous) 'stuffy' in Japanese) compounds in these languages are productive, just like 'noun-noun' compounds are . According to Lieber (1983), these types are productive, since neither of the constituent stems (roots within the present analysis) takes arguments.

According to Higginbotham (1985), adjectives serve as predicates in the same way as nouns. It is proposed that an 'adjective' denotes a property the content of which is given by the root, as an adjective does assign a property to something. In order to distinguish the P(x) of the noun from the property of an adjective, the latter is represented as A(x)[70]. When an adjective merges with a noun, forming an NP, and this NP merges with a D, forming a DP (e.g., *the big house*), the noun and the adjective have the same referential index from the D. However, I propose that the adjective does not get it directly from D, but gets it via the noun (cf. Higginbotham 1985).

How are 'adjective-noun' and 'adjective-adjective' compounds analysed? According to the proposed analysis, a compound word, like *black+bird* or is derived in the following way.

(394)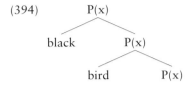

The 'left-hand' member of the above compound is a root. The above structure is constructed as follows: First, a root without word class features is merged with a P (x). Since the P (x) feature is unsaturated in the sense that it needs a referential index from a D, it percolates. Then, another root is merged to form a compound word. As P (x) is the only unsaturated feature before and/or after the root is merged, it percolates and it is thereby the head of the whole compound.

Similarly, an 'adjective-adjective' compound, such as *hot-brown* is derived in the following way.

(395)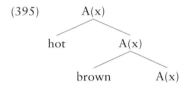

In the compound above, too, the 'left-hand' is a root without word class features. The structure above is derived in the same way as the structure (394). The head of the whole compound is the A(x) as it is the only unsaturated feature before and/or after the root *hot* is merged.

The derivation seen above can be certainly true for Japanese and Scandinavian compounds in the same way. The followings show the derivation in these languages.

The derivation of *usugitanai* (thin-dirty) 'dirty' in Japanese

(396)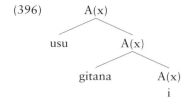

Since the derivational suffix -*i* is an adjectival suffix, it is proposed that it has an A(x) feature. This feature percolates up until the x is assigned a value through agreement with a valued P(x)[71]. Moreover, as discussed in 2.1.1, there is another type of adjective in Japanese with a –*na* suffix. The derivation of *ko-girei* (small-tidy) 'neat' is as follows.

(397)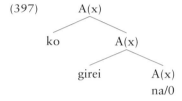

The difference between the suffixes –*na* and –*i* is that the former cannot have a phonetical realisation when it occurs in a predicate position (**John wa ko-girei na* (John TOP small-tidy) vs. *John wa ko-girei da* (John TOP small-tidy COP) 'John is neat', where the *da* is a [-Tense] particle), whereas the latter does (*John no heya wa usu-gitanai* (John GEN room TOP thin-dirty) 'John's room is untidy' vs. **John no heya wa usu-gitana.*(John GEN room thin-dirty). In both cases, there is an A(x) feature heading the compound.

Similarly, in Scandinavian languages, the derivation of adjectival compound words is as follows.

(398)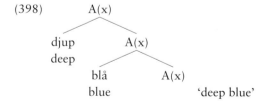

The above structure is derived as follows. The morpheme *blå* 'blue' is merged with an A(x) feature. Since the A(x) feature is unsaturated, it percolates. Another morpheme, *djup* 'deep' is merged. Since this morpheme is a root without a word class feature, the A(x) percolates and is the head of the whole compound.

4.3.4 Structure for synthetic compounds

As discussed in 2.1.1, this kind of compound word is different from the root compound. Synthetic compounds are headed by deverbal nouns and the head usually has an argument whereas a root compound word does not (Roeper & Siegel 1978).

(399)

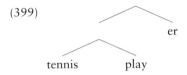

This structure shows that the derivational suffix is merged after the whole compound word is derived. The following examples have this structure.

(400) a. book lov-er
b. picture paint-ing
c. truck-drive-r

Let us propose a more sophisticated structure for this type of deverbal compounds. Is the non-head of nominal root compound in these languages different from that of synthetic compound words involving a nominal root? For example, is the compound word *tennis club* in the languages in question different from *tennis player*? One difference between the non-head in nominal root compounds and that in the synthetic compound words is that there is no theta-role argument assigned by a 'verbal element'[72], in the nominal root compounds. On the other hand, in the synthetic compound word *tennis* has a complement theta-role assigned by the base 'verb element', *play*. The interpretation of the compound word, *tennis player* is restricted to 'a person who plays tennis' and no other interpretation. According to Lieber (1983), the structure for this type of compound is as follows:

CHAPTER 4 PROPOSED STRUCTURES OF COMPOUND WORDS   159

(401)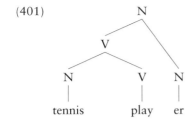

According to Lieber (see 3.1.2), the structure above shows that the 'verbal element'[73] *play* is first merged with a lexical item. When the verbal element is merged with another lexical item, the lexical item needs to satisfy the internal argument structure or semantic argument structure of the verbal element. The lexical item can be, for example, *tennis*.

Then, the nominal suffix *–er* is attached and as a result, the interpretation of the whole compound is 'a player who plays tennis', since there is only one argument in the argument position. Thus, the non-head of synthetic compound words is different from that of nominal root compound word which requires no argument structure[74].

In contrast to the type of compound seen in *tennis player*, where the base 'verbal element' takes its argument, there is another type where the base does not take any argument. One example Lieber cites is *green-driver* (Lieber 1983: 268), where the interpretation would be 'driver who wears green', but not 'someone who drives green'. For this type, Lieber (1983) proposes the following structure.

(402)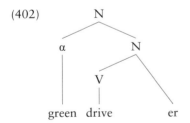

This structure shows that if the 'verbal element' is merged with the suffix *–er* first, it does not assign a theta-role. Moreover, since the verbal element is contained within a noun, it is not possible to for the argument structure of the 'verbal' element to percolate to any node higher in the compound tree.

Let us propose structures for synthetic compounds within Bare Phrase Structure theory. It is important to note that the standard Internal Subject Hypothesis has been rejected within the Bare Phrase Structure and instead, following Hale & Keyser (1993), the external argument is introduced by v (a light verb), the head of an upper projection in VP shell structure (see also Chomsky 1995). The internal argument is introduced and assigned a theta-role by V, the head of the lower projection in VP shell structure.

Within the proposed theory, it has been argued that the elements involved in compounding are roots without a word class feature. Henceforth, the elements will be called roots, instead of verbs. Moreover, it is also necessary to assume that a theme-role (henceforth Theme) is also a merged feature, not an inherent property of the root. This is clear when one considers compounds such as *green-driver* (as above), *play-leader*, and *play-maker* and so on, where the root *play* does not assign any theme-roles.

According to Levin & Hovav (1992), the nominal suffix *–er* specifies that its open position is identified with the open position in N', yielding an N' restricted to refer to an entity corresponding to the external argument of the base verb, *play*. Within the Bare Phrase Structure, since there is no N-bar projection, the open position is on the nominal suffix itself. However, within the BPS, there is no agent theta-role feature assigned by a root.

Based on these assumptions, a structure for synthetic compounds like *tennis-player* is as follows:

(403)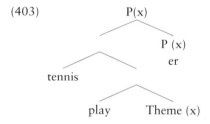

In the structure of the compound *tennis player*, first, the root *play* is merged with a Theme feature (x). It is assumed in this thesis that the Theme feature is an unvalued feature. It is assigned its value by the root *tennis* when this root is merged and the root *tennis* is thereby interpreted as having the theme role assigned by *play*. Here, there is an agreement relation between the root *tennis* and the Theme. Since there is no categorical feature on the resulting 'compound' *tennis-play*, a derivational suffix *-er* which has a P(x) is merged. This feature is unsaturated, so the head of the compound *tennis player* is the P(x), which needs a referential index from a D or DP[75, 76].

On the other hand, the following is a structure for synthetic compounds like *green-driver* where no thematic argument is assigned to the 'left-hand' element.

(404)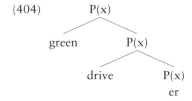

The verbal root *drive* is merged with a suffix *–er* first. Since the suffix has a P(x) feature, which is not saturated when merged, it is percolated up. Another root of any kind can be merged. The interpretation of the resulting compound is not restricted to something like a driver who drives green, because the root, *green*, does not have to value a Theta feature.

Is a synthetic compound such as *tennis player* different from its corresponding nominalization, *player of tennis*? Yes, it is. According to Levin & Hovav (1992) and van Hout & Roeper (1997), the nominalization implies an event, whereas the compound with the nominal suffix does not. A player of tennis must have played tennis; a trainer of dogs is someone who has trained dogs. On the other hand, no tennis needs to have been played by a tennis player; a dog trainer is someone who may not have trained any dogs, but simply finished dog-trainer school. Thus, there is no Event or Aspect associated with the synthetic compound, whereas there is with its corresponding nominalization.

The following differences between nominalization and compounding support this argument:

(405) a. the destruction of the city *for hours/in an hour.
 b. They destroyed the city *for hours/in an hour.
 c. the destruction of cities for hours/*in an hour.
 d. They destroyed cities for hours/*in an hour.
(van Hout & Roeper 1997)

The quantized or non-quantized nature of the object noun phrase is mapped onto the event structure as it is expressed by the predicate: telic or atelic, respectively. The distinction between telicity and non-telicity is represented with the temporal modifiers *for an hour* and *in an hour*. Nevertheless, there is no telicity feature in the corresponding compounds, such as *city-destruction*. Thus, it is not possible to say the following with the temporal modifiers.

(406) city-destruction *for hours/*in an hour   (van Hout & Roeper 1997)

In parallel, Roeper and van Hout propose that – *er* nominals do not project any aspectual features either. It is not possible to say the following.

(407) a. the lawn-mower *for hours/*in an hour
      b. ?The mower of lawn for hours needs a rest.
      c. ?The mower of the lawn in an hour is very swift.

(van Hout & Roeper 1997)

The grammaticality is marginal, but it is possible in nominalizations, however not in compound words. To see whether a predicate entails an event, an event-modifier can be used.

(408) a. the destruction of the city completely
      b. *city-destroying completely   (cf. van Hout & Roeper 1997)

The noun phrase (408a) with a quantized object has telic aspect, and thereby admits the adverb *completely*, which modifies the end point of an event.

As a result of these observations on the differences between the synthetic compounding and their corresponding nominalizations, I argue that a synthetic compound word does not have any Event feature merged, but a P(x). On the other hand, nominalizations do have an Event (x) feature. The Event (x) percolates up until it is bound by Aspect. In the syntax-semantics interface, therefore, Event is valued as either telic denoting that the Event reaches a natural completion, or atelic, meaning that the Event does not reach such a completion[77]. The Event (x) feature is similar to the 'v' in the VP-shell analysis. The proposed structure for synthetic compounding is valid for other types of derivational suffixes, such as *–ing* or *–ion* and zero suffixes. The nominal suffix is identified with the root which is merged with a Theme feature and the P(x) percolates up until it gets bound by a D or DP, not Asp since there is no Event (x) feature to bind. Whether the whole compound refers to a state or an event is an effect of the LF-lexicon.

The structure (403) can be valid if one considers Selkirk's First Order Projection Condition (1982). The First Order Projection Condition claims the following:

(409) The First Order Projection (FOPC)
      All non-SUBJ arguments of a lexical category X_i must be satisfied within the first order projection of X_i.   (Selkirk 1982: 37)

The following examples show cases of synthetic compounding, some of which violate FOPC.

(410) *player off-season trading
(411) *child+making of sandcastles

(412) *boy+eat
(413) *baby+crying
(414) *girl+swim
(415) tree+felling
(416) brick+laying
(417) fund+raising

Within the proposed structure in this thesis, the ungrammaticality of the compounds (411)–(414) can be explained.

(418) *

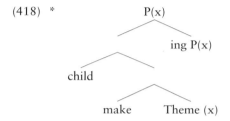

The 'left-hand' root *child* cannot be interpreted as the subject (i.e as the one who makes something, such as a sandcastle). The root merged with the 'compound' *make+ Theme* has a Theme feature assigned. On the other hand, the examples (410)–(414) are grammatical, since the 'left-hand' root gets a Theme feature assigned[78]. It follows from the principle that an unsaturated/unvalued feature must be valued as soon as it can (see Collins 2002, Pesetsky 1995), so that the root *child* must value Theme (x). Another argument requires merge of another unvalued theta-feature. But this cannot happen before the Theme (x) feature is valued. It is not possible to wait until another root is merged.

(419)

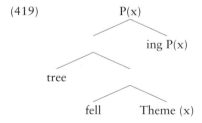

The corresponding examples in Japanese can be analysed within the present analysis. The following are examples.

(420) *(kodomo no) oya+sodate   vs.   (oya ni yoru) ko+sodate
      (children GEN) parent+rear   (parent GEN by) children+rear

'parent-rearing of children'   'child-rearing (by parents)'
(421) *kodomo+asobi   vs.   kodomo+damasi
      child +play   child+ cheat
      'children playing'   'mere child's play'
(422) *akanboo+naki   vs.   kodomo+atsukai
      baby+ cry   child+ treat
      *'baby crying'   'treat me as if I were child'

The following examples have an underlying internal argument as the non-head of the compound.

(423) heart+burn
(424) rain+ fall
(425) land+ slide
(426) jord+ skælv   [D]
       'earth+quake'
(427) pris+stop
       price+ stop
       'price freeze'
(428) mune+yake   [J]
       heart+burn
(429) ne+ sagari   [J]
       price+drop
       'fall in price'
(430) kata+ kori   [J]
       shoulder+grow-stiff
       'the state of one's shoulder being stiff'

However, the above examples clearly have different characteristics from the ones represented in (420) – (424). They are 'unaccusatives' which have only an internal argument, not an external argument. The structure for these compounds is (418) except that P(x) is phonetically null.

It is also important to examine whether cases like *kaeru+oyogi* (frog+swim) 'swim like frog', *usagi+tobi* (rabbit+jump) 'jumping along in a squatting position' in Japanese and *horse+laugh* and *cat+call* in English can be accounted for within the present theory. They are perfectly grammatical. Kageyama (1999) claims that the interpretations of these examples are metaphorical. For example, the interpretation of *kaeru+oyogi* is not that of 'frog swims', but 'swim like frog'. This argument is supported. Within the present analysis, it is not possible to explain the ungrammaticality of the compounds in (420) – (424) on one hand and the grammaticality of compounds like the examples mentioned above on the other on the basis of syntactic structure. Presumably, the grammaticality is due to the interpretation, not the structure[79]. It is possible to say that in these cases, the non-head is not an argument at all, so there is no theta-role. However, cases like *rain+fall* as opposed to **rain+fall-ing* are still problematic. Is *rainfall* another root compound without any Theme feature?

4.3.5 Recursive compounds

As discussed in 1.3, compound formation can be recursive, just as phrase formation. This is especially true for noun-noun compound words. The main characteristic of this type of compound words is that a compound noun freely becomes the base of another compound noun (Namiki 1988). Before discussing the structure of recursive compounds in the languages in question, let us define what recursive formation of words can be.

As said in the last paragraph, noun-noun compounds can be recursive in that a compound noun can be the base of another compound noun. In other words, recursivity can happen as there is, in principle, nothing preventing Merge from applying over and over again, merging more lexical items or trees (see Josefsson 1997, Roeper, Snyder & Hiramatsu 2002). Recursion is considered as a process of enlargement or expansion of a linguistic entity carried out by means of the addition of a new constituent that must be identical in category to the one of the given entity.

Bisetto (2010), following Parker (2006), argues that what we all call recursion can be categorised into recursion and iteration. Recursion is embedding at the edge or in the center of an action or object of an instance of the same type. On the other hand, iteration, is simple unembedded repetition of an action or object. To show the difference of the two types let us consider the English compounds.

(431) a. [student [film society]]
 b. [American [student [film society]]]
 c. [[[[student [film society]] committee] scandal] inquiry]
(Bisetto 2010: 20)

In the a example, the compound *film society* is expanded on the 'right' side by means of the merger of a new constituent, *student*, and in the a the compound *student film society* is enlarged through addition on the non-head side of the adjective *American*. These are iterated compounds (right-recursive compounds in my words), as the adjunction of these constituents enables the denotation of the head constituent more restricted, by adding specification or modification.

On the other hand, the b example is recursion, since each process of constituent addition implies the preceding object/action the base constituent refers to. The merger of a new head, in fact, introduces a new referent bound to the preceding one (Bisetto 2010). However, in this book I would like to argue that both right-branching and left-branching recursive compounds are called recursive compounds (Mukai 2017).

There are definitions of recursive compounds by a number of linguists, such as Bauer (2009) and Booij (2009), who take a broad definition. In contrast Haider (2001) and Pöll (2007) take narrower definition. In this book from these definitions and by summarising recursive compound is defined as follows: a compound of embedding compounds within compounds in cyclic fashion to create words, as complex and long as we like. Here 'complex' means embedding of words within words of the same kind.

With the above definitions of recursive compounds in mind recursive compounds can be derived merging root after root with a P(x) in the present analysis.

(432) barn-bok-klub

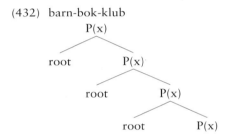

The following are some examples of this type in the languages in question.

(433) barnbogklub   Scandinavian[80]
(434) #child book club   English
       (children's book club)
(435) #kodomo hon kurabu   Japanese
       (kodomo no hon kurabu)
(436) voksenbogklub   Scandinavian
(437) adult book club   English
(438) #otona hon kurabu   Japanese
       (otona no hon kurabu)
(439) aften computer klass   Scandinavian
(440) evening computer class   English
(441) #yoru konpyutaa kurasu   Japanese
       (yoru no konpyutaa kurasu)
(442) restaurantkaffekop   Scandinavian

CHAPTER 4 PROPOSED STRUCTURES OF COMPOUND WORDS   167

(443) restaurant coffee cup   English
(444) resutoran koohii kappu   Japanese
(445) studentfilmkomité   Scandinavian
(446) student film committee   English
(447) gakusei eiga kurabu   Japanese

The examples marked with the symbol # do not exist, but they are grammatical. Native speakers of the languages seem to prefer the corresponding phrases of the examples[81].

The above examples are iterated compounds in Parker's words. It is also possible to derive left-branching or recursive compounds. The difference in the branching corresponds to a meaning difference (Section 3.2.2). For example, the example *restaurant coffee cup* means 'a coffee cup for restaurants'. In contrast, the recursive compound *gourmet coffee cup* is a cup of the kind associated with gourmet coffees. In the current analysis, the following structure is proposed for left-branching recursive compounds.

(448)
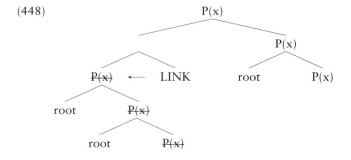

The above structure is constructed in the following way: First a root without word class features is merged with a P(x). Then, another root is merged to form a compound word. The P(x) feature needs to be checked somehow. So a linking element is merged and checks the P(x). The resulting structure is possible to merge with another [root + P(x)], which is constructed in parallel. As the P(x) on the 'rightmost element' is the only feature unsaturated, it percolates and as a result, it is the head of the whole compound. The existence of the linking element between the constituents can be always seen in left-branching compounds in Swedish, and less consistently, in Danish and Norwegian (see Josefsson 1997). Typical examples are as follows.

(449) fot-boll-s-domare   Swedish
       foot-ball-LINK-referee
       'football referee'   Swedish

(450) bo-stad-s-kvarter
live-place-LINK-area
'residential area'

(451) land-mand-s-forening   Danish
country-man-LINK-association
'farmers' association'

The linking morpheme is realized phonetically in Scandinavian left-branching compounds, whereas in English and Japanese left-branching compounds, it is generally not. The examples are as follows.

(452) [[gourmet coffee] cup]
(453) [[gekijoo ticket] uriba]
                                    Japanese
(454) [[theatre ticket]   shop]
       'a shop for theatre tickets'
(455) [[coffee maker] maker]
(456) [[coffee maker] seigyoosya]   Japanese
       coffee maker maker
(457) [[Labour Union] president]
(458) [[roodoo kumiai] choo]   Japanese
(459) labour union   president

For some reason, right-branching compounding is more restricted than left-branching compounding. It is hard to construct right-branching compounds with more than three roots. This is also the case in Scandinavian (Josefsson 1997), although ambiguity is not a problem due to the presence of an overt linking element. The explanation may be constraints on processing. A compound with too much recursivity without constituents (right-branching compounds) may cause processing problems. In left-branching compounds, the speaker forms a constituent out of adjacent roots earlier than in right-branching compounds, where a constituent cannot be formed until the last root is pronounced (Hawkins 1990)[82].

Let us see structures for four-member compounds in the languages in question.

(460) [[[Water Resources] Research] Centre]

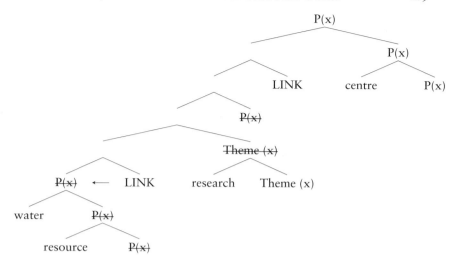

The above structure is constructed in the following way: First a root *resource* is merged with a P(x) feature. Since the P(x) feature is the unsaturated feature it percolates. Then, another root *water* is merged. The P(x) is the only unsaturated feature before and/or after the root *water* is merged, so it is the head of the compound *water resource*. Then, a linking element is merged with the compound *water resource*. The P(x) feature of the compound is checked, so that the compound can be merged with another element. In parallel, another root *research* is merged with a Theme (x) feature. The Theme (x) feature is an unvalued feature. It is assigned its value by the compound *water resource* and the compound is thereby interpreted as having the theme role assigned by *research*. Here, there is an agreement relation between the compound *water resource* and the Theme. Since there is no categorical feature on the resulting 'compound' *water-resource-resesarch*, a P(x) feature is merged. Then, a linking element is merged and checks the P(x) feature. As a result, it is possible to merge another structure, *centre* merged with a P(x) feature. Since the P(x) merged with *centre* is the only unsaturated feature of the whole compound, it percolates and needs a referential index from a D or DP. This P(x) is the head of the whole compound.

(461) [[anzen hoshoo] [[rizi]kai]]   Japanese
 safety-security-board directors
 'Security Council'

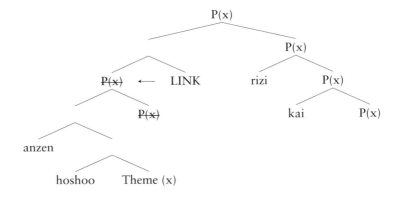

Similarly, the above structure is constructed in the following way: a root *hoshoo* is merged with a Theme (x) feature. The Theme (x) feature is an unvalued feature. It is assigned its value by the root *anzen* after the root is merged, and *anzen* is thereby interpreted as having the theme role assigned by *hoshoo*. Here, there is an agreement relation between the root *anzen* and the Theme. Since there is no categorical feature on the resulting 'compound' *anzen+hoshoo*, a P(x) feature is merged. Then, a linking morpheme is merged to check the P(x) feature on the 'compound'. It is now possible to merge another merged structure [*rizi-kai-P(x)*], which has been constructed in parallel. Since the P(x) on the 'rightmost' element of the whole compound is the only unsaturated feature, it percolates, and thereby it is the head of the whole compound.

(462)   fot +boll+s+plan+s+gräss
        foot+ball+LINK+pitch+LINK+grass
        'grass of a football pitch'

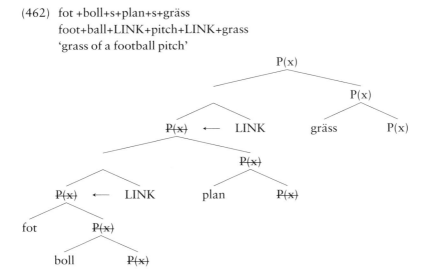

Similarly, in the above structure, a root *boll* is merged with a P(x) feature first. Since the P(x) feature is the unsaturated feature it percolates. Then, another root *fot* is merged to make a compound. The P(x) feature is the only unsaturated feature before and/or after the root *fot* is merged, so it is the head of the compound *fotboll*. Just like in (448), a linking morpheme is merged with the compound *fotboll*. The P(x) feature of the compund is checked, so that the compound can be merged with another element. In parallel, a root *plan* is merged with a P(x) feature. This *[plan+P(x)]* is merged with the *[fot+boll+P(x)+LINK]*. The P(x) feature merged with the root *plan* is unsaturated before and/or after it is merged with the *[fot+boll+P(x)+LINK]*, so it percolates. Later, another linking morpheme is merged with the *[plan +P(x)]* to check the P(x) feature. In parallel, another root *gräss* is merged with a P(x) feature. The *[grass + P(x)]* is merged with the *[plan +P(x)]*. The P(x) feature merged with the root *gräss* is unsaturated before and/or after it is merged with the other elements, so it percolates and thus, it is the head of the whole compound.

The structures seem to be applicable for all types of compounds in the languages.

4.4 Recursion in other languages for Noun-Noun compound words

It is assumed in this thesis that the existence of a linking element in between the constituents in compounds enables the language to have recursiveness. In Scandinavian languages, the linking element is generally overt in recursive compounds. This is true only in left-branching, not right-branching, compounds. Let us consider other languages, too, to see if this claim can be right.

In Dutch, there is sometimes a linking element between the two constituents in 'N-N' compounds and recursivity of compounding can be seen (Booij 2002). According to Booij (2002), an extended form of noun with an additional schwa or *–s* exists in compounds. Typical example is *schaap-s-kop* (sheep-S-head) 'sheep's head'. Like the linking morphemes in Scandinavian languages, the schwa and the /s/ in Dutch do not contribute to the meaning of the compounds. Another similar characteristic of the linking elements in Dutch to those in Scandinavian languages is that they both are historically a genitive suffix.

In contrast to Scandinavian languages, plural nouns in *–en* can occur in the non-head of compounds in Dutch. There is a semantic opposition with similar compounds with *–s*. See the following contrasts.

(463) a. bedrijf-s-terrein 'company's area'
      b. bedrijv-en-terrein 'companies'
(464) a. school-gemeenschap 'school community'
      b. schol-en-gemeenschap 'schools' community, comprehensive school'
(465) a. stad-s-raad 'city council'
      b. sted-en-raad 'cities' council'

The semantic contrast between the above examples shows that what I have claimed about English compounds with a plural morpheme is not seen in the Dutch examples above. I will not discuss the case of the Dutch examples here. Evidently, there needs to be more research on this case to see how they can be accommodated in the present theory.

In Dutch, there is sometimes a linking element between the two constituents in 'N-N' compounds and recursivity of compounding can be seen (Booij 2002). According to Booij (2009), there are recursive compounds with a linking morpheme inbetween. Let us see one example from Booij 2009.

(466)   weer -s- voorspelling -s- deskundigen - congress
        weather LE forecast LE experts conference   (Booij 2009: 205)

Similarly, in German, a linking morpheme occurs in 'N-N' compound words. Like in Dutch, the inflectional class of the 'left-hand' constituent decides whether a linking morpheme occurs and what kind (see more details in Montgomery 2001). For example, -er- only ever occurs in classes where it is licensed in the nominative plural. Let us see some typical examples of compounds with linking elements in German.

(467) Kind+er+wagen
      child+PL+cart
      'buggy'   (Wiese 1996b: 143)
(468) Schwein+e+braten[83]
      pig   +PL+roast
      'roast pork'   (Collins German Dictionary 2004: 708)
(469) Frau + en+held
      woman+PL+hero
      'womanizer'   (Collins German Dictionary 2004: 968)
(470) Tag+es+zeit
      day+PL+time
      'daytime'   (Wiese 1996b: 143)

The 'Plural' morpheme in the above examples is analysed as a linking element.

Booij claims that "only N+N compounding (and under certain conditions [....] V+N compounding as well) is recursive, both in the head position and the non-head position [....]". The following examples show this is true.

(471) a. [[[[ziekte]N[verzuim]N]N[bestrijdings]N]N[programma]N]N
illness absence fight programme
'*programme for reducing absence due to illness*'
b. [[zomer]N[[broed]V[gebied]N]N]N
summer breed area
'*breeding area for the summer*'
c. [[[grond]N[vater]N]N[[over]P[last]N]N]N
ground water over burden
'*groundwater problems*' (Booij 2009: 205)

They represent, respectively, cases of constituent addition on the right (a), constituent addition on the left (b) and (c) what Booij calls recursiveness on both constituents.

In addition to recursive compounds and 'N-N' with a linking element, there is another type of compounds in Dutch. In contrast to Scandinavian languages, plural nouns in –*en* can occur in the non-head of compounds in Dutch. There is a semantic opposition with similar compounds with –*s*. See the following contrasts.

In Romance languages, there are no linking morphemes inside compound words. This in turn is due to the fact that the genitive in general is prepositional. In addition, recursive compounds are not so widespread as in Germanic languages or Japanese (Bisetto 2010). Let us see first what kinds of compound words exist in these languages. When compounding exists in these languages, it appears to be a syntactic phrase rather than true compounding. In French, for example, there are two main types of construction. One is formed from syntactic phrases, such as *pomme de terre* (apple from tree) 'potato', *les hors d' œuvre* (outside of work) 'hors d'oeuvre', and *la mise-au-point* (put-towards-point) 'putting in point'. For this type of compound, there is a prepositional element, such as *au, de*, in between the constituents. The following is the structure for this type of compounds.

(472)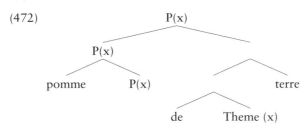

I argue that the prepositional element is like a verbal element (Section 4.3.4) in that it is merged with a Theme feature. The Theme feature is an unvalued feature and assigned its value by the root *terre* when this root is merged. The effect of this is that *terre* is interpreted as having the role Theme. There is an agreement relation between the root *terre* and the Theme. Since there is no categorical feature on the resulting 'compound' *de-terre*, another root *pomme* is merged with a P (x) categorical feature. This feature is unsaturated, so the head of the compound *pomme de terre* is the P(x). As a result, these features need a referential index from a D or DP.

The second type of compounding in Romance languages consists of a verbal element followed by its object: 'V-N' compounds. Typical examples are *le porte-parole* (carries-word) 'spokesman', *le pince-nez* (pinches-nose) in French and *el saca-corchos* (the pull-corks) 'corkscrew' in Spanish (Spencer 1991: 312, Clements 1987, Contreras 1985). This type of compound does not have a head in the traditional sense, so it is called exocentric. How can we analyse this type of compound? Is it really headless? Let us examine the verbal constituent. This constituent looks like a verbal stem in the form of third-person indicative singular (Clements 1987, Contreras 1985). However, the verbal element is not a 'verb' (with an Event category feature) but a deverbal nominalization of some kind. This argument is supported by the following points. Firstly, if it were a verb, it should inflect like a verb in the singular and plural. However, the following shows that this is not the case.

(473) a. el   saca   corchos
         the-SG   pull-INDIC-3SG   corks
         'corkscrew'
     b. los
         corchos   saca   corchos/*sacan
         the-PL   pull-INDIC-3SG corks   pull-INDIC-3PL corks

Secondly, if the 'verbal' element were a verb, it would have subject, since a normal third person singular has a subject, which may be phonetically null (except in French). But in the compound, there is no antecedent. The category of the whole compound is the P(x), unsaturated and waiting to be checked. In the proposed theory, it is possible to assume that when the root is numerated from the lexicon, it does not have any word class features of Event. When it is merged with the nominal element, the Event feature is not there. However, the issue of head has not been solved yet.

Following Zuffi (1981) and Bisetto (1994)(both cited in Guevara & Scalise 2004), Guevara & Scalise (2004) claim that this type of compounds is analysed as a special kind of endocentric compounding: the construction is headed by the 'left-hand' constituent, interpreted as a 'verbal element' plus a non-realised nominalizing suffix. The underlying form of this type of compound, such as *portalettere* (Italian) is actually something like *porta(tore di) letter* 'lit. carry(er of) letters'. The suffix *–tore* is equivalent of *–er* suffix in English and only selects 'verbal elements' with an agentive subject, but not raising verbs or verbs with a non-agentive subject. Some arguments supporting this analysis are given by Guevara & Scalise (2004). Firstly, *-tore* nouns often have an ambigious semantic reading between instrumental and agentive and that is also found in 'V-N' compounds (e.g. *miscelatore* 'mixer', *collaboratore* 'collaborator', *contagiri* 'lit. count-turns, tachometer', *portalettere*). Finally, the issue of head can be solved. Following Guevara & Scalise (2004), I propose the following structure for this type of compound in Romance languages.

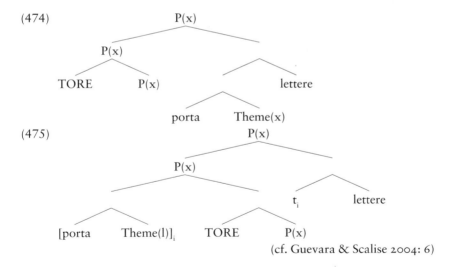

(cf. Guevara & Scalise 2004: 6)

The structure above shows that the element *porta* is merged with a Theme feature and the feature is assigned its value by the root *lettere* when the root is merged, indicated by the letter *l*[84]. Since *–tore* selects a 'verbal element' which it attaches to, it attracts *porta* which is moved and merged with the *–tore*. As argued above, the verbal element is not merged with an Event categorical feature. However, it is merged with the features [indicative, 3 person singular] (the vowel –*a*). The *–tore* is similar to the English equivalent *–er*, so I propose that the *–tore* has a P(x) feature which needs a referential index from a D or DP. Thus, the head of the whole compound is the P(x) feature. Thus, the proposed theory is also applicable for compounds in Romance languages.

Although, Romance languages do not have 'recursive' compounds like Germanic languages or Japanese do (Bisetto 2010), some of 'V-N' compounds can be recursive. A 'verb' can be adjoined on the 'left-hand' side.

(476)   porta-stuzzicadenti lit. carry-pick-teeth = toothpick-holder
(477)   porta-asciugamani lit. carry-dry-hands = towel-holder
(478)   proteggi-reggiseno lit. protect-bra = bra-protector

In these examples, the base compounds (*stuzzicadenti*, *asciugamani*, *reggiseno*) work as the internal direct object of the added verb, just like the nouns (*denti*, *mani* and *seno*) in the base 'V-N's do. Evidently, this construction needs more research (cf. Bisetto 2010).

Latin compounding is not so productive as English, Greek or Sanskrit (Fruyt 2002). Usually, when the other languages have compounding, Latin has affixation and agglutination and fewer sub-types of compounding. For example, Latin determinative compounds (normal type) and bahuvrīhi or exocentric compounds, (such as *pickpocket, loudmouth*, which refer to persons) are limited. When compounding exists in the language, the words are either influenced by Greek or in fields like science or created words by poets. Just like in Romance languages, compounding in Latin is not recursive. There are no genitive compounds either in this language.

Greek compound words also have a linking element (Johannessen (2001)). It is similar to linking elements in Scandinavian languages. The 'left-hand' constituent appears in different form in compounding than from when it appears on its own. Thus, the head of the compound is the P(x) which is unsaturated and features on the non-head are checked by the linking morpheme. According to Agathopoulou (personal communication)[85], Greek compounding can be recursive. Examples are as follows.

(479)   a.   aghrot-o-dharni-o-dhótisi
             farmer loan giving
             'money-lending to farmers'
        b.   pedh-o-odhont-íatros
             child   tooth doctor
             'a children's dentist'

c. asvest-o-polto-píisi
      lime   pulp making
      'lime-pulp-making'

The above examples, however, are not recursive compounds or left-branching compounds as such found in Modern Scandinavian languages, English or Japanese, but iteration or right-branching compounds (cf. Ralli, 2009: 457). This is contradictory to what I have just proposed: right-branching or iteration compounds are not recursive because there is no linking element between them. Is the linking element in Greek compounds not the same as those ones we see in Scandinavian languages, English or Japanese? Evidently, further research needs to be done for this language.

What is interesting and different from compounding in Scandinavian languages is that there is a linking element after each constituent, whilst in Scandinavian languages, there is a linking morpheme after embedded compounds[86], not each constituent.

According to Agathopoulou (personal communication)[87], for Greek native speakers, multi-stemmed compounds like the above (479) in which the two initial constituents are in a hierarchical relation are relatively rare in the language. The example (a) has been made up by Di Sciullo & Ralli (1994), cited in Agathopoulou personal communication). They maintain that it is acceptable by native speakers, and the examples in (b) and (c) are among the very few of this kind in the data given by Agathopoulou. More frequent are similar compounds in which the relation between the two initial constituents is coordinate, like the ones shown next.

(480) a. ot-o-rin-o-laring-o-lóghos
         ear nose throat expert
         'ear, nose, and throat specialist'
      b. kafe-zith-estiatório
         coffee ale restaurant
         'a coffee- and ale-shop'
      c. skulik-o-mirmingh-ó-tripa
         worm   ant   hole
         'a worm- and ant-hole'

Whatever the characteristics of the linking element in compounding in this language, these data support the hypothesis that when there is a linking morpheme, the language has iterated compounding.

Finnish (Karlsson 1987) has compound words similar to that of Germanic languages and Japanese. The most common type of compound word is made up of two non-derived nouns; e.g. *kirja+kauppa* (book+store) 'bookshop', *vesi+pullo* (water+bottle) 'water+bottle', *pallo+peli* (ball game) 'ball game' and many others. However, it is not just juxtaposition of two nominal elements. The 'left-hand' constituent of these compounds is often in genitive case (Spencer 2003). Also, fairly common are compounds with more than two elements, such as *maa+talous+tuotanto* (land+cultivation+production) 'agricultural production', *elo+kuva+teollisuus* (live+picture+industry) 'film industry', *huone+kalu+tehdas* (room+thing+factory) 'furniture factory', *koti+tarve+myynti* (home+need+scale) 'household sale' and so on. This language seems to be a case where compounding is productive and recursive.

In Hungarian, there is a construction of 'bare noun + verb' sequences which behave very much like compounds (Kiefer 1990): they constitute of a single phonological unit and can easily get lexicalised, and the bare noun is non-referential and non-modifiable. At the same time, they are not syntactic islands in that they can be affected by certain syntactic rules, such as focusing and negation. Moreover, auxiliaries may split up the sequences. Typical examples are as follows.

(481) a. Jancsi házat épít.
Johnny house-acc build
'Johnny is engaged in house-building'.
b. Pisti levelet ír.
Steve letter-acc write
'Steve is engaged in letter-writing'. (Kiefer 1990: 151)

As these examples demonstrate, the bare noun in this sequence is always case-marked and theta-marked just like the corresponding constructions in Japanese and English. Also, Hungarian compounding is recursive[88], just like in English, Japanese and Scandinavian languages. There seems to be a correlation between the linking element and the recursiveness of compounding within a language.

One might say that there is a contradiction against my proposal in Turkish. It has in principle unrestricted right-branching compounds but left-branching compounds is constrained by the ban against multiple adjacent occurences of the linking element. However, this is due to the fact that the linking element is final (e.g. roman+karhraman+i 'onvel+hero-LE ' character of a novel. So this is not really a contradiction, but we can say that a linking element actually plays a role for recursivity (Bisetto 2010).

Word formation in Slavic languages is similar to that of Romance languages in that word formation is from derivation rather than compounding (Clark 1993[89]). This is also true in children's spontaneous speech. Children seem to prefer coining new nouns through derivation rather than compounding (Clark

1993). However, there is some compounding in these languages. For example, in Polish, when compounding takes place, a linking element, similar to that in Greek and Scandinavian languages, does appear between the two constituents of compound words. If compounding in these languages is not productive, it is not recursive either.

In Latvian (Spencer, personal communication), 'N-N' compounds are formed from uninflected stem forms. For example, *gramata* 'book', *grāmat veikals* 'bookshop'. The form *grāmat-* is a stem (or a root) which cannot surface as such in the syntax. However, in addition to this construction Latvian has a wide range of NN compounds whose first member is in the genitive (either singular/plural) case. The examples are *grāmat-a veikals* 'bookshop' (literally. of-book shop), *latvieš-u valoda* 'Latvian language' (lit. of-the Latvians language) and *ziemasvētki* 'Christmas' (lit. of-winter festival) (Mathiassen 1997: 55-56, cited in Spencer 2003: 12). These are in the same form as normal genitive construction but thought of as compounds and have left-stress. The basic types are uninflected root + word and N-gen.pl + word and the examples are given below.

(482) gra'mat-a
      'book'
(483) veikal-s
      'shop'
(484) gra'matveikals
      gra'mat-u veikals
      book-gen.pl shop
      'bookshop'   (Spencer (personal communication))

Semantically these compounds do not really mean things like 'the shop of (the) books'. The genitive is used purely in a modifying function. They represent a species of compound in which the 'left-hand' member is inflected. In this respect they are like the internally inflected compound nouns of Finnish. Thus, compounding formation in Latvian is slightly similar to that of Swedish, English and Japanese genitive compounds. The genitive case marker checks the categorical feature on the 'left-hand' element of the compound.

Similarly, but a little bit differently from Latvian, Lithuanian has Greek-style compounds with a meaningless linking element like the one in Greek compounds. It is not homophonous with an inflected form of the compounded word, unlike in Germanic compounds. Lithuanian also has compounds consisting of N-gen.pl + N (see briefly Mathiassen 96 p. 1179-180, 181 points (a), (f)). Thus, to translate 'Lithuanian', 'Latvian' in the sense of 'the Lithuanian/Latvian language' into these languages.

(485) Lithuanian: Lietuv-is 'Lithuanian (man)-nom.sg.'
                    Lietuv-iu   kalba
                    Lithuanian.man-gen.pl language
(486) Latvian: Latviet-is 'Latvian (man)-nom.sg'
                    Latvies'-u   valoda
                    Latvian.man-gen.pl language

According to Spencer (personal communication) compounding in both Latvian and Lithuanian is very productive, much as in Germanic (in this respect Baltic languages are completely different from Slavic languages, but very similar to the Finnish and Germanic languages that surround them)[90]. Similarly to compounding in Germanic, therefore, the linking morpheme is there to check features on the non-head of the compound.

Let us observe compounds in non-Indo-European languages. Chinese according to Duanmu (1997) has two different kinds of nominal structures; [NN] and [N de N] where *de* is a particle. There is good evidence that NN and N de N are syntactically different. Especially, [NN] is not a phrase but a compound (Duanmu 1997) (*gao shan* tall mountain 'tall mountain') vs. *gao de shan* tall DE mountain 'tall mountain'). He uses productivity, conjunction reduction and adverbial modification to distinguish these two constructions[91]. Possibly, Chinese is a language where productive and recursive compounds (e.g., *mei5mei6 gaa3fel buil*[92] (gourmet coffee cup), *huk6sang1 din6jing2 wui2* (student film club), are the norm (Packard 2000), but there is no genitive compound. More examples of recursive compounds are listed below.

(487)   fèiwù chǔ zhì jìhuà
        waste disposal plan
        'waste disposal plan'   (Tokizaki 2008: 9)
(488)   zhongguo gongchan dang
        China communist party
        'Communist Party of China'
(489)   zhongguo gongchan dang zhongyang zhengzhiju
        China communist party central authorities politbureau
        'central politbureau of the CPC[93]'

As the above examples show, there seem to be recursive compounds in Chinese and they are productive, too. However, as discussed above, Chinese does not seem to have genitive compounds and so the existence of a linking element does no have anything to do with its recursion in the language.

In Korean there seems to be genitive compound words. For example, there is a word such as *kwukkwun-uni nal* 'soldier's day' with the genitive case marker *uni* inside functioning, I assume, as a linking element. In this type of compound word, in this language, the feature on the non-head is checked by the linking element. Korean 'N-N' compounding is very productive. I have not been able to find whether compounding in Korean is recursive or not. However, in the serial verb constructions, where two verbal roots are combined, a linking element appears after the left-hand verbal root. Serial verbs are lexicalised (*contra* Chung 1993), not syntactic verbs, in that the two verbal roots have the same subject, they denote one single event, not a sequence of events. Between the two constituents, the linking element exists without any meaning. In the Principle and Parameters approach, the linking element is argued to be inserted for the lack of fullness in the verbal root (Kang 1988, cited in Chung 1993). So presumably within the Minimalist Program, the linking element is merged in the narrow syntax, just like the linking element in Scandinavian languages.

In contrast, according to Chung (1993), lexical 'compound verbs' also exist in Korean and there is no linking element between the two verbal elements. Another difference from the serial verb construction is that the meaning of the whole compound word is usually figurative (Chung1993: 45). For example, compare the following two sentences.

(490) a. lexical compound verb
Mary-ka ku kay-lul cal tol-po-ess-ta.
Mary-N the dog-A well turn-around-see-Pst-Dec
'Mary looked after the dog well'.
b. serial verb
Mary-ka ku kay-lul tol-e po-ess-ta.
Mary-N the dog-A turn around-E see-Past-Dec
'Mary turned around and saw the dog'.   (Chung 1993: 45)

In (487a) and (487b), the lexical 'compound verb' and the 'serial verb' constructions contain the same component verbal roots, *tol-* 'turn around' and *po-* 'see'. The lexical 'compound verb' construction in (487a) has a figurative meaning, 'look after', but the 'serial verb' construction in (487b) retains the meanings of its component verbal roots, 'turn around/see'. The meanings of the lexical 'compound verbs' are often not predictable from the component verbal roots, although there are cases where meaning can be predicted. Within the proposed theory, 'serial verb' construction and lexical 'compound verb' are both assumed to be derived in the narrow syntax , the difference being that the LF-lexicon has the meaning of the compound verb stored[94].

In the Akan language, spoken in Ghana, compounding is recursive and there are genitive compounds, just like in the Germanic languages[95]. It is possible to have a recursive compound, such as *[[[nyamesEm] ka]* '[[[God] story] say]' or *[[[asEm] pa] ka]* '[[[story] God] say] both meaning 'evangelism'. There are examples, such as *awofoda* (*awofoO* 'mothers' + *Eda* 'day') meaning 'mother's day'. However, since this language does not have overt case markers, the case marking does not show in genitive compounds. Again, compounding in this language shows that my claim is on the right track.

Hebrew relies mainly on derivation for word formation. According to Clark (1993), the main word-formation device is the association of consonantal roots with patterns of vowel infixes, plus prefixes or suffixes. For example, the root *g-d-l* 'grow' has given rise to established nouns like *gidul* 'growth, tumor,' *gódel* 'size', *gdila* 'growing, growth', *gdula* 'greatness', *migdal* 'tower', and *hagdala* 'enlargement' (Berman 1978, both cited in Clark 1993: 172). Compound word formation does exist. However, many types of head nouns need some modification since they must appear in bound form in compounds. For instance, the free form *mexona* 'machine', when in a compound, occurs in the form *mxonat*, as in *mxonat-htiv*' 'a type writer. The full-form *bayt* 'house' appears *bet-* in compounds like *bet-sēfer* 'school'. Compounding is more common in written Hebrew than in spoken Hebrew.

In contrast to Clark's claim, Pereltsvaig (1998) argues that compounding in Modern Hebrew is productive unlike in other Semitic languages. Pereltsvaig gives a list of compound types in Hebrew and the list tells us how productive each types is. It seems like 'N-N', 'N-A', 'A-N', and 'A-A' are all common and the other types, such as 'N-V', 'N-P', 'V-N', 'V-A', 'V-V', 'V-P', 'P-N', 'P-A', 'P-V', and 'P-P' types are either rare or non-existent. According to Pereltsvaig, the impossibility of 'V-V' is not due to the Argument Linking Principle proposed by Lieber (1992) but the non-concatenative nature of verbal morphology. In order to form a well-formed verb in Hebrew some non-concatenative morphology must apply. In contrast, nominal compounds are possible in Hebrew. However, as argued by Clark and Pereltsvaig, there is some derivational nominal morphology which is non-concatenative.

According to Pereltsvaig (1998) and Borer (1988), there are compound words and construct state nominals in Hebrew or Semitic languages. Compound words contranst with construct state nominals which are considered non-compound strings. Let us compare the two constructions. The (a) examples are of compounds, whereas the (b) examples are of corresponding construct state nominals.

(491) a. beyt sefer
house book
'a school'
b. beyt more
house teacher

CHAPTER 4 PROPOSED STRUCTURES OF COMPOUND WORDS 183

    'a teacher's house'
(492) a. yom tov
    day good
    'a holiday'
  b. yom yafe
    day beautiful
    'a nice day'
(493) a. yafe to'ar
    beautiful image
    'handsome'
  b. yafe ʔeynaim
    'with beautiful eyes'   (Pereltsvaig 1998: 4)

The constructions share many properties. Firstly, they both form one prosodic word. In other words, the head of both constructions does not bear main stress, but the non-head does.

Secondly, other properties shared by the constructions follow from the fact that compounds and construct state nominals form one prosodic word.

(491) a. *beyt xadaš sefer
    house new book
    'a new school'
  b. *beyt xadaš more
    house new teacher
    'a teacher's new house'   (Pereltsvaig 1998: 6)

The above examples show that no other material can intervene between the head and the non-head in the constructions.

Another similarity is that the non-head is obligatory, with the weak form of the head standing alone being ungrammatical: *beyt 'house' (construct form). Also, in both constructions it is not possible for the head to bear the definite article.

(492) a. (*ha-) beyt sefer
    the house book
    'the school'
  b. (*ha-) beyt more
    the house teacher
    'the teacher's house' or 'the house of a teacher' (Pereltsvaig 1998: 6)

Moreover, the definiteness marked on the non-head member of both compound words and construct state nominals spreads to the head member. In other words, the whole compound word and construct state nominal is understood as definite.

(493) a. Ra' iti'et beyt ha-sefer.   b. Ra'iti (* 'et) beyt sefer.
         saw-I acc house the-book   saw-I   acc house book
         'I saw the school'.   'I saw a school'.
     c. Ra'iti 'et beyt ha-more.   d. Ra'iti (* 'et) beyt more.
         saw-I acc house the-teacher   saw-I acc   house teacher
         'I saw the teacher's house'.   'I saw a teacher's house'.

(Pereltsvaig 1998: 6)

Let us see how to distinguish the two constructions. As one can see from the (a) examples of compound words and the (b) examples of construct state nominals, the difference between them is semantic compositionality. Whilst construct state nominals are semantically compositional, compound words are not. In addition, construct state nominals are recursive and productive due to the compositionality.

Another interesting difference between the two constructions is that when the definiteness is marked on the non-head and spreads to the head, the non-head marked with a definiteness marker in compounds but not in construct state nominals may have a non-specific interpretation. In other words, the compound *beyt ha-sefer* 'the school' does not refer to a particular book. On the other hand, the construct state nominal *manhigey ha-kita* (leaders the-class) means 'the leader of the class', but not 'the leaders of a class'.

Another interesting property of construct state nonimals is that they have an exclusively left-branching structure. In other words, the head must be bare, and cannot be modified by a determiner (493a) or by an adjective (493b). Any attempt to modify the head directly must use the *shel* strategy of possession in (494). Alternatively, the head can be modified indirectly.

(494) a. *ha- cə if ha-yalda
          the-scarf the-girl
      b. *cə if (ha-) yafe ha-yalda
          scarf the pretty the-girl   (Borer 1988:48)
(495) a. ha-ca if ha-yafe (shel ha-yalda)
          the-scarf the-pretty of the-girl
          'the girl's pretty scarf'
      b. cə if ha-yalda
          scarf the-girl
          'the scarf of the girl'

c. '*a scarf of the girl'
   '*the scarf of a girl'
   d. cə if ha-yeled ha-yafe
      scarf the-boy the-pretty
      'the boy's pretty scarf'
      'the pretty boy's scarf'   (Borer 1988:47)

Since construct state nominals sometimes behave like a word and sometimes behave like a phrase, Borer (1988) states that the construct state nominal becomes a word at a stage no later than S-Structure in the syntax. Within the Minimalist Program, since there is no S-Structure, it is possible to claim construct state nominals may be pronounced as words but have a syntax similar to phrases. This is why they can be recursive.

(496) a. madaf sifrey ha-yalda
         shelf books the-girl
         'the shelf of the books of the girl'
      b. madaf sifrey ha-yalda ha-xadash
         shelf books the-girl the-new
         'the new shelf of the books of the girl'
      c. madaf sifrey ha-yalda ha-yafim
         shelf books the-girl the nice-pl
         'the shelf of the nice books of the girl'
      d. madaf sifrey ha-yalda ha-ktana
         shelf books the-girl the-little
         'shelf of the books of the little girl'   (Borer 1988: 59)

The non-head of this construction is referential (Pereltsvaig 1998). Thus, the P(x) feature of the non-head noun is checked by a D within the construction. This means that it is not a compound.

Arabic is well known for not having compound words (personal communication with Peter Sells). In contrast to this claim, Emery (1988) concludes that there are a number of compound words in Arabic, just like in English. As for productivity of compounding, however, Emery has no comment. Many sources within the literature claim that compounding is a strictly morphological process distinct from the indigenous syntactic process of complex NP formation and is scarcely used in any form of Arabic (Holes 1990, cited in Pereltsvaig 1998: 22). There are some examples from Holes given below and according to Holes and Pereltsvaig, these examples are complex noun constructions, not compound words.

(497) aHmar il-loon
     red   the-colour
     'red coloured'

An expression like (497) is a complex phrasal noun construction, since the definite article is inside it. Pereltsvaig claims that the unproductivity of compounding in Arabic is due to its non-concatenative morphology. I conclude in this thesis that there is neither recursive compounding nor genitive compounds in Arabic.

Further support for the interaction of non-concatenativity and compounding is provided by an examination of Maltese. This is also another Semitic language with rich non-concatenative morphology (Pereltsvaig 1998: 24). There is a 'N-N' construction in this language. However, these constructions are generally transparent semantically, as well as syntactically (see Pereltsvaig 1998 for further details).

The Table 5 is a summary of the observation of the languages above. The second column shows whether the language has productive and recursive compound words and the final column shows whether there is a linking element or not in the language.

Table 5: Productive and Recursive compounds

Languages	Productive/Recursive?	Linking element?
Japanese	Yes/Yes Especially 'noun-noun' compounds	Genitive compounds
English	Yes/Yes, especially 'noun-noun' compounds	Genitive compounds
Scandinavian languages	Yes/Yes, especially 'noun-noun' compounds	Genitive compounds
Dutch	Yes/Yes	A linking element between 'noun-noun' compounds
German	Yes/Yes	A linking element between 'noun-noun' compounds.
Greek	Yes/Yes.	A linking element after each constituent involved in iterated compounding.
Romance languages	Yes/Not recursive	Lexicalised 'noun-noun', 'V-N' and 'noun + preposition + noun' compounds. No genitive compounds or linking element.
Latin	No/no	No
Finnish	Yes/yes	The non-head in partitive case

Hungarian	Yes/Yes	Case-marker in 'N-V' compounds, which is both lexical and syntactic.
Slavic	Not very productive/not recursive	Yes, in Polish with a linking element in compounds. Prefers derivation
Latvian	Yes/recursive?	A case-marker-like linking element
Lithuanian	Yes/recursive?	A linking element
Chinese	Yes/Yes	No genitive compounds/no linking element
Korean	Yes/Yes?	Genitive compounds/ dummy linking element in the 'serial verb' construction, none in compounding.
Akan	Yes/Yes	Genitive compounds
Hebrew	Yes in written language, but not recursive due to semantic opacity. Construct state nominals behave like a word phonologically and the head cannot be modified by a determiner or by an adjective. But the non-head is referential, so it behaves differently from 'normal' compound words.	Not so much in spoken because of disjunctive morphology. No linking element or no genitive.
Arabic	Not recursive	No genitive compounds.
Maltese	Not productive, because of disjunctive morphology.	

The table above shows that there are languages which allow and languages which do not allow recursive compounding. I have proposed above that there is a linking element which checks the features of the head of the 'first' compound in Scandinavian languages, English and Japanese. If my claim is true, left-branching recursive compounding or more generally, recursion of the non-head of the compound must be universally dependent on the existence of a linking element. The linking element is there for the sake of asymmetry. If the linking element does not check the categorical features of the non-head, the structure will be impossible, having two heads. Thus, in the languages without recursive compounding, there is no projection of a linking element. Even though the languages do have productive two-member compounding, it is not possible to produce more than two-member compound words.

(498)

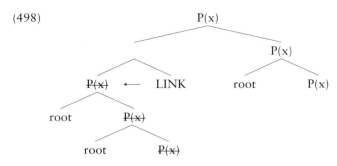

It seems that languages without productive compounding have more complex compound-like constructions without any linking element inside them. However, more work needs to be done within the proposed theory for other languages.

4.5 Phrasal compounds

Within this framework, phrasal compounds in the languages in question can also be analysed. In phrasal compounds, as discussed in 2.4, the non-head is a maximal projection. Lieber (1992) proposed that there is interaction between syntax and lexicon for this type of word formation. It is also significant to state that the phrasal constituent of the compounds is always the non-head, not the head (Namiki 2001) and so it is similar to left-branching compounds (see 4.3.5). Based on the Lexical Integrity tests in Section 2.4, I assume that the whole compound is different from a DP or NP.

Let us see the derivations of some phrasal compounds in the languages in question.

(499) 'an I-long-for-you-message'

CHAPTER 4 PROPOSED STRUCTURES OF COMPOUND WORDS   189

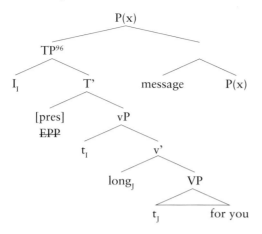

Whatever the projection of the non-head of the compound is (TP or CP), there are no more features to be checked, because it is a complete main clause (for an argument that it is a main clause see footnote 89 below). Thus, the derivation is completed and it is possible to merge another head. The root *message* is merged with a P(x) feature and this category can merge with the TP forming a compound. The P(x) feature needs a referential index from a D, so the head of the whole compound is P(x).

Another example with phrasal non-head is as follows.

(500) 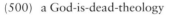 a God-is-dead-theology

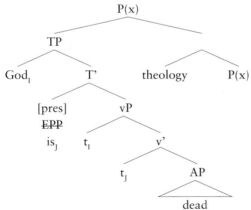

Again, the non-head is a complete clause with no features to be checked, so it can merge with a head forming a compound.

Let us see some examples in Scandinavian languages.

(501) ett jag-längtar-efter-dig-brev[97]   (Swedish)
    a I long for you letter

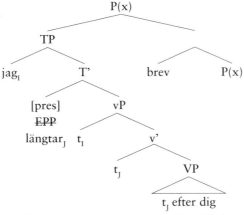

(502) ett skicka-mera-pengar-brev   (Swedish)
    a send more money letter

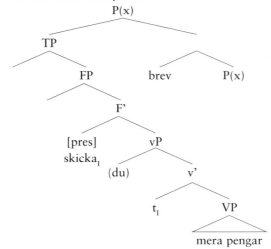

The non-head of the example above is imperative. In this example, I assume Platzack & Rosengren's (1998) theory of imperatives in the Mainland Scanedinavian. According to Platzack & Rosengren, there are several positions available for the imperative subject in these languages: *Spring (du) alltså (du) hem (du) meddetsamma (du)!* (Run (you) thus (you) home (you) immediately (you)). Thus, it means 'you run home immediately!'. Based on this phenomenon, they argue that the subject can either stay in the Spec VP or move to intermediate positions between TP and VP (e.g. FP) and this phenomenon can be explained by the strength of EPP. Whatever the position of the subject is, just like the sentential non-head, the derivation of the non-head imperative is completed before another root is merged. This root is merged with P(x), which percolates to the dominating node.

Japanese can have sentential non-heads in compound words, too, and the structure is similar to that of Germanic languages. Let us see the structure for some examples.

(503) (boku[98] ga) kimi-o-aisiteiru-message
  I   NOM you-ACC-love-message
  'I-love-you-message'

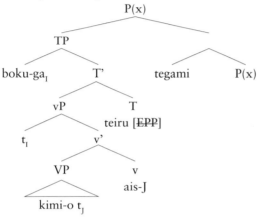

As in Germanic languages, there is no more features to be checked, because it is a complete main clause. Thus, the derivation is completed and another root can be merged. *Tegami* is merged with a P(x) and the P(x) needs a referential index from a D, so the the head of the whole compound is P(x).

(504) (anata-ga)- nandemo-tabe-rareru-restoran
  (you-NOM)-anything eat-can restaurant
  'you-can-eat-anything-restaurant'

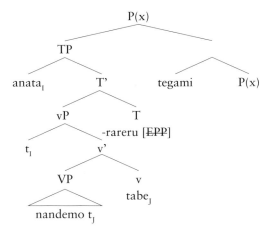

The non-head of this compound is also TP or CP and has no more features to be checked. It is therefore possible to merge another head.

I assume that a similar structure is applicable for the other examples of phrasal compounds cited in 2.4, since the non-head is a maximal projection, i.e. no more features need to be saturated. The proposed theory seems to work for a wide variety of compounds. Compound words are derived in the same way as phrases are, which is why the proposed theory is applicable for phrasal compounds.

What about examples such as below?

(505) strict-word-order-language

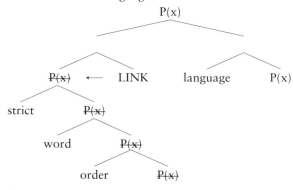

In the 'compound', *strict-word-order* (*very-strict-word-order-language*), as the P(x) is the head, it percolates. It needs to be checked by a linking morpheme, since there is no D or DP inside this compound (*[a-strict-word-order]-language*). Then, another root can be merged with a P(x) feature. The head of the whole compound is P(x) of the 'right-most' element.

(506) [maborosi no chosha] sagasi
phantom GEN author research
'search of a phantom author'

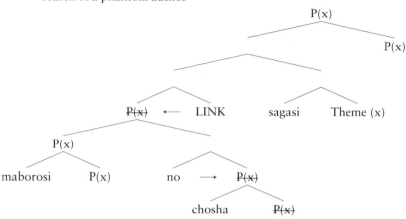

What makes this compound different from the other compunds represented above is that one cannot easily tell what the head is in the non-head *'maborosi-no-chosha* as the individual in question can be both a kind of an author and a phantom (metaphorically). I assume that the head of this construction is the P(x) merged with *maborosi*. The above structure is derived in the following way. Firstly, *chosha* is merged with a P(x) feature which is valued with *no*. The *no* is merged as a linker (den Dikken & Singhapreecha 2000) and checks the P(x) feature of *chosha*. Then, *maborosi* is merged with a P(x) which is the head of the construction *maborosi no chosha*. To check this P(x) feature, a linking element is merged. Since the derivation of the non-head is not complete (it is not possible to have an accusative case marker: *maborosi-no-chosha-o-sagasi*, a linking element is merged and checks the feature P(x). Then, another root, *sagasi*, is merged with a Theme (x) feature. The unvalued Theme feature is valued with the non-head, and the P(x) is merged, as there is no categorical feature on the whole compound. It is the head of the compound.

The proposed theory seems to work for a wide variety of compounds. If the non-head is not complete (i.e. not a maximal projection in the sense of Collins (2002)), a linking element is merged and checks the remaining unvalued feature[99].

4.6 Copulative compounds and Dvandva compounds in these languages

The previous sections have looked at compound words with two constituents in a modifier-modified relationship. As discussed in 2.5, there are compounds in Japanese as well as in English and Scandinavian where the relationship between the two constituents is coordination.

Examples of (146)–(148) are repeated below. (509), (510), and (511) are examples of coordinative compounds; (512) and (513) are examples of appositional compounds[100].

(507) Japanese
    a. saru + kiji
       monkey+ pheasant
    b. jishin+ kaji
       earthquake+fire
    c. oya+ ko
       parent+child
    d. yama+ kawa
       mountain+river
    e. ame+kaze
       rain+wind
    f. ama+tsuchi
       heaven+earth
    g. kusa+ki
       grass+tree
    h. ta+ hata
       paddy-field+field

(508) English
    a. mother+daughter relationship
    b. the doctor+patient gap   (from Plag 2003: 146)
    c. the nature+nurture debate   (from Plag 2003: 146)
    d. a modifier+head structure   (from Plag 2003: 146)
    e. the mind+body problem   (from Plag 2003: 146)

(509) Scandinavian
    a. moder+datter forhold
       mother+daughter relationship

(510) English
    a. mother+daughter
    b. blue+black

CHAPTER 4 PROPOSED STRUCTURES OF COMPOUND WORDS   195

    c. poet+translator   (from Plag 2003: 146)
    d. singer+songwriter   (from Plag 2003: 146)
    e. scientist+explorer   (from Plag 2003: 146)
    f. hero+martyr   (from Plag 2003: 146)
    g. dunch (dinner and lunch combined together)[101]

(511) Scandinavian
    a. nord+vest
    b. North+west
    c. Østrig+Ungarn
        Austria+Hungary
    d. Svensk+russisk
        Swedish+Russian   (Mellenius 1997: 22)
    e. blå+gul
        blue+yellow   (Mellenius 1997: 22)
    f. bonden+advokaten
        farmer-the+lawyer-the
        'the farmer and lawyer'   (Mellenius 1997: 22)

I propose coordinative compounds are structured in the following way.

(512)

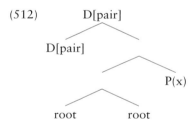

The above structure accounts for coordinative compounds. Two roots are merged and then this merges with P(x). This expresses the fact that the property which is assigned to the D or DP is neither that of being a parent or that of a child, if we take (511c)[102] as example, or a combination of being both a parent and a child assigned to one individual. Instead, it is a property assigned to a pair of individuals.

(513)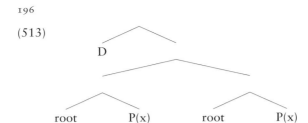

On the other hand, the structure (513) is for the appositional compounds. This structure shows that the case of *poet-translator* in (510c) is not the property of poet or that of translator, but a combination of the two properties assigned to one person. So the D has a referential feature which is assigned the property of parent and the property of child. The interpretation of the whole compound would be 'one person with two properties'[103].

4.7 Weak points in other theories and analyses solved in my theory

As the previous sections have shown, many of the problems found in the other theories and analyses can be solved in by the theory proposed in this thesis. Regarding the headedness of compound words, all of the other authors rely on some version of Williams' (1981) headedness. Williams argues the following: In morphology, we define the head of a morphologically complex word to be the right-hand member of that word (Williams 1981: 248). However, given that the place of Morphology is outside the Lexicon and after the Narrow Syntax, the Righthand Head Rule does not determine the head and has no place in the Narrow Syntax. It is still important to assume the asymmetry of the structure of compounds. Within the present theory, Collins' (2002) definition of head has been used. According to Collins, a head is a category which has one or more unsaturated features. Another stipulation taken from Collins (2202) is that when a lexical item is chosen from the lexical array and introduced to the derivation, the unsaturated features of this lexical item must be satisfied before any new unsaturated lexical items are chosen from the lexical array. The effect of these two assumptions is that when two categories α and β are merged, only one of them, say α, can have an unsaturated feature (which is not saturated by β), so α will be the head.

Also in the theory proposed in this thesis, the non-head of a compound is either a root without word class feature or any unsaturated feature, or it is merged with a linking morpheme, which checks its unvalued feature. The problems of headedness in transformationalist accounts in Lees (1960) and

Levi (1978) and the Minimalist account in Spencer (2003), Roeper, Snyder, & Hiramatsu (2002) and Josefsson (1997), therefore, are resolved.

Another problem, the unnecessary movement in Holmberg (1992) and Roeper, Snyder & Hiramatsu's theories is also resolved by the theory proposed in this thesis, since there is no unnecessary movement involved. The Extension Condition, which is violated in Roeper et al's theory by insertion of a new item in the empty 'Clitic' position, is not violated in the proposed analysis, since every new element is merged with the top node of the tree.

Another deficiency of Williams (1981), Selkirk (1982), and Spencer's (2003) theories is that these theories do not analyse the whole range of of compound words, such as lexicalised compounds, neoclassical compound words, genitive compounds, phrasal compounds and dvandva compounds. In the theory proposed in this thesis, all these kinds of compound words can be analysed in the same way. Lexicalised compounds and productive compounds have the same structures. The List of Morphemes together with the LF-lexicon, proposed by Platzack (1993), can account for the difference between the meanings of lexicalised and productive compounds. The conventionalised meaning is there in the LF-lexicon, whereas the meaning of the productive compound is composed of the meaning of the lexical entries.

Moreover, unlike in the previous theories, the theory proposed here seems to account for compounding in a variety of languages. There are languages which allow recursive nominal compounding and in these language, it has been hypothesised that there is a linking element which can be abstract, but which is sometimes spelled out as a genitive case affix, as is the case in Japanese, English and the Scandinavian languages. However, more work needs to be done in order to support the hypothesis that there is a relationship between the linking element and recursive compounding in a given language.

4.8 Problems in this theory

Even though the present theory works for many types of compounds in a range of different languages, there is a problem with this theory. As has been extensively argued, the non-head of compound words is a root without word class features. However, the non-head of a 'verb-verb' compound in Japanese needs to be merged with a Theme (x) feature before it is merged with another root, because the constituents involved in this type of compounds need to have compatible argument structures (Kageyama 1999, 2001, Matsumoto 1996 and many others). Thus, it is a problem for the present theory that the argument structure of the non-head matters. The non-head is supposed to be a root without theta-features, but in the cases of a 'verb-verb' compounds, it does not seem to be true.

For instance, the following examples illustrate that this claim is right.

(514) osi + taos+u
push+topple+Present
'push down'
a. John ga Bill o osi+taosi+ta.
   John NOM Bill ACC push+topple+Past
   'John pushed Bill down'.
b. *John ga Bill o osi+taore+ta.
   John NOM Bill ACC push+fall+Past
   *John pushed Bill and Bill fell.

The examples show that the argument structures of the left-hand and right-hand constituents need to be the same: *John* and *Bill* are arguments of the two constituents *osi* and *taosi* in the example (a), whereas *John* cannot be an argument of the right-hand constituent, *taore+* in the example (b). This shows that the argument structures of the left-hand as well as the right-hand constituent does matter. Consequently, the former is not a root without word class features. More research is required to determine how these compounds can be accommodated in the present theory.

Conversion being non-directional is discussed by Lieber (1980, 1981), whereas it being directional is discussed by Don (2005). If a root has no word class features the noun-verb pairs are both derived from an underlying root. However, in Dutch, verbs and nouns are derived from a common root. However, according to Don (2005), we may also assume that a noun is derived from a verb. Dutch has a gender distinction between neuter and non-neuter and Dutch verbs also fall into two main classes: regular verbs, using the same stem in all tenses; and the so-called "strong" or irregular verbs which have different stems in different tenses and in some cases deviant inflectional endings. As there are two types of nouns and two classes of verbs, we expect four types of conversion pairs to occur.

(515) a. regular verb- non-neuter noun
       b. regular verb- neuter noun
       c. irregular verb-non-neuter noun
       d. irregular verb – neuter noun   (Don 2005: 4)

However, no convincing examples of the fourth type can be given. If a root has no word class features, the gap in the Dutch pair cannot be explained. However, if a root has word class features, namely, it having syntactic feature of, say, noun, we could explain the gap in the Dutch pair. More research is required to answer this question, along with many other questions.

In many languages the productivity of compounding is partly determined by the existence of a linking element. Also, English has productive N-N compounding, but A-N compounding is rarer, while V-N compounding is absent. In addition, Japanese, Korean and Chinese allow V-V compound words. If the left-hand of a compound has no word class features, there are no syntactic restrictions of compounding. However, this is problematic. Category needs to be specified to capture the productivity of compounding in a given language. Or the root involved in V-V compounds is different from that in N-N compounds.

Notes

55 For the status of the two types of adjectives in Japanese, see Miyagawa (1987) and Ohkado (1991).
56 See also Section 2.4.1 for Lexical Phonology.
59 Other phonological differences between the two kinds of affixes within Lexical Phonology are vowel shortening and shift in the Stratum 1 affixes, but not in Stratum-2, and a syllabic base-final consonant in the Stratum-2 affixes but not in the Stratum-1 affixes. However, Giegerich argues that these two are not necessary conditions.
58 In this approach, then, there is no problem of dual membership, which is a problem in the affix-driven approach. For instance, the affix –able has dual membership and can be categorised as a Stratum 1-affix as well as a Stratum 2-affix, according to the phonological criteria (stress-shift/stress-neutral), as the bases can both be free (the examples in (b) below) as well as bound (the examples in (a) below).

a. affable	b. debatable
arable	dependable
capable	noticeable
formidable	perishable
probable	manageable

However, if one takes the Root-to-Word Conversion rule and the base-driven approach, it is possible to derive the above examples without considering the dual membership of the affix.

a. affable
   aff→-able
   Root to Word Conversion
   *[aff]$_r$ → [[aff]$_r$]$_L$
b. debatable
   debate→able
   [debate]$_V$ → [[debate]$_V$]

The inputs to all stratum-1 affixation are members of the category Root and those to all stratum-2 affixation are Word. In this approach, both Root and Word are recursive categories; e.g. it is possible to derive another word after the stratum-1 affixation in *sensation-sensational, sensationality* as well as after the stratum-2 affixation in *home-homeless, homelessness*.

59 NOM stands for *nominaliser*.
60 I would like to thank Jorgen Staun for his data in Danish.
61 The fact that tense cannot be found inside compounds is not clear-cut; it does not exist at least in the languages in question.
62 Giegerich assumes the Blocking Effect of Kiparsky (1982) in his theory.
63 Klavans (1982, 1985) argues that there are five parameters for clitics. One of the parameters is 'the domain of cliticization'. After observations of clitics in several languages, she claims that clitics seem to attach to entire phrases, not just to words. *–tati* is also a phrasal affix just like clitics.
64 Collins (2002) proposes to eliminate labels from the syntax, so he does not assume the idea of percolation. However, I am assuming a more traditional phrase structure theory with percolation.
65 So the idea that the determiner is the head of the noun phrase is natural at conceptual level as well as empirical level. In Japanese, too, according to Saito & Murasagi (1991) a D exists in Japanese, too. They take nominalisation as an example and argues that this is parallel with the English counterparts.
66 The translations into Danish and Japanese are my own.
67 Baker (2003) proposes a syntactic definition of the lexical categories, noun, verb and adjectives, after considering several languages. He argues that "nouns have criteria of identity, whereby they can serve as standards of sameness" (Baker 2003: 95). This is a semantic version of nouns. In short, he claims that only nouns, but not adjectives or verbs, occur in 'X is the same as Y'. Moreover, he claims that the syntactic version is that a noun X is a noun if and only if X is a lexical category and X bears a *referential index*, expressed as an ordered pair of integers. The question of whether Baker's theory is compatible with the present theory is left here for future research
68 Shimamura (1986) proposes a structure for genitive compounds. However, it is not applicable in the GB theory.
69 However, as discussed in 4.1.2, there is an exception for compound words with a regular plural marker: *parks commissioner*. In at least some native speakers' lexicon, both *park/parks commissioner* exist and there is semantic difference between them: singular and plural. For this compound, the structure is as follows.

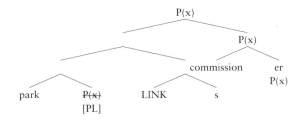

The category spelled out as *–s* is a complex morpheme, a LINK with a plural feature. If it does not have any unvalued feature, it will not percolate, so the tree [park, PL] can merge with the P(x)-headed tree [*commission, -er*].

70 Baker (2003) argues that one difference between adjective and the other lexical categories, nouns and verbs is that only adjectives are gradable and can have their grade specified by a functional head that projects its own phrase. Moreover, he claims that predicates which can

have degree heads, such as *too, such,* or *how* are not simple one-place predicates that hold of an entity; they are actually two-place relations that hold of an entity-degree pair. Thus, the sentence, *John is too hungry* is true if the person John is hungry to a degree x that exceeds the standard given in the context. This means that a degree head or comparable adverb saturates the extra position in the theta-grid of the lexical head by establishing a relationship of theta-role binding (Higginbotham 1985). Therefore, it is possible to predict the ungrammaticality of examples like, *Seven is as prime as two,* or *How three-legged is the stool?* These do not have a grade position in their theta-grid. Interestingly, the lexical item, *prime* cannot be a predicate. So it does not assign a theta-role feature. Although Baker's arguments about adjectives are valid, his arguments will not be used in this thesis, since there are adjectives which cannot be gradable, such as *closed, supreme, atomic, potential, three-legged, blue-eyed.* It is argued here that all these adjectives have the Property feature and they all have (x) feature which needs to be valued by agreeing with a valued P(x).

71 This type of adjective in Japanese is called an *–i* adjective and it has its own inflectional paradigm for tense. The suffix is a present tense feature. So if the past tense suffix, *-katta* is merged with the *kitana-*, its feature A(x) is percolated up. Since it is possible to say things like '*heya wa 5 hunkan kitanakatta*' (the room was dirty for five minutes) but not possible to say it in the non-past tense, I believe that the tense feature needs to be checked by an Aspectual head. However, the difference between verbal elements and this kind of adjective is that the latter is not merged with a Theme feature (see 4.3.4). On the other hand, there is another type of Japanese adjective with the *–na* suffix. This suffix does not have its own inflectional paradigm for tense and behaves more similarly to nouns in Japanese.

72 In this section, the term 'verbal' or 'verbal element' is used when it is not clear whether the element involved in compounding is a root or a stem. On the other hand, the term 'verbal root' is used when it is clear that a root, not a stem or a word is used in compounding.

73 Lieber (1983) assumes that this element is a stem.

74 According to Lieber (1983), synthetic compounds with *-ing* are different from those with the *–er* suffix in that the *-ing* forms lexical items belong to several categories, progressive ('verb'), 'noun' and 'adjective'. In adjectival or nominal root compounds with-*ing*, it is not necessary to have an argument. So in the present framework, the non-head of this type of compounds does not have any arguments either. Thus, the structure of this type of compound would be the same as the one proposed in (403). Also in the synthetic compounds with progressive, no argument is required by the progressive verb *-ing*. Thus, the non-head has no argument structure. Therefore, the structure is the same.

75 Josefsson (1997) argues that a reason that a compound like *tennis+ play* which projects an Event feature is not possible in English is that the root *play* does not assign any case to the root *tennis* (e.g. *I tennis+play+ed yesterday.*). I agree with her argument, since the verbal root does not assign any case feature to the root. Moreover, it is not necessary for the nominal root to be incorporated to the verbal root, because there is no motivation for the incorporation.

76 Within the present theory, in a case where a root like *play* is merged with a DP, not a root, the root *play* is first merged with a Theme (x) feature. Then, a DP with a referential index is merged. As a result, the (x) in the Theme feature and the referential index in the DP are exchanged. However, the 'lefthand' root in a synthetic compound does not need a referential index, so it is not merged with a DP.

77 van Hout and Roeper claim that the structure of synthetic compounds is different from that of nominalization. They propose a structure based on the Abstract Clitic Hypothesis. However, since in this thesis, I have claimed that the structure based on the Abstract Clitic Hypothesis does not account for the headedness of derivation of a compounding, I am arguing

the structure I have proposed is more valid. The readings that the *tennis player* has to be an agentive argument and the *lawn-mower* could be either an agent or instrumental argument are, I claim, in effects of the LF-lexicon, not effects of the syntax.

78 How about ungrammatical examples like **tree-falling,* *brick-lying and *fund-rising? The head roots are presumably merged with a Theme theta-feature, since they are 'unaccusative'. In Swedish, too, there are *barngråt* (child-crying), or *kvinnogråt* (women crying) but not *barngråtande (child-crying) or *kvinnogråtande. For the moment, there is no solution for these cases.

79 Not every kind of animal can be in the 'left-hand' position of this type of compounds, though. The unproductivity might be due to the LF-lexicon and the world knowledge. More work into this type of compound needs to be carried out.

80 This implies that the data shown is same in all Scandinavian languages, except sometimes for spelling.

81 In addition Kösling and Plag (2008), using acoustic data from several hundred pertinent compounds from the Boston University Radio Speech Corpus, found that the predictions of the Lexical Category Prominence Rule (Lieberman and Prince (1977), see Footnote 22) are borne out for the majority of the data.

82 Hawkins (1990) proposes the Early Immediate Constituents principle which states that the parser prefers those orders of words that enable it to recognise all Immediate Constituents of a mother node as rapidly as possible. This proposal is supported with real-time psycholinguistic experiments on alternative orderings of Immediate Constituents in languages that allow such alternatives; from text-frequency counts for these alternative orderings; from native speaker acceptability judgments; and from the grammaticalised word orders of the world's languages (Hawkins 1990: 230). For instance, Extraposition, such *as It surprised Mary that Bill was frightened* is motivated, because it brings forward the VP, making a very short constituent recognition domain for IP. In addition, as there are three daughter Immediate Constituents, the V, NP, and CP, the VP stays efficient in this construction. Moreover, an eye-movement experiment proves the difficulty of processing the corresponding construction of the Extraposition, *That Bill was frightened surprised Mary* (Frazier and Rainer 1988, cited in Hawkins 1990: 231).

83 I would like to thank Stefanie Reissner for helping me with these data in German.

84 See a similar analysis of this type of compound in Italian in Gračanin-Yuksek (2005).

85 I would like to thank Dr. Agathopoulou for her comments.

86 More precisely, after every left-branching constituent in a word, as derived words also require the linker (see Josefsson 1997) *barn+dom+s+minne* (child+hood+LINK+memory) in Swedish.

87 I would like to thank Dr Agathopoulou for her comment on nominal compounds in Greek.

88 I would like to thank Mr Fejes for his comments on this matter.

89 I would like to thank Prof. Wayles Browne for his comments on this topic.

90 I would like to thank Professor Spencer for sharing his knowledge on compounding in these languages.

91 As far as I know, Chinese equivalent word *Mother's day* do not use the genitive marker inside them, since Chinese does not have a Case marker. N de N is a possessive construction.

92 The numbers show the tones. I would like to thank Ms Winnie Yiu for the data.

93 I would like to thank Prof. Shäfer for giving me these data in Chinese.

94 Chung convincingly claims that the Korean serial verb construction is different from the verbal coordinate construction, too. The first difference is seen in the interpretations of the negation scope.

a. John-i ku chayk-ul ani ilk-ko   pannapha-ess-ta.
   John-N the book-A NEG read-CONJ return-Past-Declarative
   'John returned the book, without reading'. (Chung 1993: 26)

In this example, the negative morpheme takes scope only over the left-hand verbal root. In contrast, however, serial verb construction sometimes shows ambiguities in the scope of negation (also supported by H.D. Ahn 1992, cited in Chung 1993: 24 footnote 24).

b. John-i ani   kel-e ka-ess-ta.
   John-N NEG walk-E go-Pst-dec
   (i) It is not the case that John went on foot.
   (ii) John went, not on foot. (Chung 1993: 39)

Another fact about serial verb construction is that it is productive. However, in contrast, Korean lexical verb compounds are not. Moreover, Chung states that the serial verb has the right-hand verbal root as its head. In order to make that argument, Chung provides the following example.

a. apeci-ka kapang-ul tul-e olli-si-ess-ta.
    Father-N bag-A take-E raise-Hon-Past-declarative
    'Father took/raised the bag'.
b.*apeci-ka kapang-ul tul-usi-e olli-si-ess-ta.
    Father-N bag-A take-HON-E raise-Hon-Past-declarative
    'Father took/raised the bag'. (Chung 1993: 100)

The agreement (honorification) marker *si* appears on the 'right-hand' verbal root, not on the 'left-hand' verbal root as shown above.
Another argument for the headship of the 'right-hand' verbal root in a serial verb construction is in the selection of adverbs. An aspectual adverb cannot conflict with the 'right-hand' verbal root head without resulting in ungrammaticality. Consider how verbal roots select aspectual adverbs:

a. John-i il cwuil tongan kwulm-ess-ta.
    John-N one week for go without food-Pst-dec
    'John went without food for a week'.
b.*John-i il cwuil tongan cwuk-ess-ta.
    John-N one week for die-pst-dec

The verbal root *kwulm-* 'to go without food' may take a durational adverbial element as in (a) because it is an activity verbal root, whereas the verbal root *cwuk-* 'die' cannot because it is an achievement verbal root. These two verbal roots combine to form a serial verb construction as shown in the following examples. However, the serial verbal construction cannot take a durational adverb, as shown below.

a. John-i il kwulm-e cwuk-ess-ta.
    John-N go without food-E die-Pst-dec
    'John went without food/died' (John died of hunger).
b.*John-i il cwuil tongan kwulm-e cwuk-ess-ta.
    John-N one week for go without food-E die-pst-dec

'John went without food/died for a week'. (Chung 1993: 103)

As the arguments show, this construction has the 'right-hand' element as the head, since the linking morpheme checks the features of 'left-hand' element. There is no tense, aspect or honorific features on the 'left-hand' element but there is on the 'right-hand element'.

95 I would like to thank Dr. Charles Marfo for his comments on this language.
96 The structure of the non-head for the examples (499) and (500) are taken from Adger (2003).
97 The non-head has the word order of a main clause with verb-second, evident if an adverb is included (Holmberg & Platzack 1995): *ett jag-längtar-ännu-efter dig brev* (a I-long-still-after you letter). If V2 clauses are derived by subject movement to Spec CP, then the non-head is a CP.
98 For the issue of pro-drop in Japanese, see Ono (2001). He argues, based on Alexiadou and Anagnostopoulou's (1998) analysis of pro-drop languages, that overt subject raising in Japanese is EPP-driven and that EPP is strong in this language. I agree with him in that the subject does raise out of VP to the IP Spec position. This argument is supported by the fact that case-marker cannot be dropped in non-theta-marked position (Ono 2001: 3); and the fact that adjuncts may intervene between floating quantifiers and the subject noun phrases, whereas internal arguments and manner adverbs may not.
99 Scandinavian does not like compounds like *strikt-ordföljdsspråk* (strict-word-order-language). This might be due to the fact that compounds with adjectival non-head are not productive. I do not have an answer to this question at the moment.
100 What does my theory say about coordination in compounds? Head deletion is possible, like in the Scandinavian examples and the Japanese examples (some of them). That means these compounds are not completely words and behave syntactically in the sense of Lexical Integrity. If they are words, the head should not be deleted. So possibly, the account might be the same as normal coordination. P(x) is deleted at the PF interface, because it is understood.
101 More examples of copulative compounds are in the Appendix.
102 After the derivation of the dvandva, it is possible to merge a classifier or plural phrasal affix – *tachi* (see 4.1.1). Then, the dvandva DP moves to a Spec higher DP to get a referential feature from the higher D.
103 Appositional compounds in Scandinavian languages have a suffixed definite article on both of the constituents. For the example (511f), there are definite articles on both the constituents, the structure is different from (513). Following Homberg & Platzack (2005: 445) I assume that the suffixed article in Scandinavian is an agreement element, a head with an unvalued D-feature, receiving a value from D which is usually, though not always, null. The P(x) features of the two constituents is then assigned its value by a higher D, which may be abstract. So this example is different from the other examples in Scandinavian languages in that it does not have any head. Based on this, I propose the following structure.

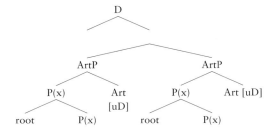

It is important to note that the two ArtP do not contain any other material, such as no complement of P(x) and that the Art is there to agree with D but does not have an index of its own. On the other hand, the P(x)s have an unvalued referential index which needs to be valued by the D.

CHAPTER 5
Conclusion

The main aim of this book has been to propose a unified structure for compound words in Japanese, English and Mainland Scandinavain within the Minimalist Program. Chapter 2 examined some characteristics of noun-noun compound words in the languages in question and observed that the left-hand constituent of compounds in English looks like a free morpheme, whereas that in the other languages does not. In addition, I have found out that neoclassical compounds and cranberry morphemes do exist in Japanese and Scandinavian languages, like in English. Moreover, it has been observed that there are genitive compounds, phrasal compounds, coordinative compounds in the languages in question, and appositional compounds in English and the Scandinavian languages. Also, this chapter has observed that there are some differences between compounds and their corresponding phrases with respect to Lexical Integrity. However, it was also shown that there are some counter-examples to Lexical Integrity.

In Chapter 3, a number of previously proposed theories of compound words were discussed and criticised. I have presented evidence that none of them is good enough and in Chapter 4 I proposed an alternative theory for compound words in the languages in question. Following Josefsson (1997), I have presented evidence that the 'left-hand' segment of compound word in these languages has no word class features, even in English, where the non-head looks like a free morpheme. With respect to the headedness of a word, Josefsson argues the inflection is the only source for word class and is therefore referred to as N^0. Inflections are carried by words, and if the inflection is a suffix, it is the head of the word. Inflections host features like number and gender, and these features are what makes a stem a noun. However, it is hard to apply this idea to NN compounds in Japanese, since there is no number inflection which can be merged with a nominal stem or a nominal root to make it a noun in Japanese.

Instead, I have proposed to use Collins' (2002) definition of head for compound words. The crucial assumptions are: (a) A head is a category which has one or more unsaturated features; (b) if a lexical item is chosen from the lexical array (Chomsky (1995)) and introduced to the derivation, the probe/selectors of this lexical item must be satisfied before any new unsaturated lexical items are chosen from the lexical array.

I have argued that the 'right-hand' constituent of a compound in the languages in question is merged with a categorical feature. In the case of nouns, this feature is represented as $P(x)$ where P stands for 'denotes a property', and where x represents an unvalued referential index. Since the $P(x)$ feature is unsaturated in the sense that it needs a referential index from either a D or DP, it percolates. Then, another root is merged to form a compound word. As the $P(x)$ is the only unsaturated feature before and/or after the root is merged, it percolates and is the head of the whole compound.

An advantage of the proposed analysis is that it is applicable to a wide range of compound types, including neoclassical compounds, phrasal compounds, recursive compounds, synthetic compounds and genitive compounds in the languages in question and compounds with a plural inflection inside in English. I have proposed that when the 'left-hand' is not merged with a categorical feature $P(x)$, the 'right-hand' element is merged with a $P(x)$ and the head of the whole compound is the $P(x)$. On the other hand, when the 'left-hand' is merged with a $P(x)$ feature, I have proposed a linking element needs to be merged to check the $P(x)$ feature merged with the 'left-hand' element. This is because a structure cannot have two heads. Before and after the $P(x)$ feature merged with the 'left-hand' element is checked by the linking element, the $P(x)$ feature merged with another root, 'right-hand' element is unsaturated. As a result, this $P(x)$ feature needs a referential index from a D or DP. Thus, the head of the compound word is $P(x)$ merged with the 'right-hand' constituent.

A compound noun can freely become the base of another compound noun in the languages in question. This type of compound word is called recursive compounds, and it is possible to have both right-branching and left-branching recursive compound words. Right-branching recursive compounds are derived by merging root after root with a $P(x)$ in the present theory. On the other hand, a left-branching compound is derived with a linking morpheme. The linking morpheme is merged after the 'left-hand' root is merged, because the $P(x)$ merged with the 'second' root needs to be checked somehow. So the linking morpheme is merged and checks the $P(x)$. As a result, the $P(x)$ on the 'rightmost' element is the head.

Based on the assumption that a linking morpheme is merged if the derivation is not complete (i.e. there are still features to be checked), phrasal compounds are also analysed within the present theory. A linking element is merged to check the non-head if there are features to be checked. If the derivation of the non-head is complete (e.g. the non-head is a main clause), it is not necessary to merge a linking element, but it is possible to merge a root with a categorical feature, which is the head of the whole compound word.

In addition, I have argued that the proposed theory is applicable to compound words in many other languages in the world. Since recursion, particularly left-recursion, in compounds is dependent on a linking element to check the P(x) of the non-head, the claim is that languages with left-recursion have a word-internal linking element which may or may not be overt. I have shown that many of them actually have an overt linking element in at least some compounds.

As a result, in this theory, I have made a universal claim. However, a question immediately arising is why not all languages seem to be subsumed under the same rules of compound word formation. For example, why are there 'verb-verb' compounds in Japanese and not in the Germanic languages? More research is required to answer this question, along with many other questions.

References

ADGER, D. 2003. *Core syntax: A Minimalist approach.* Oxford: Oxford University Press.
AGATHOPOULOU, G. 2003. On functional features in Second Language Acquisition of nominal compounds: Evidence from the Greek-English Interlanguage. In J.M. Liceras et al (Eds.), *Proceedings of the 6th Generative Approaches to Second Language Acquisition Conference.* (pp. 1-8). Somerville Mass; Cascadillia Proceedings Project.
ALEGRE, M. A. & GORDON, P. 1996. Why parks commissioners aren't rats eaters: Semantic constraints on regular plurals inside compounds. Unpublished manuscript, Teacher's College, Columbia University.
ALEXIADOU, A. & ANAGNOSTOPOULOU, E. 1998. Parameterizing AGR: Word order, V-movement and EPP-checking. *Natural Language and Lingusitic Theory*, 18, 491-539.
ALLEN, M. 1978. Morphological Investigations. Unpublished doctoral dissertation, University of Connecticut.
ANDERSON, S. 1982. Where's Morphology? *Linguistic Inquiry* 13, 571-612.
———. (1985). Inflectional Morphology. In T. Shopen (Ed.), *Language typology and syntactic description: Grammatical categories and the lexicon*, 3 (pp. 15-201). Cambridge: Cambridge University Press.
———. 1992. *A-morphous morphology.* Cambridge, Cambridge University Press.
ARAD, M. 2003. Locality Constraints on the interpretation of roots: The case of Hebrew denominal verb. *Natural Language and Linguistic Theory*, 21, 737-778.
ARONOFF, M. 1976. *Word formation in Generative Grammar.* Cambridge, Mass: MIT Press.
ASHER, R.E. 1994. *Encyclopaedia of language and linguistics.* Oxford: Pergamon Press.
BAKER, M. C. 1988. *Incorporation: A theory of grammatical function changing.* Chicago: Chicago University Press.
———. 2003. *Lexical categories –verbs, nouns, and adjectives.* Cambridge: University of Cambridge Press.
BARKER, C. 1998. Episodic –ee in English: A thematic role constraint on a new word formation. *Language*, 74, 695-727.
BAUER, L. 1978. *The grammar of nominal compounding with special reference to Danish, English and French.* Odense: Odense University Press.
———. 1983. *English word-formation.* Cambridge: Cambridge textbooks in Linguistics.
———. 1998a. When is a sequence of two nouns a compound in English? *English Language and Linguistics*, 2, 65-86.
———. 1998b. Is there a class of neoclassical compounds, and if so is it productive? *Linguistics*, 36, 403-422.
BAUER, LAURIE. 2009. Typology of compounds. In The Oxford handbook of compounding, eds. Rochelle Lieber and Pavol Stekauer, 343-356. Oxford: Oxford University Press.
BENNETT, P. 1996. English adjective-noun compounds and related constructions. available at www.ccl.umist.ac.uk/staff/paul/adjn.html.
BERMAN, R. A. 1978. *Modern Hebrew Structure.* Tel Aviv, Israel: University Publishing Projects.
BISETTO, A. 1994. Italian compounds of the 'accendigas' type: A case of endocentric formations? *Working Papers in Linguistics*, 4, 1-20.
———. 2010. Recursiveness and Italian compounds. SKASE *Journal of Theoretical Linguistics*, 7, 14-35.
BLOOMFIELD, L. 1933. *Language.* New York: Holt.
BOOIJ, G. 1993. Against Split Morphology. *Yearbook of Morphology*, 27-49.

———. 2002. *The morphology of Dutch.* Oxford: Oxford Linguistics.

———. 2009. Compounding and construction morphology. In Rochelle Lieber and Pavol Stekauer (eds.), *The Oxford Handbook of Compounding.* Oxford: Oxford University Press, 201-216.

BORER, H. 1988. On the morphological parallelism between compounds and constructs. *Yearbook of Morphology,* 1, 45-64.

BOTHA, R. 1981. A Base Rule Theory of Afrikaans synthetic compounding. In R. Borsley (Ed.), *The Natural and Function of Syntactic Categories* (pp. 101-31). New York: Academic press.

CHIERCHIA, G. 1998. Reference to kinds across languages. *Natural Language Semantics,* 6, 339-405.

CHOMSKY, N. 1965. *Aspects of the theory of syntax.* Cambridge, Mass: The MIT Press.

CHOMSKY, N. & HALLE, M. 1968. *The sound pattern of English.* New York: Harper& Row.

CHOMSKY, N. 1970. Remarks on Nominalization. In R. Jacobs & P. Rosenbaum (Eds.), *Readings in English transformational grammar* (pp. 184-221). Waltham, Mass.

CHOMSKY, N. & H. LASNIK. 1977. Filters and Control. *Linguistic Inquiry,* 8, 425-504.

CHOMSKY, N. 1981. *Lectures on Government and Binding.* Dordrecht: Foris Publications.

———. 1993. A Minimalist Program for Linguistic Theory. In K. Hale & S. J Keyser (Eds.), *View from Building 20. Essays in Linguistcs in Honour of Sylvain Bromberger* (pp.1-52). Cambridge, Mass, London: The MIT Press.

———. 1994. Bare Phrase Structure. *MIT Occasional Papers in Linguistics,* 5, 1-52.

———. 1995. *The Minimalist Program.* Cambridge, Mass: The MIT Press

———. 2000. Minimalist Inquiries: The framework. In R. Martin, D. Michaels, & J. Uriagereka (Eds.), *Step by Step. Essays on Minimalist Syntax in Honour of Howard Lasnik* (pp. 1-59). Cambridge MA: MIT Press.

———. 2001. Beyond Explanatory Adequacy. unpublished manuscript, MIT.

———. 2002. *On Nature and Language.* Cambridge: Cambridge University Press.

CHUNG, T. 1993. Argument structure and serial verbs in Korean. Ph.D. dissertation. The University of Texas at Austin.

CLARK, E.V. 1993. *The lexicon in acquisition.* Cambridge: Cambridge University Press.

CLEMENTS, J. C. 1987. Lexical category hierarchy and 'head of compound' in Spanish. In C. Laeufer & T. A. Morgan (Eds.), *Theoretical analyses in Romance linguistics* (pp. 151-166). John Benjamins Publishing Company.

COLLINS, C. 2002. Eliminating Labels. In S.D. Epstein & T. D. Seely (Eds.), *Derivation and explanation in the Minimalist Program* (pp. 42-64). Oxford: Blackwell.

CONTRERAS, H. 1985. Spanish exocentric compounds. In F. H. Nussel, Jr (Ed.), *Current issues in Hispanic phonology and morphology* (pp. 14-27). University of Louisville.

DAHLSTEDT, K.-H. 1965. Homonym i nusvenskan [Homonym in present Swedish]. *Nusvenska studier [Studies of present Swedish],* 45, 52-192.

DELSING, L-O. 1993. *The internal structure of Noun Phrases in the Scandinavian languages: A comparative study.* Department of Scandinavian languages, University of Lund.

DEN DIKKEN, M & P. SINGHAPREECHA. 2000. Complex Noun Phrases and linkers. available at www.gc.cuny.edu/dept.lingu/dendikken/thai glow.pdf

DI SCIULLO, A & A. RALLI. 1994. Argument structure and inflection in compounds: Some differences between English, Italian and Modern Greek. In Pi. Bouillon-Dominique Estival (Ed.), *Proceedings of the Workshop on Compound Nouns: Multi lingual aspects of nominal composition,* (pp. 61-76). Geneve: ISSCO.

DI SCIULLO, A. & E. WILLIAMS. 1987. *On the definition of Word.* Cambridge, Mass: MIT Press.

Don, J. 2005. Roots, Deverbal Noun, and Denominal Verbs. In G. Booij, E. Guevara, A. Ralli, S. Sgroi & Scalise (Eds.), *Morphology and Linguistic Typology, On-line Proceedings of the Fourth Mediterranean Morphology Meeting* (MMM4) (pp. 1-13). Catania 21-23 September 2004. University of Bolognia 2005. available at www.morbo.lingua.unibo.it/mmm/.

Downing, P. 1977. On the creation and use of English compound nouns. *Language* 53, 810-842.

Duanmu, S. 1997. Recursive constraint evaluation in Optimality Theory. *Natural Language and Linguistic Theory* 15, 465-507.

Embick, D. & R, Noyer 2004. Distributed morphology and the syntax/morphology interface. In G. Ramchand & E. Reiss (Eds.), *The Oxford handbook of linguistic interfaces* (pp. 289-324). Oxford: OUP.

Emery, P. 1988. Compound Words in Modern Standard Arabic *ZAL,* 19, 32-43.

Emonds, J. E. 1970. *Root and structure preserving transformations.* Indiana University Linguistics Club.

Frazier, L. & K, Rainer. 1988. Parameterizing the language processing system: Left- versus Right-branching within and across Languages. In J.A. Hawkins (Ed.), *Explaining Language Universals* (pp. 247-279). Oxford: Basil Blackwell.

Fruyt, M. 2002. Constraints and productivity in Latin nominal compounding. *Transactions of the Philological Society,* 100: 3, 259-287.

Fudge, E. 1984. *English word-stress.* London: Allen and Unwin.

Giegerich, H. J. 1999. *Lexical Strata in English.* Cambridge: Cambridge University Press.

———. 2003. Compound or phrase? English noun-plus-noun constructions and the stress criterion. Cambridge University Press, 8, 1-24.

Giegerich, H. 2015. *Lexical Structure: Compounding and the Modules of Grammar*, Edinburgh: Edinburgh University Press.

Gil, D. 2002. Ludlings in Malayic languages: An introduction. *PELBBA 15 Pertemuan Linguistik (Pusat Kajian) Bahasa dan Budaya Atma Jaya: Kelima Belas.* Pusat Kajian Bahasa dan Budaya, Unika Atma Jaya, Jakarta, 2002.

Gračanin-Yuksek, M. 2005. V-N compounds in Italian: Agreement in word formation. available at www.mit.ed/~mgracani/gracnin.pdf

Grigson, G. 1973. *A dictionary of English plant names.* London: Allen Lane.

Grimshaw, J. 1990. *Argument structure.* Cambridge, Mass; London: MIT Press

Guevara, E, & S. Scalise. 2004. V-Compounding in Dutch and Italian. In Cuadernos de Lingüiistica del Instituto Universitario Ortega y Gasset-Madrid-XI (2004). available at www2.facli.unibo.it/scalise/papers/NL-IT-24-02-04-final.htm

Haider, H. 2001. Why are there no complex head-initial compounds? In Ch. Schaner-Wolles, J. Rennison and F. Neubart (eds.) *Naturally!: Linguistic studies in honour of Wolfgang Ulrich Dressler presented on the occasion of his 60th birthday.* Torino: Rosenberg & Sellier, 165-174.

Hale, K & S. J. Keyser. 1993. On Argument Structure and the lexical representation of syntactic relations. In H. Keyser & S. J. Keyser (Eds.), *The view from Building 20: Essays in linguistics in honor of Sylvain Bromberger,* 53-109. Cambridge, Mass: MIT Press.

Halle, M. 1973. Prolegomena to a theory of word-formation. *Lingusitic Inquiry* 4, 3-16.

Halle, K. & A. Maranz. 1993. Distributed Morphology and the pieces of inflection. In Hale, Keyser & S. J. Keyser (Eds.), *The view from building 20: Essays in linguistics in honor of Sylvain Bromberger,* (pp. 111-176). Cambridge, MA: MIT Press.

Halle, M. & K. P. Mohan. 1985. Segmental phonology of Modern English. *Linguistic Inquiry* 8, 611-625.

HARRIS, J. W. 1985. Spanish Word Markers. In F. H. Nussel (Ed.), *Current issues in Hispanic phonology and morphology* (pp. 34-54). University of Louisville.

HASKELL, T. R, MARYELLEN, C. MACDONALD, & M. S. SEIDENBERG. 2003. Language learning and innateness: Some implications of *compounds* research. *Cognitive Psychology*, 47, 119-163.

HAUSER, MARC. D., CHOMSKY, N., & W. FITCH, TECUMSEH. 2002. The Faculty of Language: What is it, Who has it, and How did it evolve? *Science* 298, 1569-1579.

HAWKINS, J.A. 1990. A parsing theory of word order universals. *Linguistic Inquiry*, 21, 223-261.

HIGGINBOTHAM, J. 1985. On Semantics. *Linguistic Inquiry*, 16, 547-593.

HIGURASHI, Y. 1983. *The accent of extended word structure in Tokyo Standard Japanese*. Tokyo: Iwanami Shoten.

HIRAKAWA, M. 2000. Unaccusativity in second language Japanese and English. Unpublished Doctoral Dissertation. Montreal: Mc Gill University.

HOLES, C. 1990. *Gulf Arabic*. London: Routledge.

HOLMBERG, A. 1992. Properties of non-heads in compounds: A case study. *Working Papers in Scandinavian Syntax*, 49, 27-57.

HOLMBERG, A & C. PLATZACK. 1995. *The role of inflection in Scandinavian syntax*. Oxford: Oxford University Press.

———. 2005. The Scandinavian languages. In G. Cinque & Kayne. R (Eds.), *The Oxford handbook of comparative syntax* (pp. 420-458). Oxford: Oxford University Press.

HORNSTEIN, N. 1999. Movement and control. *Linguistic Inquiry* 30: 69-96.

VAN HOUT & T. ROEPER. 1997. Events and aspectual structure in derivational morphology. available at www.people.umass.edu/roeper/online-

ISHII, Y. 2000. Plurality and Definiteness in Japanese. available at www. coe-sun.kuis.ac.jp. coe/public/paper.html.papers/Event%20van%20Ho%2097%20mitwpl.pdf.

JACKENDOFF, R. 1977. *X' Syntax: A study of Phrase Structure*. Cambridge: MIT Press.

———. 1985. *Semantics and cognition*. London, Cambridge, Mass: MIT.

———. 1990. *Semantic structures*. Cambridge: MIT Press.

———. 1997. *The architecture of the language faculty*. Cambridge, Mass: MIT.

JOHANNESSEN, J. B. 2001. Sammensatte ord (Compound word). *Norsk LIngvistisk Tidsskrift (Norwegian Linguistic Periodical)*, 19, 59-91.

JOSEFSSON, G. 1993. Noun incorporating verbs in Swedish. *LAMBDA* 18, 274-304.

———. 1997. *On the principles of word formation in Swedish*. Lund: Lund University Press.

———. 2005. How could Merge be free and word formation restricted: The case of compounding in Romance and Germanic. *Working Papers in Scandinavian Syntax* 75, 55-96.

JOSEPH, B.D. & I. P-PHILIPPAKI-WARBURTON. 1987. *Modern Greek*. London: Cloom Helm.

KAGEYAMA, T. 1983. Word formation in Japanese. *Lingua*, 56, 215-258.

———. 1993. *Bunpoo to gokeisei (Grammar and word formation)*. Tokyo: Hituzi Press.

———. 1999. *Keitairon to imi (Morphology and meaning)*. Tokyo: Kuroshio Publishers.

———. 2001. Word plus: The intersection of words and phrases. In Jeroen van de Weijer & Nishihara, T (Eds.), *Isseus in Japanese phonology and morphology* (pp. 245-270). Berlin: Mouton de Gruyter.

KANG, M-Y. 1988. Topics in Korean syntax: Phrase structure, variable binding, and movement. Ph.D. Dissertation. MIT.

KARLSSON, F. 1987. *Finnish Grammar*. Werner Söderström Osakeyhtiö.

KATAMBA, F. 1993. *Morphology*. London: The Macmillan Press Ltd.

KAWASHIMA, R. 1994. *The structure of noun phrases and the interpretation of quantifica-*

tional NPs in Japanese. Michigan: UMI Dissertation Information Service.

KAYNE, R. 1994. *The antisymmetry of syntax*. Cambridge, Mass, London, England: The MIT Press.

KEYSER, S. J. & T. ROEPER. 1992. Re: The Abstract Clitic hypothesis. *Linguistic Inquiry*, 23, 89-125.

KIEFER, F. 1990. Noun Incorporation in Hungarian. *Acta Linguistica Hungarica*, 40, 149-177.

KIPARSKY, P. 1982. From cyclic phonology to lexical phonology. In H. van der Hulst, & N. Smith (Eds.), *The structure of phonological representations* (pp. 131-175). Dordrecht, The Netherlands: Foris.

KLAVANS, J. L. 1982. *Some problems in a theory of Clitics*. Indiana University Linguistics Club, Lindley Hall 310, Bloomington, in 47405.

———. 1985. The independence of syntax and phonology in cliticization. *Language* 61, 95-119.

KUBOZONO, H. 1993. *The organisation of Japanese Prosody*. Tokyo: Kurosio Publishers.

———. 1995. *Gokeisei to onin kozo. (Word formation and phonological structure)*. Tokyo: Kurosio Publishers.

KÖSLING, K. & I. PLAG. 2008. Does branching direction determine prominence assignment? An empirical investigation of triconstituent compounds in English. *Corpus Linguistics and Linguistic Theory* 5 (2): 205-43.

LADD, D.R. 1984. English compound stress. In D. Gibbon & H. Richter (Eds.), *Intonation, accent and rhythm* (pp. 253-266). Berlin and New York: de Gruyter.

LASNIK, H & M. SAITO. 1992. *Move [alpha]: conditions on its applications and output*. Cambridge, Mass; London: MIT Press.

LEES, R. 1960. *The grammar of English Nominalizations*. The Hague: Mouton.

LEVI, J. 1978. *The syntax and semantics of complex nominals*. New York, San Francisco, London: Academic Press.

LEVIN, B & M. R. HOVAV. 1992. Wiping the slate clean: A lexical semantic exploration. In B. Levin & S. Pinker (Eds.), *Lexical & Conceptual Semantics* (pp. 123-152). Cambridge, Oxford: Blackwell.

LIEBER, R. 1980. On the organization of the lexicon. Doctoral dissertation. MIT, Cambridge, Massachusetts. Distributed by the Indiana University Linguistics Club, Bloomington, Indiana.

———. 1981. *On the organization of the lexicon*. Bloomington, IN: Indiana University Linguistics Club.

———. 1983. Argument linking and compounds in English. *Linguistic Inquiry*, 14, 251-86.

———. 1992. *De-Constructing Morphology*. Chicago and London: The University of Chicago Press.

———. 2005. English word-formation processes: Observations, issues, and thoughts on future research. In P. Stekauer & R. Lieber (Eds.), *Handbook of Word-formation* (pp. 375-427). Springer: Dordrecht.

LIEBERMAN, M. & A. PRINCE. 1977. On stress and linguistic rhythm. *Linguistic Inquiry*, 8, 249-336.

LIEBERMAN, M. & A. SPROAT. 1992. The stress and structure of modified noun phrases in English. In I. A. Sag & A. Scabolsci (Eds.), *Lexical matters* (pp. 131-181). Stanford.

LIPKA, L. 2002. *English Lexicology: Lexical structure, word semantics & word-formation*. Tübingen: Narr.

MARANTZ, A. 1984. *On the nature of grammatical relations*. Cambridge: MIT Press.

———. 1997. No Escape from Syntax: Don't try morphological analysis in the privacy of your own lexicon. In A. Dimitriadis et al. (Eds.), *Proceedings of the 21st Annual Penn Linguistics Colloquium* (pp. 201-225). "UPenn Working Papers in Linguistics" 4.

MARCHAND, H. 1969. *The categories and types of present-day English word formation*, 2nd edition, Munich: Beck.

MATHIASSEN, T. 1997. *A short grammar of Latvian*. Slavica.

MATSUMOTO, Y. 1996. *Complex predicates in Japanese: A syntactic and semantic study of the notion of 'Word'*. Stanford, CA; Kurosio.CSLI.

MATTHEWS, P. H. 1991. *Morphology*. 2nd ed. Cambridge: Cambridge University Press.

MELLENIUS, I. 1997. *The acquisition of nominal compounding in Swedish*. Lund University Press.

MIYAGAWA, S. 1987. Lexical categories in Japanese. *Lingua*, 73, 29-51.

MIYOSHI, N. 1999. Compounds and complex predicates: Japanese evidence for a "global" parameter. In *Proceedings of BUCLD 23*. Somerville, Mass: Cascadilla Press.

MONTGOMERY, B. 2001. Studies in German and English Morphology with special reference to 'linking elements'. Unpublished doctoral dissertation. University of Edinburgh.

MUKAI, M. 2004. A comparative study of compound words in English and Japanese. *Durham Working Papers in Linguistics*, 10, 151-167.

———. 2017. Semantic characteristics of recursive compounds, in M. Sheehan and L. R. Bailey (Eds.), *Order and Structure in syntax II*, 2017 (pp. 285-288).

MUYSKEN, P.C. 1983. Parameterizing the notion Head. *The Journal of Linguistics Research*, 2, 57-76.

NAKAMURA, M, Y. KANEKO & KIKUCHI. A. 2001. *Seiseibunpoo no shintenkai: Minimalist Program (New development of the Generative Grammar: Minimalist Program-)*. Tokyo: Kenkyuusha.

NAMIKI, T. 1988. Fukugogo no nichiei taisho (A comparative study of compound words between Japanese and English). *Nihongo gaku (Japanese Linguistics)*, 7, 68-78.

———. 2001. Further evidence in support of the Right-hand Head Rule in Japanese. *Issues in Japanese Phonology and Morphology*. Hague: Mouton De Gruyter.

OCHI, M. 2003. How come and other adjunct wh-phrases: A cross-linguistic perspective. to appear in *Proceedings of GLOW in Asia 2002 (2003)*.

OHKADO, M. 1991. On the status of adjectival nouns in Japanese. *Lingua*, 83, 67-87.

OLSEN, S. 2000. Copulative compounds: A closer look at the interface between syntax and morphology. *Yearbook of Morphology*, 279-320.

ONO, H. 2001. EPP-driven XP Movement in Japanese. In *Proceedings of WECOL '99*. Department of Linguistics, California State University, Fresno.

OTHMAN, Z & S. ATMOSUMARTO. 1995. *Colloquial Malay. A complete language course*. London: Routledge.

OTSU, Y. 1980. Some aspect of Rendaku in Japanese and related problems. In A.K. Farmer & Y. Otsu (Eds.), *Theoretical Issues in Japanese Linguistics*, MIT Working Papers in Linguistics, 2, 207-228.

PACKARD, J. L. 2000. *The morphology of Chinese*. Cambridge: University of Cambridge Press.

PARKER A. R. 2006. Evolving the narrow language faculty: Was recursion the pivotal step? In A. Cangelogi, A: D, M. Smith & K. Smith (Eds.), *The evolution of language: Proceedings of the 6th International Conference on the Evolution of Langurage* (pp. 239-246).

PERELTSVAIG, A. 1998. Compounding in Semitic, and why English mice are not like Arabic 'roofs'*. Unpublished manuscript., University of Tromsø.

PESETSKY, D. 1995. *Zero syntax: Experiences and cascade*. Cambridge, Mass: MIT Press.

PINKER, S. 1999. *Words and rules*. New York: Basic Books.
PLAG, I. 2003. *Word-formation in English*. Cambridge: Cambridge University Press.
———. 2004. Productivity. *Encyclopedia of Language and Linguistics* 2nd Ed., Elsevier May 17, 2004.
PLATZACK, C. 1993. A triune lexicon: An approach to a lexical description. In M. Herslund & F. Sørensen (Eds.), The Nordlex Project: Lexical Studies in the Scandinavian Languages, *Lambada* 18, 305-318. Institu for Datalingvistik, Handelshøjskolen i København.
PLATZACK, C. & I. ROSENGREN. 1998. On the subject of imperatives: A Minimalist account of the imperative clause. *The Journal of Comparative Linguistics*, 3, 177-224.
PÖLL, B. 2007. Restricted recursion in N-N compounding: some thoughts on possible reasons. *Linguistische Berichte*, 23, 141-163.
RADFORD, A. 1988. *Transformational Grammar. A First Course*. Cambridge: Cambridge University Press.
———. 2004. *Minimalist Syntax*. Cambridge: Cambridge University Press.
RAINER, F. 1988. Constrants on Productivity. In Stekauer P & R. Lieber (Eds.), *Handbook of Word-formation* (pp. 335-352). Verlag: Springer.
RALLI, A. 2009. IE, Hellenic: Modern Greek. In R. Liebe, Stekauer, P. (Eds.), *The Oxford Handbook of Compounding* (pp. 453-463). Oxford: Oxford University Press.
ROEPER, T. 1988. Compound syntax and head movement. *Yearbook of Morphology*. Dordrecht: Foris.
ROEPER, T, SNYDER, W & K. HIRAMATSU. 2002. Learnability in a Minimalist framework: Root compounds, merger, and the syntax-morphology interface. In I. Lasser (Ed.), *The process of language acquisition*, 25-35. Frankfurt: Peter Lang Verlag.
ROEPER, T. & SIEGEL, D. 1978. A lexical transformation for verbal compounds. *Linguistic Inquiry*, 9, 199-260.
ROEPER, T. & SNYDER, W. 2002. Language learnability and the forms of recursion. In A. M. Di Sciullo & R. Delmonte (Eds.), *UG and External Systems*. Amsterdam: John Benjamins.
ROSE, J.H. 1973. Principled limitations on productivity in denominal verbs. *Foundations of Language*, 10, 509-526.
ROSEN, T.S. 1989. Two types of noun incorporation: a lexical analysis. *Language*, 65: 2, 294-317.
SAITO, M, & K. MURASAGI. 1991. N'-deletion in Japanese: A preliminary study. *Japanese/Korean linguistics*, 1, 285-302.
SCALISE, S. 1984. *Generative morphology*. Foris Dord Lecht.
———. 1988. The notion of 'head' in Morphology. *Yearbook of Morphology*, 1, 229-246.
SCALISE, S, A. BISETTO, & GUEVARA, E. 2004. Selection in compounding and derivation. *Proceedings of the XI Morphology Meeting*-Vienna, February 2004. Benjamins-Amsterdam.
SCHULTINK, H. 1961. Productiviteit als morfologisch fenomeen. *Forum der Letteren*, 2, 110-125.
SELKIRK, E. 1982. *The syntax of words*. Cambridge: Mass: MIT Press.
SHIMAMURA, R. 1986. Lexicalization of syntactic phrases: The case of genitive compounds like woman's magazine'. *English Linguistics*, 3, 20-37.
———. 2015. Eiko no "meishi+meishu" wa ku ka go ka (Is "noun+noun" in English a phrase or a word?). In T. Nishihara and Tanaka S (Eds.), *Gendai no keitairon to Onseigaku oninron no shiten to ronten (Aspects and Discussions of modern Morphology and Phonetics Phonology)*, 21-41. Tokyo: Kaitakusha.
SIEGEL, D. 1974. Topics in English morphology. PhD thesis. MIT.

SLABAKOVA, R. 1999. The complex predicate/N-N compounding relation in L2 acquisition. In A. Greenhill, H. Littlefield, & C. Tano (Eds.), *Proceedings of the Boston University Conference on Language Development 23*. Somerville, MA: Cascadilla Press.

SMITH, C. 1964. Determiners and relative clauses in a Generative Grammar of English. *Language*, 40, 37-52; in D. Reibel and S. Schane, eds. (1969), 247-263.

SNYDER, W. 1995. Language acquisition and language variation: The role of morphology. Doctoral Dissertation. MIT. The Department of Brain and Cognitive Sciences.

———. 1996. The acquisitional role of the syntax-morphology interface: Morphological compounds and syntactic complex predicates. *Proceedings of the 20th Annual Boston University Conference on Language Development*, Volume 2, 728-735. Sommerville, MA: Cascadilla Press.

SNYDER, W. & D. CHEN. 1997. The syntax-morphology interface in the acquisition of French and English. In K. Kusumoto (Ed.), *Proceedings of NELS, 27*. Amherst, Mass: GLSA.

SPENCER, A. 1991. *Morphological theory*. Blackwell: Oxford.

———. 2003. Does English have productive Compounding? In G. Booij, J. de Cesaris, A. Ralli & A, Scalise (Eds.), *Proceedings of the 3rd Mediterranean Morphology Meeting. Institute of Universitali de Linguistics Applicada, Universitat Pompeu Fabra*, Barcelona. 21 September 2001.

STOWELL, T. 1981. *Origins of Phrase Structure*. Cambridge, Mass: MIT dissertation.

SUGISAKI, K. & M. ISOBE. 2000. Resultatives result from the Compounding Parameter. Amhest, MA: GLSA. On the acquisitional correlation between resultatives and N-N compounds in Japanese. *Proceedings of the West Coast Conference on Linguistics 19*.

TAYLOR, J. R. 1996. *Possessives in English: An exploration in cognitive grammar*. Oxford: Clarendem Press.

TELEMAN, U. 1969. *Om svenska ord (About Swedish words)*. Lund: Gleerups.

TOKUZAKI, H. 2011. The nature of linear information in the morpho-syntax-PF interface. English linguistics, 28 (2), 227-257.

TSUJIMURA, N. 1996. *An introduction to Japanese linguistics*. Massachussets: Blackwell.

VANCE, T. 2015. Rendaku. In H. Kubozono (Ed.), The Handbook of Japanese Phonology and Phonetics. Berlin: Walter de Gruyter.

WARD, G., R. SPAROAT & G. MCKOON. 1991. A pragmatic analysis of so-called anaphoric islands. *Language, 67*, 439-74.

WIESE, R. 1996a. Phrasal compounds and the theory of word syntax. *Linguistic Inquiry, 27*, 183-193.

———. 1996b. *The phonology of German*. Oxford: Claron Press.

WILLIAMS, E. 1981. On the notions "Lexically Related" and "Head of a Word". *Linguistic Inquiry*, 12, 245-274.

ZUFFI, S. 1981. The nominal composition in Italian. Topics in generative morphology. *Journal of Italian Linguistics, 6-2*, 1-54.

The data are taken from:

Collins COBUILD English Dictionary for Advanced Learners 3rd edition first pulibhsed 2001. Harper Collins Publishers 1987, 1995, 2001.

Collins German Dictionary, 5th Edition (2004), In P. Terrell, V. Schnorr, W.V.A. Smith and R.O. Breitsprecher (Eds.). Glasgow: Harper Collins.

Engelsk-dansk ordbog. Gyldendals røde ordbøger. Copenhagen: Nordisk Forlag A/S.

New College English-Japanese Dictionary, 6th edition (C) Kenkyusha Ltd. 1967,1994,1998).

GRISSON, G. 1973. A dictionary of English plant names. London: Allen Lane.

HOLMES, P.& SERIN, G. *Colloquial Swedish*. London and New York: Routledge.
JOSEFFSON, G. 1997. *On the Principles of Word Formation in Swedish*. Lund: Lund University Press.
Koojien·Genius English-Japanese Dictionary, Japanese-English Dictionary. (Sharp Electronic dictionary).
NAMIKI, T. 1988. Fukugogo no nichiei taisho ('A comparative study of compound words between Japanese and English). *Nihongogaku (Japanese Linguistics)*, 7, 68-78.
www.google.co.uk, www.google.co.jp, www.google.co.dk and Google internet sites in Italy, Spanish, French and Scandinavian countries.

Appendix

Appendix I
More tests for the anaphoric island

English

The following sentences show the difference between compounds and their corresponding phrases.

(1) coffee+cup
   *At the Whittard I bought a coffee+cup and drank some yesterday.
(2) wine+bottle
   a. ?Pat had a winebottle and spilled some of it on the table.
   b. Pat had a bottle of wine and spilled some of it on the table.
(3) match+box
   a. *When I saw a match$_i$+box on the table, I lit one$_i$ very carefully.
   b. When I saw a box with matches$_i$ on the table, I lit one$_i$ very carefully.

Interestingly, two native speakers (an American and British) said that the pronominal *one* refers to *box* in (b) example.

(4) lamp+post
   a. *When John looked at the lamp+post it had gone off.
   b. When John looked at the post which holds a lamp had gone off.

A question mark for the sentence (b) as native speakers would not say *post which holds a lamp* instead of *lamp-post*.

Japanese

The following sentences show the difference between compounds and their corresponding phrases.

(5) koohii+kappu
   coffee+cup
   a. *omise de koohii$_i$+kappu o kai sore$_i$ o sukoshi nonda.
      shop at coffee$_i$+cup ACC buy-and that$_i$ ACC little drank
      'I bought a coffee cup and drank some of the coffee'.
   b. omise de koohii$_i$ no kappu o kai sore$_i$ o sukoshi nonda.
      shop at coffee GEN cup ACC buy-and that ACC little drank

'I bought a cup of coffee and drank some of the coffee'.
(6) cha+wan
tea+bowl
a. *cha$_i$+wan o kattekite sore$_i$ o nonda.
   *Tea$_i$+bowl ACC bought-and that$_i$ ACC drank
   'I bought a teabowl and drank that'.
b. cha$_i$ o nomu tame no o wan o kattekite sore$_i$ o nonda.
   tea$_i$ ACC drink for GEN POL bowl ACC bought-and that$_i$ ACC drank
   'I bought a bowl for drinking tea and drank that'.
(7) hana+mi
flower+watch
'cherry-blossom viewing'
a. *hana$_i$+mi ni itta-kedo sorera$_i$ wa zenbu moo kareteita.
   flower-watch GEN went-but those$_i$ TOP all already withered
   'I went to see the cherry blossoms but they all had already withered.'
b. hana$_i$ o mi-ni-itta-kedo sorera$_i$ wa zenbu moo kareteita.
   flower$_i$ ACC watch-DAT went-but those$_i$ TOP all already withered
   'I went to see some flowers but they all had already withered.'
(8) hon+dana
book+shelf
'book-shelf'
a. *hon$_i$+dana o motteitaga sono$_i$ naka no ju-ssatu to mo
   book$_i$+shelf ACC possessed-and that$_i$ inside GEN ten-CL and too
   moeteshimatta.
   burned-unfortnately
   'I had a bookshelf, but ten of them unfortunately burned'.
b. *hon$_i$+dana o motteitaga sore$_i$ wa moetteshimatta.
   book$_i$+shelf ACC possessed-but that$_i$ TOP burned-unfortunately
   'I had a bookshelf, but it unfortunately burned'.
(9) shokki+todana
tableware+cupboard
'cupboard/sideboard'
*shokki+todana no naka kara i-kko toridashita.
tableware-cupboard GEN inside from one-CL took-out
'I took one piece of tableware out from the table-ware.'

The grammaticality of the following sentences shows that anaphoric island is not violated in the compound word in question. Lexical Integrity is not clear-cut in Japanese either.

(10) rekoodo+keesu
record+case

    a. rekoodo$_i$+keesu o mituke-te sono$_i$ naka no ichi-mai o kaketa.
        record$_i$+case ACC found-and that$_i$ inside GEN one-CL ACC put-on
        'I found a record case and played one piece of record'.

    b. ?rekoodo$_i$+keesu o mitukete sore$_i$ o kaketa.
        record$_i$+case ACC found-and that$_i$ ACC put-on
        'I found a record case and played that'.

(11) hon+dana
book+shelf
'bookshelf'

    a. ?hon+dana ni te o dasite i-ssatu o toridasita.
        book-shelf DAT hand ACC hand-and one-CL ACC took-out
        'I stretched my hand and took one (book) out'.

    b. ?hon$_i$+dana ni te o dasite sore$_i$ o toridasita.
        book$_i$+shelf DAT hand ACC hand-and that$_i$ ACC took-out
        'I stretched my hand and took that out'.

Appendix II
Compound words

Underlined: phonological change
Bolded: neoclassical element
Bracket: not a compound in the language
Novel compound: shaded
-not accepted by native speakers of the language
Person, people, organisation

Japanese	English	Scandinavian
ginkoo+in	bank+clerk	bank+tjenestemand
hoan+tai	security+forces	sikkerhed+s+styrker
gaado+man	security+man	sikkerhed+s+mand
himitsu+keisatsu	security+police	sikkerhed+s+politi
bideo+ kurabu+liidaa	video club chairman	video+klub+formand
#kodomo+hon+kurabu (kodomo no hon klub)	#children+book+club children's book club	barn+bog+klub
#otona hon kurabu (otona no hon klub)	adult+book+club	voksen+bog+klub
#yoru+kompyuutaa+kurasu (yoru no computer class)	evening+computer+class	aften+computer+klass
gekijoo+kippu+uriba	theatre+ticket+office	teater+billet+kontor
yuubin+kozutumi+zeikan kokuti+choo	parcel+post+customers declaration	
roodoo+kumiai+choo	Labour+union+president	fag+forening+ præsident
coffee+meikaa+seigyoosha	coffee+maker+maker	kaffe+brygger+ fabrikant
indo+yooroppa+gozoku	(Indo-European family)	(den indoeuropæiske familie)
sekai+hoken+kikan	World+Health+Organisation	Verden+s helse+organisation
sekai+kishoo+kikan	World+Meteological+Orga.	(Det meteorologisk verdensorganisation)
sekai+kokusai+hukkoo kaihatu+ginkoo	(International bank of Reconstruction and Development)	
sekai+ginkoo	World+Bank	
joosetsu+kokusai+sihoo+ saibansho	World+Court	
sekai+kankyoo+dei	World+Environment+Day	
sekai+renpoo+shugi	World+Federalism	
sekai+shokuryoo+rizikai	World+Food+Programme	Verden+s+mad+vare+ Program
sekai+ roodoo+kumiai+ renmei	(World Federation of Trade Unions)	(Verdensforbundet af fagforeninger)
sekai+booeki+sentaa	World+Trade+Centre	
sekai+kanshi+keikaku	World+Weather+Watch	
waarudo+kappu	World+Cup	Verden+s+cup
sekai+yasei+seibutsu+kikin	World+Wildlife+Fund	Verden+s+natur+fondet
sekai+heiwa+kyoogikai	World+Peace+Council	Verdens+fred+s+rådet

sekai+kaiyoo+hunkan zikken	World+Ocean+circulation+experiment	
minshu +too	(Liberal Democratic party)	Liberal+demokratiske+partiet (two words) (det liberaldemokratiske partie)
roodoo+too	Labour+Party	Arbejder+partiet
(midori no too)	Green+Party	Grøn +Partiet
sinpo+too	Progress+Party	Fremskridt+s+partiet
chuuoo+minshu+too	Central Democrat	Centrum+ demokraterne
roodoo+kumiai	Labour+association	Arbejder +forening
kyoosei+roodoo+shuuyoo+jo	labour+camp	arbejd+s+lejr
roodoo+ichiba	labour+market	arbejder+marked
roodoo+undoo	labour+movement	Arbejder+bevægelse
roodoo+soogi	labour+conflict/dispute	arbejd+s+konflikt
booei+choo	The Defence+Minister	Forvar+s+ministeriet
zaimu+sho	*Finance+Minister (Minister of Finance)	Finans+ministeriet
monbu+shoo	*Education+Minister (Minister of Education)	Undervisning+s+ministeriet
*	*	Kirke+ministeriet
naimu+shoo	Home+Office	Indenrig+s+ministeriet
gaimu+shoo	Foreign+Office	Udenrig+s+ministeriet
Kankyoo+choo	#Environment+ Ministry (Ministry of Environment)	Miljø+ministeriet
zaimu+shoo	#Finance+Ministry (Ministry of Finance)	Skatte+ministeriet
hana+yome	bride+groom	brud+gom
hana+yome/hana+muko	(bridal couple)	brud+par
kenchiku+ka	building+worker	byggning+s+arbejdere
piisu+meikaa	peace+maker	Fred+s+mægler
poppu+guruupu	pop+group	pop+gruppe
oo+ken	royal+authority	konge+magt
#busu+gyooretsu (bus no gyooretsu)	bus+queue	bus+s+kø
noogyoo+kumiai	#farmer+association farmer's association farming association/farmers association	landmand+s +forening
heiwa+kaigi	peace+conference	fred+s+konference
heiwa+butai	Peace+corps	fred+s+korps
kyookai+sinja	church+man	kirk+e+mand
*	*	Kirk+e+ministeriet
naimu+shoo	Home+Office	Indering+s+ministeriet
kankyoo+choo	#Environment+Ministry (Ministry of Environment)	Miljø+ministeriet
zaimu+shoo	#Finance+Ministry (Ministry of Finance)	Skatte+ministeriet
ha+isha	(dentist)	tand+læge
me+gasira	(eye)	(øje)

mono+usa	spring+fever	forår+s+fornemmelser

animal, person, event, object, place

mitsu+bachi	honey+bee	honningbi
(hachi no su) hachi+su (old usage)	honey+comb	bikage
sa+doo	tea+ceremony	te ceremoni
hanii+moon	honey+moon	hvede+brød+sdage
hun+soo	tea+fight	te+slabbearads
tii+bureiku	tea+break	te+pause
u+ki	rain+season	regn+tid
kurisumasu+paatii	Christmas+party	jul+e+fest
yama+kazi	mountain+fire	bjerg+e+brand
piisu+kyanpu	peace+camp	fred+s+lejr
kyookai+ranchi	church+lunch	kirk+e+frokost
rei+hai	church+service	gud+s+tjeneste
yobi+bi	rain+date	
zange+ kayoobi	Shrove+Tuesday	hvid+e+tirsdag
bizin+ konkuuru	beauty+competition	skønhedskonkurrence
bodii+chekku	security+check	sikkerhed+s+kontrol
i+sshun	(moment)	øje+blik
taipu+raitaa	type+writer	skrive+maskine
denki+suihanki	(electronic rice cooker)	
match+bako	match+box	tænd+stik+mappe+æske
daidokoro+ kigu	kitchen+equipment	kok+s+maskin
tii+potto	tea+pot	te+potte
tii+baggu	tea+bag	te+brev
(cha no ha) cha+ppa/ cha+ha	tea+leaf	te+blad
tii+kappu	tea+cup	te+kop
cha+zutsu	tea+caddy	te+dåse
mahoo+bin	coffee+thermos	kaffe+termos
cha+bako	tea+chest	te+kiste/skrin
tii+potto+kabaa	tea+cosy	te+pann+s+össa (tea-post-hat)
biniiru+bukuro	plastic+handbag	plast+handtag
tii+booru	tea+ball	te+æg
tii+roozu	tea+rose	te+rose
cha+bon	tea+tray	te+bakke
tii+wagon	tea+wagon	te+vagn
hana+wa	flower+garland	blomster+krans
denki+sutando	table+lamp	bord+s+lamp
kompyuta+insatsuki	computer+printer	computer+printer
kureditto+kaado	credit+card	kredit+kort
sen+kan	war+ship	krig+s+skib
zikayoo+**sha**	private+car	person+bil
shokudo+sha	buffet+car	restaurant+vagn
ryukku+sakku	ruck+sack	ryg+sæk

zikan+wari+hyoo	time+table	køre+plan/togplan(schema)
ni+guruma	(cart)	vogn, arbejd+s+vogn
sukin+kuriimu	skin+food	hud+creme
mado+garasu	glass+window	glas+vindue
ya+ziri (arrow-hip)	arrow+head	pil+e+spids
anzen+beruto	safety+belt	sikkerhed+s+bælte
inu+goya	(kennel)	hund+e+hus
tori+kago	bird+cage	fugl+e+bar
kuuki+juu	air+rifle	luft+gevær
jooki+kikan+**sha**	steam+engine	damp+maskine
suisoo+bakudan	hydrogen+bomb	brint+bombe
mizu+dokei	water+clock	vand+ur
huu+sha	wind+mill	vind+møller
chika+**sui**	underground+water	undergrund+s+vand
hon+dana	book+shelf	bog+reol/skab
satoo+kibi	sugar+cane	sukker+ror
kiken+tooka+sihon	venture+capital	risiko+villing
yubi+wa	(ring)	(ring)
gai+too	street+light	gade+lys
cha+wakasi	tea+urn	te+maskine
cha+kosi	tea+strainer	te+si
me+gusuri	eye+drop	øje+drop
ha+burasi	tooth+brush	tand+borste
yuki+daruma	snow+man	sne+mand
kyookai+kiroku	church+register	kirk+e+bog
kittin+teiburu	kitchen+table	køk+s+bord
kinyuu+bumon	marketing+department	marked+s+afdeling
ame+mizu	rain+water	regn+vand
bane+juu	spring+gun	selv+skud
#ame+booshi (ame yo no boshi)	rain+hat	regn+hat
#kaba+eda (kaba no eda)	birch+twig	bjor+kris
#kippu+nedan (kippu no nedan)	ticket+price	billet+pris
zi+sho	(dictionary)	ord+bog
(sakkaa)	foot+ball	fod+bold
si+kka+**kei**	(rectangle)	fire+kantig
si+**gai**	city+centre/town+centre	(centrum)
hai+**en**	(pneumonia)	lung+betændelse (inflammation;swedish)
huraido+poteto	(chips)	pommes+ frites
bunka+men	arts+page	kultur+side
otokonoko+(no) +huku	boy's+clothes	dreng+e+tøj
seimei+hoken	life+insurance	liv+s+forsikring
cha+bata	tea+garden	restauration+s+have/te+plantage

kissa+ten	tea+shop	te+restaurant/te+salon
ryoo+son	fishing+village	fiske+by
san+ iki	mountain+area	skæle+trakt (scale)
kuu+koo	air+port	fly+plads
hoiku+sho	nursery+school	dag+hjem
gasorin+sutando	petrol+station	bensin+station
kita+airurando	North+Ireland	Nord+irland
o+huro+ba	bath+room	bad+værelse
kosaku+nooka	peasant+cottage	bond+stuga
yuubin+kyoku	post+office	post+kontor
omocha+koojoo	toy+factory	lege+tøj+fabrik
kagaku+zikken+situ	chemistry+labatory	chemi+labotrium
spootsu+hooru	sport+hall	sport+hall
ho+kkyok+ken	(arctic)	nord+kalotten
chi+ka	under+ground	tunnel+bane
bijutsu+kan	art+museum	kunst+museum
#kyookai+bochi (kyookai no bochi)	grave+yard	kirk+e+gård
hon+ya	book+shop	bog+handler
rakuseihin+chozosho	spring+house	
huyu+gesiki	winter+scenery	vinter+landskabe
roodosha+kaikyuu+chiiki (phrase)	working+class+area	arbejder+kvarter
	peace+pipe	fred+s+pibe
#kyookai+too (kyookai no too)	church+tower	kirk+e+tårn
choosen+minshushugi kyoowa+koku	#Democracy+People Republic Korea	#Demokratiske Folkrepubliken Korea
#chikatetsu+eki+kiosk (chika-tetsu no baiten)	tubestation kiosk	tunnel+bane+kiosk
chika+tetsu	tube+train	tunnel+bane+tog
sakura+n+boo	(cherry)	kirse+bær/kors bar
haru+maki	spring+roll	forår+s+rulle
insutanto+koohii	instant+coffee	pulver+kaffe
oranzi+juusu	orange+juice	appelsin
shakai+men	social+page	familje+sida
paasonaru+sutereo	personal+stereo	free+styl
juukyo+chi	residential+area	bo+stad+s+kvarter
otoko+shakai	(male-dominated society)	mand+s+samhed
ka+gaku	physical+science	natur+videnskab
shakai+kagaku	social+science	samhed+s+videnskab
kootsu+shudan	#transport+means (means for transport)	transport+medel
#ki+kyookai (mokuzai de…)	#tree+church (wooden church)	træ+kirk
denki+kamisori	electric+shaver	elektrisk barber+maskine
denki+kikan+sha	electric+train	elektrisk tåg
nettai+shokubutsu	tropical+vegetation	tropisk vegetation
sakkaa+tiimu	football+team	fod+bold+slag

sakkaa+joo   football+pitch   fod+bald+s+plan
#daigaku+honya   university+bookshop   akakemi+bog+handel
(daigaku no hon-ya)
#kokumin+kyuuzitsu   public+holiday   almen+helg+dag
sangyoo+tosi   industrial+land   industri+land

NP-N

balm of Gilead
bacon and Eggs-lotus corniculatus
beauty of Bath –dessert apple
forget-me-not
jack-go-to-bed-at-noon
tragopogon pratensis
lily-of-the-valley –convallaria majalis
lords-and-ladies—arum maculatum
love-in-idleness-voila tricolor, pansy
love-lies-bleeding-amarathus caudatus
love-in-a-mist-
pellitory-of-the-wall –parietaria diffusa
star-of-bethlehem
tree of heaven-ailanthus altissima Chinese,
York and Lancaster Rose-rosa damascena

Copulative compounds
English (from Olsen 2000)
writer+director
producer+writer
director+producer
producer+screenwriter
producer+composer+musician
screenwriter+lycricist
actor+author
actor+writer+impressionist
actor+stantman
comedy writer+performer
director+choreographer
dancer+choreographer+actor+designer
singer+guitarist
singer+songwriter
composer+pianist+singer
dancer+singer
singer+bassist
singer+actor+entertainer
jazz composer+arranger+band leader

pianist+singer+composer
conductor+composer
rock singer+pianist
saxophonist+actor+songwriter+screenwriter
editor+publisher
writer+performer
writer+artist+publisher
author+journalist
novelist+professor
newswoman+author
philosopher+poet
musician+poet+pop icon
poet+historian
poet+philosopher+politician
lawyer+author
philosopher+scientist
scientist+inventor
astronomer+author
adventurer+author+sicentist
scientist+researcher
scientist+business consultant
sailor+scientist
salesman+artist
artist+photographer
artist+designer
artist+waitress
artist+explorer
philosopher+physician
explorer+linguist
hunter+scavengers
screenwriter+volunteer
actor+bodybuilder
patriot+poet
play-wright+activist
singer+spy
songwriter+producer+arranger+friend
diplomat+playboy
architect+prophet
poet+drunkard
actor+friend
producer+boyfriend

nerd+genius
scoundrel+savior
hero+martyr
participant+observer
lawyer+son
doctor+daughter
attorney+husband
lawyer+husband
producer+director+husband
engineer+father
singer+father
admiral+grandfather
actor+brother
kindergartner+brother
actress+wife
producer+cousin

Spencer's examples with stress
A. Technical and geographical terminology
A1. NN compounds with Compound Stress

Van der Gráaf generator, Márch band, Púrkinje cell, Wóulfe bottle, Líe algebra, Gödel number, Póisson distribution, Chómsky hierarchy, Féinman diagram, Chérnyshev polynomial, Fráuenhofer lines, Állen key, Stánley knife

X island: Wrángel island, Báffin Island, Éaster Island, Vírgin Islands, Chrístmas Island, Fálkland Islands (exceptions: Long Ísland, Staten Ísland, Treasure Ísland)

A2. NN compounds with Phrasal Stress (right-stress)
Wheatstone brídge, Markov cháin, Bessemer convérter, Bunsen búrner, Dyson vácuum cleaner, Rolls Royce éngine, Pirelli týres, Phillips (or Phillips'??) scréwdriver, Magellan, Bering stráits, Baffin báy (cf. Báffin Island), Wrangle Móunt (cf. Wrángle Island), Hudson Báy, Victória Falls, Drake Pássage

A3. N's N expressions with Compound Stress
Bróca's aphasia, Ásperger's syndrome, Párkinson's disease, Schróedinger's equation, Stóke's (Pythagoras's, Euler's, ...) theorem, Chúrch's conjuncture, Kúndt's tube, Líebig's condenser, Fresnél's lens, Van der Wáal's force, Hígg's particle (Hígg's boson), Pláto's (Órwell's) Problem.

A4. N's N expressions with Phrasal Stress;
Newton's crádle, Archimedes' (s) scréw, Descartes' (s) cógito, Halley's cómet, Beecham's pówders, Foucault's péndulum, Young's slíts, Ayer's róck, Cook's stráit (cf. Cóok Island), Fisherman's cóve, the Giant's Cáuseway.
and most animal names (Lieberman and Sproat 1992: 154): Swainson's thrúsh, Thomson's gazélle

B. Chess terminology
B1. NN/AN expressions with Compound stress
Three Kníghts, Vienna, ... Opening, King's Índian Defence, Schéveningen Variation, Richter-Ráuzer Attack, Látvian Gambit (but Greco Cóunter Gambit—the term Cóunter Gambit is always stressed)
Quéen/Kíng Pawn; Páwn, Quéen, etc. sacrifice; páwn centre

B2. NN/AN expressions with Phrasal Stress
Queen's/King's side áttack; isolated páwn; minor exchánge
Note that a declined gambit always gets right-stress;
Látvian Gambit ~ Latvian gambit Declíned
King's Gámbit ~ King's Gambit Declíned
Greco Cóunter Gambit ~ Greco Counter Gambit Declíned

B3. N's N expressions with Compound Stress:
Chess terms:: Lásker's (Bénko's, Kére's, ... Gambit; but King's/Queen's Gámbit), Aljoxin's (aka Álekhine's, Phílidor's, Pétroff's, ...) Defence; Bírd's (Bíshop's, Réti's...)
Opening; Nimzowitsch's (Botvínnik's, ...) System; Gligóric's (Nimzowitsch's, ...)
Variation; Romaníschin's Line.
Note: these often appear without the possessive marker; the Phílidor, Pétroff etc. Defence, Réti Opening etc.
Quéen's/Kíng's side, Quéen's/Kíng's rook's file

B4 N's N expressions with Phrasal Stress:
Queen's/King's Gámbit; Queen's/King's Páwn, Bíshop, Kníght, Róok

C. musical terminology
C1. NN/AN expressions with Compound Stress
Names of symphonies, concertos etc.
Tóy (Lóndon, Farewéll, Surpríse, Prágue, Háffner, Júpiter, Pástoral, Eróica, Chóral, Resurréction, Mánfred, Léningrad, Tulangalîla) Symphony,
Fífths, Sún, Émperor, Díssonance, Húnt, Razumóvsky, Américan, 'Intimate

Létters' quartet
(note that this compounded from a phrase, which is stressed internally as a phrase, but which bears the main stress because it is the left component of the compound).
La Fólia, Góldberg, Diabélli, Enígma, Frank Brídge variations,
Frénch, Énglish (Unaccompanied) Céllo, Pulcinélla, Hómberg, Cápriol Suite.
Brandenburg, Italian, Émperor, Ébony concerto; violín, piáno, clarinét, mandolín concerto
Rósary, Gólden, Spríng, Kréutzer, Pathétique, Wáldstein, Hammerklavíer sonata; violín, piáno, flúte, Arpeggióne sonata (but Moonlight sonáta?)
Archdúke, Ghóst, Dúmky trio; piáno trio/quartet/quintet, stríng quartet/quintet (but string trío; also string quartét/quintét)
Égmont, Leonóra, Fingal's Cáve, Midsummernight's Dréam, Lóhengrin overture
Gréensleeves, Tállis, Fantasia (but also Tallis Fantásia?),
Names of instruments: vóice flute, kéttle drum (exceptions to C2 below).

C2. NN/AN expressions with Phrasal Stress:
Christmas/Easter Oratório (an exception to the general pattern seen under C1).
Specified types of instrument: B-flat clarinét, bass víol, tenor sháwm, portative órgan,
French (English) hórn, pedal hárpsichord; string trío/quartét (exceptions to pattern above)
Names of cadences, intervals and chords: Landini, Burgundian, English cádence;
Neapolitan Sécond, French Síxth, perfect fóurth, diminished séventh; G major arpéggio
Unique sets or types of work modified by a composer's name:
a Debussy étúde, a DuParc sóng, a Mahler sýmphony, a Vivaldi concérto, a Haydn quartét,
a Bach cantáta (fúgue, prélude, ária…), a Telemann trío sonata, a Purcell ánthem, a Gabrieli canzóna, a Josquin motét, a Machaut vírelai, a Mozart quintét, a Chopin balláde, a Schubert sóng, a Wagner Síngspiel, a Handel ópera, a Ravel orchestrátion, the Pachalbel Cánon (and Gigue), the Mendelssohn Octét, the Schubert Quintét, the Franck Sonáta, the Bruch concérto, the Ravel Boléro, the Verdi Réquiem, the Monteverdi Vespers, the Tallis Lamentátions, the Byrd fíve-part (or the Byrd five-part máss.).

C3. N's N expressions with Compound Stress:
These seem to be very rare. Examples are cases in which a character in an opera etc. has an aria named after them: Sólveig's song, the Cóuntess's aria, the

Pickled Boys's song. However, this does not happen with laments: the lover's, Ariadne's, Dido's etc. lamént

C4. N's N expressions with Phrasal Stress:
This seems to be the common pattern:
Beethoven's Séventh (cf Beethoven's Seventh Sýmphony), Schubert's Unfínished, Nielsen's Inextínguishable, Monteverdi's Vespers;
The Earl of Essex's Galliard, Sir John Smith's Álmain, the King of Denmark's Pávan, Worcester Bráwles, Mistress Winter's Jump, cf. also, Selinger's Róund, Kemp's Jígge, Ariadne's Lamént.
The comparative lack of N's N expressions with Compound Stress in musical terminology stands in marked contrast to the situation with technical and chess vocabulary.

Names of bands, etc. show vacillation, determined it seems by the head noun:
Compound stress:
chámber orchestra/ensemble/group
the Hánover Band, the Énglish Concert, the Palládian (Hílliard, etc) Ensemble, the Early Músic Consort, the Róse Consort (but the full title would be the Rose Consort of Víols), the (London) Bách Choir, the Concértgebouw orchestra

Phrasal stress
Halle Órchestra, the King's Cónsort, the King's Nóyse, Henry's Eight, the Cardinal's Musick, His Majesty's Sackbutts and Córnetts, the BBC Síngers, Vienna State Ópera
Note that the head nouns orchestra, consort and singers may give either stress pattern. Names of bands which are clearly phrases are given normal phrasal stress: the Parley of Ínstruments, the Orchestra of the Age of the Enlíghtenment, the Fires of Lóndon

Quartets are given phrasal stress with full name X Stríng Quartet, but compound stress with truncated name, e.g. the Alban Bérg, Amadéus, Bórodin, Hungárian, Gabriéli, ... quartet

Index

A

'A that is a B'   33
abstract Case   88, 90
adjectival compounds   130, 157
adjectival and verbal left-hand segments of compounds   12
agreement   157
Alegre & Gordon   41
Allen's Variable R condition   22
A (x) feature   157
abstract WM[case]   91
Agreement-linking Principle   75, 76
Akan language(the)   181
anaphoric relationship   26
Anderson   15, 45
any word class feature   132
appositional compounds   91, 196
Arad   120
assigning x a value that is an index   151
asymmetry of syntax (the)   119, 196

B

Baker   3
bare nominal   141
bare noun   143
Bare Phrase Structure (the)   100
Bauer   2, 6, 12, 16, 18, 49, 56
Bisetto   165, 166, 175
Bloomfield   11
borderline between compounds and phrases(the)   59
Borer   185
both from a new word from existing words   11
bound morphemes as constituents   23
BPS framework   99

C

case   179
checking the P(x) feature   152, 154
Chierchia   123
Chomsky   1, 7, 8, 64, 92–94, 96, 98, 108, 119, 120, 145, 146
Clark   182
clitic position   111
Collins   VIII, 145, 146, 163
Compound Accent Rule   34
compound formation   37
Compound Stress Rule   38
compound words in English, Japanese and Mainland Scandinavian   1, 2, 83
compounding is the combination of two independent words   11
compound word(s)   28, 50, 111, 179
construct state nominals   184
coordination   53
cranberry morphemes   16, 59, 117

D

derivational suffix -er   160
derivation in Japanese   131
determiner phrases   28
devil's advocate   88
devoid of features   76
Di Sciullo & Ralli   177
Di Sciullo & Williams   5, 24
Distributed Morphology   116
does not refer to specific elements   50
Don   198
Downing   64
driver's license   88
Dutch   171, 198
dvandva compounds   72, 195

E

economical 100
Emery 185
Emonds 67
end-stress 33
English 20, 30, 38, 63, 68
Event (x) feature 162
Extension Condition (the) 101

F

feature percolation 69
Feature Percolation Conventions 75
Finnish 17
free morphemes 14, 59

G

gender distinction 198
general concept 48
generic 49
Genitive compound words 88, 180, 181
German 172
Giegerich 31–33, 132–134
goal 95
Greek compound words 176
green-driver 159
Grimshaw 148, 149
Guevara & Scalise 175

H

Hale & Keyser 159
Hale & Marantz 116, 118
Haskell, Maryellen, Mac Donald & Seidenberg 40, 41
head of the word vii, viii, 9, 72, 76, 95, 129, 145, 153, 156, 167, 189
heads are final with respect to modifiers 80
Higginbotham 123, 155
Holmberg 15, 68, 84, 86
Hungarian compounding 178

I

idiosyncratic 29
idiosyncratic formation 4
imperative 191
indefinite null noun 27

J

Jackendoff 121, 123
Japanese 15, 23, 38, 41, 63, 99, 111, 129, 138, 168, 191
Josefsson 4, 14, 71, 97, 115, 118, 119, 121, 124, 140, 141, 152, 165

K

Kageyama 12, 13, 28, 43, 51, 68, 71, 148, 164
Karlsson 177
Keyser & Roeper 105–108, 110
Kiefer 178
Kiparsky 140, 141
Klinge 31
Korean 180
Kubozono 34–36

L

label 91, 93
lack a base 39
Latvian 179, 180
Lees 64
left-branching recursive compounds 112, 167, 187
left-hand/non-head of a compound 42, 49, 50, 63, 90, 101, 129, 131, 132, 184, 192, 193
Levi 65, 67
Levin & Hovav 161
lexical 32
lexicalised compound 2, 3, 29
Lexical Integrity 47
lexicon 3, 39, 138
LF lexicon (the) 117

Lieber 52, 53, 70, 73–75, 77, 79, 81, 158, 188
Lieber's Licensing Condition 83
Lieberman & Sproat 64, 99
linking element 3, 14, 23, 46, 76, 112, 113, 137, 152, 167, 168, 170, 171, 172, 173, 176, 178, 186–188, 193, 197, 199
Lithuanian 179, 180
Lyman's Law 37

M
MADE OF 154
Mainland Scandinavian languages 16, 20, 23, 28, 30, 38, 44, 63, 81, 84, 129, 168
Marantz 120
Maximal projection 192
Mellenius 31, 54, 58, 195
merge 93
merge recursively combines elements 92
merged twice with the same head noun 114
merging root after root with a P(x) 166
Minimalist Program 91
Miyoshi 17
more restricted than left-branching compounding 168
morphological criterion 130
Morphology is outside the Lexicon 196
moved noun (the) 114
Mukai 21, 166

N
N de N 180
Namiki 52, 56, 68, 110, 188
neoclassical compounds 17, 18, 20, 22, 59, 72, 90, 117, 153
no 48

no direct relation 8
no feature to be checked 114, 189
no linking element 173
nominalisation 162
non-compositional 29
non-head of a 'verb-verb' compound in Japanese 197
non-head of compounds and derivations in Japanese 130
not an inflectional morpheme 48
Noun Phrase 28
numeral classifier 143

O
Ochi 96
Olsen 55
one or more unsaturated features VIII
Otsu 37

P
P(x) feature 156, 157, 160, 162, 167, 169, 170, 185, 191, 193, 195, 189
paraphrase of 'N for N' 32
park/s commissioner 42, 131
Pereltsvaig 183, 184
Pesetsky 163
PF 151
phonologically null 164
phonological feature 37
phrasal compounds 192
phrase-like compounding in Japanese 44
Pinker 40
Plag 5, 6, 16–19, 54–56, 194
Platzack 4, 115, 116
plural marker or plural tantamn 39, 42
possessive marker 46, 152
prepositional element 174
probe 95

productivity or productive compounds   4, 5, 56, 98, 99, 180, 186, 188, 199
pronominal reference   26
property feature   VIII
properties of word formation   7

R

real-world knowledge   33
recursivity or recursive compounds   5, 71, 172–182, 186, 197, 238
referential feature   196
referential index   147, 189
regular plurals   114
renyokei or 'an infinitive form'   13
right-branching recursive compounds   113, 168
right-headed   81
Roeper & Siegel   11, 158
Roeper & Snyder   112
Roeper, Snyder & Hiramatsu   97, 102, 104, 108, 110, 165
Romance languages   103, 173, 174
root   90

S

Scalise   17
Selkirk   41, 70, 72
semantic features   101
semantic relationship   53
Shimamura   45, 46
Snyder   104, 105
sound and meaning   8

Spencer   32, 98
'stems' rather than affixes   19
Sugisaki & Isobe   57
syntactic features   101
syntax/X'- theory   69
synthetic compound word   162

T

-tachi   142, 143
Taylor   45, 46
theme (x) feature   146, 160, 169, 170, 193
theta feature (the)   147
triune lexicon (the)   115

U

'unaccusatives'   164
uninflected adjective   13
universally dependent   187
unsaturated feature   146, 156

V

van Hout & Roeper   161
'V-N' compounds   176
vowel morpheme   14

W

Wiese   51
Williams   VII, 67, 71, 98, 196

Z

Zuffi   175

向井真樹子（むかい まきこ）

略歴

1976年広島生まれ。1990年父の転勤で渡英。1999年英国イースト・アングリア大学（北欧研究卒業）、2000年英国ウォーリック大学院（修士号取得）、2002年英国ダーラム大学大学院（修士号取得）、2006年英国ニューカッスル大学大学院英文学英語学言語学科博士課程修了（Ph.d.）。2008年高知女子大学文化学部講師を経て、現在高知県立大学文化学部准教授。

Makiko Mukai was born in Hiroshima, Japan in 1976. She moved to Great Britain in 1990 because of her father's job. She graduated from University of East Anglia in 1999 (BA Scandinavian Studies), University of Warwick in 2000 (MA Translation Studies), University of Durham (MA Teaching Japanese as a Second Language), and received a Ph.D. in Linguistics at University of Newcastle in 2006. She started working at Kochi Women's University in 2008 and now, Associate Professor at University of Kochi.

主な論文

- Semantic characteristics of recursive compounds. *Order and structure in syntax II: Subjecthood and argument structure* (2017).
- Word formation in Phase Theory. *Newcastle and Northumbria Working Papers in Linguistics*, 21.1, (2015).
- Recursive compounds in Phase Theory, *papers from the Conference and from the International Spring Forum of the English Linguistic Society of Japan*, 311–317, (2014). 52.(2011)
- Recursive compounds and Linking Morpheme, *International Journal of English Linguistics*, 3. 4, 36–49, (2013).

Hituzi Linguistics in English No. 25
A Comparative Study of Compound Words

発行	2018年2月16日 初版1刷
定価	13000円＋税
著者	©向井真樹子
発行者	松本功
ブックデザイン	白井敬尚形成事務所
印刷所	株式会社 ディグ
製本所	株式会社 星共社
発行所	株式会社 ひつじ書房

〒112-0011 東京都文京区千石2-1-2 大和ビル2F
Tel: 03-5319-4916
Fax: 03-5319-4917
郵便振替 00120-8-142852
toiawase@hituzi.co.jp
http://www.hituzi.co.jp/
ISBN978-4-89476-900-7

造本には充分注意しておりますが、落丁・乱丁などがございましたら、小社かお買上げ書店にておとりかえいたします。ご意見、ご感想など、小社までお寄せ下されば幸いです。

刊行のご案内

ファンダメンタル英語学　改訂版
中島平三 著　定価 1,400 円＋税

ファンダメンタル認知言語学
野村益寛 著　定価 1,600 円＋税

ファンダメンタル英語史　改訂版
児馬修 著　定価 1,600 円＋税

刊行のご案内

ひつじ研究叢書（言語編）

第143巻 相互行為における指示表現
須賀あゆみ 著　定価 6,400 円＋税

第151巻 多人数会話におけるジェスチャーの同期
「同じ」を目指そうとするやりとりの会話分析
城綾実 著　定価 5,800 円＋税

第152巻 日本語語彙的複合動詞の意味と体系
コンストラクション形態論とフレーム意味論
陳奕廷・松本曜 著　定価 8,500 円＋税

刊行のご案内

英語コーパス研究シリーズ
堀正広・赤野一郎監修　定価 各3,200円＋税

第1巻　コーパスと英語研究（近刊）
第2巻　コーパスと英語教育
第3巻　コーパスと辞書（近刊）
第4巻　コーパスと英文法・語法
第5巻　コーパスと英語文体
第6巻　コーパスと英語史（近刊）
第7巻　コーパスと多様な関連領域

刊行のご案内

Hituzi Language Studies

No. 1 Relational Practice in Meeting Discourse in New Zealand and Japan
村田和代 著　定価 6,000 円 + 税

No. 2 Style and Creativity
Towards a Theory of Creative Stylistics
斎藤兆史 著　定価 7,500 円 + 税

No. 3 Rhetorical Questions
A Relevance-Theoretic Approach to Interrogative Utterances in English and Japanese
後藤リサ 著　定価 10,000 円 + 税

刊行のご案内

Hituzi Linguistics in English

No. 24 Metaphor of Emotions in English
With Special Reference to the Natural World and the Animal Kingdom as Their Source Domains
大森文子 著　定価 9,500 円＋税

No. 26 Grammatical Variation of Pronouns in Nineteenth-Century English Novels
中山匡美 著　定価 12,000 円＋税

No. 27 *I mean* as a Marker of Intersubjective Adjustment
A Cognitive Linguistic Approach
小林隆 著　定価 8,500 円＋税